# Noël Coward
## COLLECTED PLAYS: ONE

### HAY FEVER, THE VORTEX, FALLEN ANGELS, EASY VIRTUE

This volume contains the plays with which Noël Coward 'arrived' on the theatrical scene in the 1920s – plays which made him, in John Gielgud's words, 'the angry young man of the day'.

*Hay Fever*, one of the best-loved of all Coward's plays, was reckoned by Tyrone Guthrie to have 'as good a chance of immortality as any work of an author now living'.

'Here is a piece,' wrote James Agate of *The Vortex*, 'which is the *dernier cri* in the theatrical mode, *un peu schoking* perhaps, but no less popular on that account.'

*Fallen Angels* was described, wrote Coward, as 'vulgar, disgusting, shocking, nauseating, vile, obscene, degenerate, etc., etc . . . All this was capital for the box-office and the play ran for several months.'

Of *Easy Virtue*, Coward wrote: 'Women with pasts today receive far more enthusiastic social recognition than women without pasts . . . It was in a mood of nostalgic regret at the decline of such conventions that I wrote *Easy Virtue*.'

# Noël Coward

# COLLECTED PLAYS

## ONE

HAY FEVER

THE VORTEX

FALLEN ANGELS

EASY VIRTUE

*Introduced by Sheridan Morley*

Methuen

METHUEN WORLD CLASSICS

10 9

This collection first published in Great Britain in 1979
by Eyre Methuen Ltd
Reissued with a new Introduction in 1989
Reissued with a new cover, revised Introduction and Chronology in 1999 by
Methuen Publishing Ltd
215 Vauxhall Bridge Road, London SW1V 1EL

*Hay Fever* was first published in 1925 by Ernest Benn
as Contemporary British Dramatists Volume 27 and republished
by Heinemann in 1934 in Play Parade Vol. 1

*The Vortex* was first published in 1925 by Ernest Benn
as Contemporary British Dramatists Volume 19 and republished
by Heinemann in 1934 in Play Parade Vol. 1

*Fallen Angels* was first published in 1925 by Ernest Benn
as Contemporary British Dramatists Volume 25 and republished
by Heinemann in 1950 in the revised Play Parade Vol. 2

*Easy Virtue* was first published in 1926 by Ernest Benn
as Contemporary British Dramatists Volume 26 and republished
by Heinemann in 1950 in the revised Play Parade Vol. 2

Copyright in all the plays is by the Estate of the late Noël Coward
Introduction copyright © 1989, 1999 by Sheridan Morley
Chronology copyright © 1987, 1999 by Jacqui Russell

The right of the authors to be identified as the authors of this work has been
asserted by them in accordance with the Copyright, Designs and Patents Act, 1988

ISBN 0 413 46060 6

Methuen Publishing Limited Reg. No. 3543167

A CIP catalogue record for this book
is available from the British Library

Typeset by Deltatype Ltd, Birkenhead, Merseyside
Printed and bound in Great Britain by
Cox & Wyman Ltd, Reading, Berkshire

CAUTION

These plays are fully protected by copyright throughout the world. All applications
for performance, etc., should be made *by professionals* to Alan Brodie Representation Ltd,
211 Piccadilly, London W1V 9LD, and *by amateurs* to Samuel French Ltd, 52 Fitzroy Street,
London W1P 9HF. No performance may be given unless a licence has been obtained.

# CONTENTS

The four plays that make up the first volume of this collection of Noël Coward's plays were all written over a two-year period in the middle 1920s; they include the drama that made his name amid considerable shock-horror press coverage, two classic light comedies and a period piece now almost totally unrevived but once made into a film by Alfred Hitchcock.

Born on December 16, 1899, just before the last Christmas of the last century (hence the name Noël), Coward was the second son of an unsuccessful piano-tuner turned salesman and a doting, ambitious mother. He grew up amid genteel poverty at a series of suburban South London addresses, and when he was ten his mother answered a newspaper advertisement for child actors. Within three months Noël was on the stage of the Crystal Palace in a play called *The Goldfish*, and moved from there to the ritual Christmas treats of *Where The Rainbow Ends* and *Peter Pan*; it was Kenneth Tynan who commented half a century later that having started out as Slightly in *Peter Pan*, Noël remained Wholly in it forever afterwards. Coward then rapidly settled with his beloved friend and partner from childhood Gertrude Lawrence into the touring life of a fairly successful juvenile player: in his own view he was 'when washed and smarmed down a bit, passably attractive, but one of the worst boy actors ever inflicted on the paying public'.

Nevertheless he survived, and by 1917 was already making his first film appearance with the Gish sisters for D. W. Griffith in *Hearts of the World*. There followed a brief and unhappy spell in the army, ignominious dismissal from a West End comedy for mocking the leading lady, and then a lengthy Birmingham and London engagement as Ralph in *The Knight of the Burning Pestle*. But by now Noël's ambitions were to be a playwright and songwriter as well as an actor, and by April 1920, at the very beginning of his own twenties and the decade with which he was to be constantly and inevitably associated, he was in rehearsal in Manchester for *I'll Leave It to You*, the first play with which he was to reach the West End as both author and leading actor.

That it was not destined to be a great success (it lasted only 37 performances and has seldom been revived) did not much matter: the author/actor double achieved at 20, was sufficient to guarantee several magazine profiles of an 'infant prodigy' and to launch Coward into a remarkable decade:

> Between 1920 and 1930 I achieved a great deal of what I had set out to achieve, and a great deal that I had not. I had not, for instance, envisaged in those early days of the Twenties that before the decade was over I would be laid low by a serious nervous breakdown, recover from it, and return to London to be booed off the stage and spat at in the streets. Nor did I imagine, faced by this unmannerly disaster, that only a few months would ensue before I would be back again, steadier, and a great deal more triumphant than before.

After the failure of *I'll Leave It to You* Noël went into a rapid revival of *Knight of the Burning Pestle* and then a Broadway comedy, *Polly with a Past*, which gave him a certain curiosity about the America he had never visited. After the show one night, about halfway through the run, he met Jeanne Eagels at a party of Ivor Novello's and the aura of American magic that she radiated made Coward decide that it was high time he took the ocean voyage to the new world, surely countless other gorgeous actresses like her were eagerly awaiting the arrival of his acting and composing and playwriting talents to amuse. Noël had in the bank about half the £100 that a crossing on the Aquitania would cost; he made the rest by selling a couple of songs to a friend and benefactor, Ned Lathom, who didn't actually want them but was charitably disposed and also very rich. At the end of May 1921 he thus set off for New York with his friend Jeffrey Amherst, a bundle of manuscripts and just over £17 in sterling.

It was Moss Hart who once noted that New York was not a city in which to be poor or unsuccessful, and Noël on his first visit there was both; he also found that all three impresarios to whom he had letters of introduction were on their way out of the city for the summer, and that he couldn't afford a hotel, though he luckily found room at a Washington Square apartment then owned by a Mrs Gabrielle Enthoven who later became the founding figure of the British Theatre Museum. To make enough to eat, Noël sold some short pieces to Vanity Fair based on a book of parody character sketches (*A Withered Nosegay*) that he had recently published in London; he also made the acquaintance of Tallulah Bankhead, Ronald Colman, Alfred Lunt and Lynn Fontanne, not to mention the actress Laurette Taylor and her husband Hartley Manners who would often invite him to gatherings at their home on Riverside Drive which is where, several years before it was actually written, *Hay Fever* was born:

'On Sunday evenings up on Riverside Drive', wrote Noël in his first autobiography *Present Indicative*, 'we had cold supper and played games, often rather acrimonious games owing to Laurette's abrupt disapproval of any guest who turned out to be self-conscious, nervous, or unable to act an adverb or an historical personage with proper abandon. There were also, very often, shrill arguments concerning rules. These were waged entirely among the family, and frequently ended in all four of them leaving the room and retiring upstairs where, later on, they might be discovered by any guest bold enough to go in search of them, amicably drinking tea in the kitchen. It was inevitable that someone should eventually utilise portions of this eccentricity in a play, and I am only grateful to Fate that no guest of the Hartley Manners's thought of writing *Hay Fever* before I did.'

Returning to London, Noël then achieved a sudden and immense success with a revue (*London Calling*), a controversial drama (*The Vortex*) and a comedy (*Fallen Angels*), all of which were running simultaneously in the West End in 1925 when one of its leading ladies, Marie Tempest, remembered being sent a play that Noël had written over one weekend on his first return from the USA and entitled *Oranges and Lemons*, before deciding that *Hay Fever* might be a more suitable title:

The idea came to me suddenly in my mother's garden, and I finished it in about three days ... however when I had finished it I read it through and was rather unimpressed ... I knew certain scenes were good, especially the breakfast scene in the last act, and the dialogue between the giggling flapper and the diplomat in the first act, but apart from these it seemed to me a little tedious. I think the reason for this was that I was passing through a transition stage as a writer; my dialogue was becoming more natural and less elaborate, and I was beginning to concentrate more on the comedy values of the situation rather than the comedy values of actual lines. I expect that when I read through *Hay Fever* that first time, I was subconsciously bemoaning its lack of snappy epigrams. At any rate I thought well enough of it to consider it a good vehicle for Marie Tempest.

In her drawing room, with Miss Tempest's husband dozing quietly in a corner, Noël read her the play only to have it immediately if politely declined; Miss Tempest was, she explained, then looking for a drama rather than yet another light comedy; there was no emotion here, and though Judith might be a good part for her, the story of a theatrical family inviting some unsuspecting outsiders for a weekend of 'get the guests' was altogether too plotless and seriously lacking in any kind of action.

The play thus disappeared into a desk for a couple of years, only to reappear when Miss Tempest called for it after Noël's subsequent trio of hits: 'but' protested the author 'she has already turned this one down once. She said she didn't like it.' 'I think,' replied her manager to the author of *The Vortex* and *On with the Dance* and *Fallen Angels*, 'you will find that she likes it now.' And sure enough Miss Tempest decreed not only that she would now do the play, but that she would have Noël himself direct it.

The prospect appalled him, as she was reputed to be a daunting lady not overly fond of directors telling her how to act. In the event he needn't have worried: early in rehearsals Miss Tempest summoned him onto the stage and announced that as Noël had written one particularly difficult scene the very least he could do would be to show her how to play it. This he did, and the two of them got along very well from then onwards: she later wrote of Noël in her diary 'he is the most stimulating and exciting personality that has come into my life in the last ten years.'

A comedy of bad manners which starts with the arrival of four guests, invited independently by different members of the Bliss family for a weekend at their country house near Maidenhead, *Hay Fever* largely concerns the way that they are alternately ignored, embraced, embarrassed, humiliated and ultimately abandoned to slink away by themselves during a blazing family row, a curtain device later echoed by the end of *Private Lives*. As a play it offers some characteristic examples of Coward's clenched wit: 'She goes about using sex as a sort of shrimping-net', and 'You should wash, darling, it's really so bad for your skin to leave things lying about on it.'

It has been the mistake of countless amateur societies and innumerable local theatres to assume that because *Hay Fever* is a comedy with few characters in one set, it must therefore also be easy to perform. Coward himself, as usual, knew better: '*Hay Fever* is far and away one of the most difficult plays to perform that I have ever encountered.' But the play's technical symmetry always appealed to him: 'It's quite extraordinarily well constructed. And as I did the whole thing in three days, I didn't even rewrite. I enjoyed writing it and producing it, and I have frequently enjoyed watching it.'

So, on the first night in June 1925, did most of the critics, though in some notices it was possible to detect already the beginning of a curiously patronising attitude which dictated that in almost all Coward comedy reviews over the next forty years or so the words 'flippant' and 'trivial' were to recur with alarming frequency, implying by comparison that in some strange way the other comedies of the time were deeper and imbued with all kinds of significance denied by Coward to his audiences. Perhaps it was because the brittle, flash nature of his writing often distracted attention from what his characters left unsaid: 'His comic creations', wrote John Russell Taylor in 1966, 'do live as people, and their lives go on behind and under and around what they are saying; the text provides only the faintest guidelines to what is really going on between the people on the stage.'

The original *Hay Fever* cast starred Miss Tempest and her husband W. Graham Browne as Judith and David Bliss, with Robert Andrews and Helen Spencer as their children and Hilda Moore, Athole Stewart, Ann Trevor and Patrick Susands as the benighted house-guests. Making his curtain speech from the stage, Noël noted, with half an eye on the critics who had complained about the risqué nature of *Fallen Angels* a few months earlier, that even if the new comedy was 'dreary', they would have to admit in the press that it was clean as a whistle. This they did, and *The Era* went so far as to hail 'the gayest, brightest and most amusing entertainment in London', though James Agate for the *Sunday Times* was rather less ecstatic:

> There is neither health nor cleanness about any of Mr Coward's characters, who are still the same vicious babies sprawling upon the floor of their unwholesome crèche . . . Mr Coward is credited with the capacity to turn out these very highly polished pieces of writing in an incredibly short time; and if rumour and the illustrated weeklies are to be believed, he writes his plays in a flowered dressing-gown and before breakfast. But what I want to know is what kind of work he intends to do after breakfast, when he is clothed and in his right mind.

*Hay Fever* ran triumphantly on its first outing for more than a year, and was revived with rather less success by Charles Cochran in 1933, when Coward again directed a cast headed by Constance Collier and Louis Hayward. At that time *The Times* noted 'the nonsense is purely nonsensical, as in *The Importance of Being Earnest*, but Wilde's play is superior to Coward's in its being sprung from a richer fable and a more elaborate verbal pattern. Yet the proof that *Hay Fever* is in the same class (and has the same rare freedom from emotional alloy) lies in the discovery that it does not date. If it had pointed an arrow at contemporary manners, it would already have lost its aim; if love, or hope, or sadness, or hatred, or ambition had, even for a moment, intruded upon its fooling, there would be parts of it already tarnished . . . but as it is in the highest mood of fantastic comedy, it is deliciously heartless and therefore deliciously alive and fresh.'

In America the play fared rather less well: 'On the morning of the first (Broadway 1925) rehearsal, I walked onto the stage of the Broadhurst Theatre and was startled to find a company of over thirty which, for a comedy of nine characters, seemed excessive. I weeded them out gradually, but one lady gave me a great deal of trouble. She was a brassy blonde in a decolleté afternoon dress of black lace, and was lying on her back on a wooden bench chewing gum with an expression of studied languor. At first she replied to my questioning laconically, but even in her monosyllables it was not difficult to detect a strong Brooklyn accent. I asked her what part Mr Shubert had promised her, and shifting the gum from one side of her mouth to the other she replied "Myra" and turned her head away wearily, as though the whole interview was distasteful to her. Out of the corner of my eye I observed Laura Hope-Crews (who was playing Judith Bliss) at the prompt table convulsed with laughter. I persevered, with as much tact as I could manage, and said that I was extremely sorry, but that as Myra was such a typically English character she could obviously not be played with such a thorough-going American accent. Whereupon the blonde rose with sudden fury, spat her gum neatly into a chiffon handkerchief, said "Accent hell, I gotta contract" and flounced off the stage.'

*Hay Fever* survived barely six weeks on Broadway, but was to live on in regular British repertory company revival despite the fact that, as Noël himself noted, 'it has no plot at all and remarkably little action. Its general effectiveness therefore depends on expert technique from each and every member of the cast.'

And that expert technique was precisely what it got when a National Theatre revival in 1964 spearheaded a remarkable rebirth of interest in Coward's stage work, one which he himself was wont to refer to as 'Dad's Renaissance'.

After suffering a kind of postwar eclipse in London, with the failure of a couple of big musicals (*Pacific 1860* and *Ace of Clubs*), Noël had taken up residence abroad and seemed for a while without much honour in his own country. But then, when Laurence Olivier (who had played in the original *Private Lives* in London and New York) chose to make *Hay Fever* the first work at the National Theatre by a living British dramatist, one moreover who would direct it himself, the tide abruptly turned in Coward's favour: 'the perennial shock of modernity', wrote Ronald Bryden in the *New Statesman*, 'is the amount of it which simply consists ' of old things looking different . . . who would have thought that the landmarks of the Sixties would include a Nobel prize for Sartre, a surge of historical interest in the Great War, and the emergence of Noël Coward as the grand old man of British drama? There he was one morning, flipping verbal tiddlywinks with reporters in that light, endlessly parodiable voice which sang *Mad Dogs and Englishmen* and *Mrs Worthington*. The next, there he was again, a national treasure; recipient of the Order of Merit, slightly older than the century on which he sits, his eyelids wearier than ever, hanging beside Forster and Eliot and the OM's, demonstrably the greatest living English playwright.'

Admittedly the National's *Hay Fever* had a cast which could have played any script in the world and made it look wonderful: Edith Evans, Maggie Smith, Lynn Redgrave, Derek Jacobi, Robert Stephens, Anthony Nicholls and Louise Purnell. 'I am thrilled and flattered', wrote Noël in reply to Olivier's offer, 'and frankly a little flabbergasted that the National Theatre should have had the curious perceptiveness to choose a very early play of mine and to give it a cast that could play the Albanian telephone directory.'

This was perhaps not the most obvious of Coward's plays for the National to honour: both *Private Lives* and *Design for Living* are more typical of the now time-honoured 'cocktails and laughter but what comes after' Coward myth. Yet of all his work, *Hay Fever* is the best suited to a talented company playing together and off each other in perfect harmony; it offers one tremendous star lead in Judith Bliss, but it also offers seven other roles that are very nearly as good. To have Coward himself direct was also a brilliant idea: not only did he recall the style of the early Twenties with an accuracy that could be rivalled by few other directors still in the business, but he also understood better than anyone the elliptical twin-level technique which he had first perfected, and which Harold Pinter later adapted to his own darker dramatic purpose: the technique of having a character say one thing while thinking and meaning something entirely different. In retrospect it was now possible to see this as Coward's greatest contribution to stage comedy in the Twenties: after the carefully orchestrated epigrams of Oscar Wilde, he brought to the theatre a style that was at once simpler and more spontaneous; a character in *Shadow Play*, written 11 years after *Hay Fever*, summed it all up: 'Small talk, a lot of small talk, with other thoughts going on behind.'

When Coward flew to London to start rehearsals for the National *Hay Fever*, he was met at the airport by a reporter who suggested it was rather old hat for the new company to be doing a revival like this in the mid-Sixties. Fixing him with that stare once described by Robert Benchley as 'the look of a dead albatross', Noël remarked acidly that if a comedy was good enough it would live over the centuries without becoming dated, like for instance *The School For Scandal* or *The Importance of Being Earnest*. 'Oh', said the reporter, 'and are they yours too?'

Rehearsals were not always smooth, with Dame Edith's memory a particular problem: when for several weeks she had rendered the line 'On a clear day you can see Marlow' as 'On a very clear day you can see Marlow', Noël finally stopped her from the stalls to correct the rhythm of his line: 'Edith', he commanded, 'the line is "On a clear day you can see Marlow." On a very clear day, you can see Marlowe *and* Beaumont and Fletcher.'

Since that National revival of almost a quarter of a century ago, *Hay Fever* has had two further West End returns, the first with Celia Johnson, Roland Culver, Simon Williams and Lucy Fleming in 1968, and the second with Penelope Keith and Moray Watson in 1983: 'When I tapped out this little comedy onto my typewriter so exuberantly in the year 1924', wrote Noël later, 'I would have been astonished if anyone had told me that it was destined to re-emerge fresh and blooming forty years later.'

Soon after his return from the first American visit that had given him the idea for *Hay Fever*, Noël had his first real adult West End success as a player and songwriter in a Charlot revue called *London Calling*: during its lengthy run, he found the time to write two other plays, one of which was *Fallen Angels* and the other *The Vortex*, a drama which had its origins, Coward later explained, in a chance meeting:

A friend of mine was a guards officer who had a problem mother, a lady whose lovers were men of her son's age. One evening I was in a supper club, the Garrick Galleries I think, with my friend when his mother walked in. 'Look over there' someone said, 'at that old hag with the good-looking young man in tow!' I tried to imagine what her son must have been thinking, and the incident gave me the idea for *The Vortex*.

The play made what was then for Coward the usual unsuccessful round of managers' offices until, in 1924, Norman MacDermott took it for his Everyman Theatre in Hampstead, once a drill hall, then a playhouse and now a cinema, but dedicated at that time to the off-West End discovery of new plays and playwrights. A near-melodrama which reaches its climax in a latterday adaptation of the closet scene from *Hamlet*, with an uneasy mother–son relationship further complicated by the fact that the son takes drugs and that the whole crisis erupts during a stately weekend in the country, *The Vortex* was, for its time, a very strong play indeed and attracted the tabloid label 'dustbin drama' exactly 50 years before anyone thought of applying it to John Osborne and *Look Back in Anger*.

But the story of its first production has most of the qualities of those backstage sagas perpetrated by Hollywood in the 1930s: the theatre itself was on the verge of bankruptcy, and only saved by Noël himself persuading the novelist Michael Arlen to make them a gift of £250. Then the original leading lady, Kate Cutler, announced a week away from the first night that the part of the mother (though written by Noël with her in mind) was in fact unsuitable and that she would be leaving the cast.

In some desperation, Coward approached Lilian Braithwaite, a tall, dark grande dame of the theatre accustomed to presiding over graceful tea-party scenes in light comedies at the Haymarket. Seeing the challenge of a totally different and vastly more neurotic role, she agreed at once to step into the breach, only then to find the Lord Chamberlain threatening to deny the play a licence for performance since its theme was 'far too unpleasant', though whether this referred to the mother's nymphomania, the son's drug-addiction or his passionate devotion to his mother remained unclear. In the event, on the morning of the first night, Noël (who was himself playing the son and co-directing with MacDermott) repaired to St James's Palace and convinced the

Lord Chamberlain that so far from being unpleasant, his play was in fact a moral tract of the highest order about the evils of drugs.

Beyond doubt, the play came as a severe shock to its Hampstead audience: here, from a writer of hitherto minor light comedies, was a play about drug-addiction at a time when alcoholism was still barely mentioned on the stage, and the reviews were both impressed and stunned as Noël recalled: 'Practically all of my notices for this play were generously adulatory, though most of them were concerned that I should choose such an "unpleasant" subject and such "decadent" types. I have come to the conclusion that an "unpleasant" subject is something that everybody knows about, but shrinks from the belief that other people know about it too ... The minor characters in *The Vortex* drink cocktails, employ superlatives, and sometimes turn on the gramophone ... Florence takes lovers occasionally and Nicky takes drugs very occasionally ... I consider neither of these vices are any more unpleasant than murder or seduction, both of which have been a standing tradition in the English theatre for many years.'

Yet, in fact, the first night had been nothing short of a triumph for Noël, who as author, star and co-director had still been forced to spend most of the afternoon on his hands and knees with his designer Gladys Calthrop and the Hampstead stage manager finishing off the set; he then got away with a nerve-strung, histrionic *tour de force* that in later weeks he was able to refine and discipline into a more subdued but perhaps no more effective reading of the part. Until then, by virtue of being his own director, he had not found time to do much about his acting, but the tension of his performance on opening night was increased by the fact that in sweeping a collection of bottles from a dressing-room table in the last act he managed to cut his wrist quite badly, which then bled effectively throughout his curtain speech. Blood, like children and dogs, can usually be relied on as an applause-raiser, though on this occasion the play would unquestionably have survived without it.

A fashionable audience led by the Mountbattens and what *The Tatler* called 'all the regular theatrical enthusiasts of *le beau monde*' made the then unusual trek to Hampstead on the strength of

Noël's light-comedy reputation, and their reaction was much akin to that which greeted Osborne at the Court half a century later: now, and in cold print, Nicky's outburst against his mother and the depraved world around her may seem a little over the top: but on stage in 1924, without even a backward glance at Pinero, there's no doubt that it came over as very startling indeed. 'If I had written that,' said Michael Arlen going backstage after the opening, 'I should have been so very proud.'

Most critics acknowledged a kind of fashionable depravity in Nicky's drug-taking and the social gossip about the weekend house-party set to whose private lives it was widely believed that Noël already belonged: but it was left to St John Ervine among the original reviewers to realise that on the contrary *The Vortex* is a highly moral tract, dedicated to the virtues of old-fashioned hard work and clean living, and to standards by which most of the characters are tried and found wanting. Like so much of Coward's later work, right through *Post Mortem* to his last *Suite in Three Keys*, *The Vortex* is concerned with standards – with what is done and not done in the best moral code of values. One is made constantly aware here of the dignities of life and of how these are being abused: 'It doesn't matter about death', Nicky tells his mother at the end of Act Three, 'but it matters terribly about life' and, by implication, the way we choose to live it.

Reviews that were simultaneously shocked and enthusiastic, plus a public titillated by the murmur of something faintly immoral, assured for *The Vortex* a sold-out Hampstead season and a rapid transfer to the West End: the feeling was that the boy wonder, 'destiny's tot' as Woollcott was later to call him, had come up with something solid and lasting which would ensure him success as a dramatist rather more powerfully than the brittle and precarious social hits that had gone before. Eight managers put in bids for the transfer, and the one that won opened it at the Royalty in December 1924 at the start of a run lasting more than two hundred performances there and at other West End homes.

Superficially, the resemblance between Noël and Nicky Lancaster was too great for him ever to escape the 'well groomed, witty and decadent' label of the neurotic misfit that he had created for his play, but to have argued with all that publicity would have been futile and Noël was astute enough to realise that gossip columnists might find the truth about his hard-working, puritan ethic a lot less exciting. At a time when the advertising industry was still in its infancy, *The Vortex* was an early example of the image becoming the reality, and on Coward's home life its effect was electric:

> With this success came many pleasurable trappings. A car. New suits. Silk shirts. An extravagant amount of pyjamas and dressing gowns, and a still more extravagant amount of publicity. I was photographed, and interviewed, and photographed again. In the street. In the park. In my dressing room. At my piano. With my dear old mother, without my dear old mother and on one occasion sitting up in an over-elaborate bed looking like a heavily doped Chinese Illusionist. This last photograph, I believe, did me a good deal of harm. People glancing at it concluded at once, and with a certain justification, that I was undoubtedly a weedy sensualist in the last stages of physical and moral disintegration, and that they had better hurry off to see me in my play before my inevitable demise placed that faintly macabre pleasure beyond their reach. This attitude, while temporarily very good for business, became irritating after a time and for many years I was seldom mentioned in the press without allusions to 'cocktails', 'postwar hysteria' and 'decadence.'

The Royalty opening of *The Vortex* was on Noël's 25th birthday, and he made a restrained curtain speech hoping that the West End would enjoy the play as much as had audiences up in Hampstead. This they did, though the *Daily Mail* was still writing of 'a dustbin of a play', and Agate after a good deal of praise ended his *Sunday Times* review 'the third act is too long, there is too much piano playing in the second, and ladies do not exhale cigarette smoke through their noses'. Still, the majority view was that of Ivor Brown who wrote that 'as actor and author Coward drives at reality'.

The play then became something of a *cause célèbre* when Sir Gerald du Maurier, at that time the effective leader of the acting profession in Britain, wrote a scathing attack on the immorality of modern drama in general and *The Vortex* in particular. Coward was immediately defended in print by Arnold Bennett and Edward Knoblock, but by now there was little doubt that the play had dragged the London theatre from Edwardian gentility or Barriesque whimsy towards the acid cynicism of social commentary for the first time since Wilde. Hannen Swaffer still deprecated 'the most decadent play of our time' while another critic noted ruefully that 'the fault, dear Noël, lies not in our Ma's but in ourselves that we are slaves to dope'.

*The Vortex* was, beyond all others, the play which typified the less attractive social characteristics of London and the mid-20's: it also achieved a footnote in theatre history as the first major production in which the cast took curtain calls only at the end of the play and not between each act as hitherto. Eventually Noël was to take his drama on to Broadway and a long American tour ('success took me to her bosom like a maternal boa constrictor') and in 1927 it was made into a silent film by Ivor Novello and Frances Doble, while Dirk Bogarde starred in a major 1952 stage revival.

During its original London run, Coward was replaced by his understudy (a young John Gielgud) so that he might oversee two other productions of his then going into rehearsal; one was the revue *On with the Dance*, the other a comedy that he had written in 1923 about two respectable middle-class married women getting progressively drunker while they await the return of an old and shared French lover. Originally written for, and rejected by, Gladys Cooper and Madge Titheradge, *Fallen Angels* had (like *Hay Fever*) lain idle until a rash of other Coward successes around 1925 suddenly brought it to the forefront of attention again. As a play it depends totally on two star performances, and the second act is almost exclusively an alcoholic duologue for them, while the first and third acts seem almost to have been tacked on in order to expand what is essentially a revue-sketch idea into a full-length play.

Edna Best and Margaret Bannerman were now cast for the leading roles, but barely a week before the first night Miss Bannerman gave way to a nervous breakdown and was replaced by the exotic Tallulah Bankhead who had herself just been dismissed by Maugham from his *Rain* in time to give Noël yet another huge commercial success. In the climate of almost hysterical morality engendered by the du Maurier row over *The Vortex*, first night reviews dismissed *Fallen Angels* as 'degenerate', 'vile', 'obscene', 'shocking' and 'nauseating', largely because the on-stage admission that both Jane and Julia have had a pre-marital affair with the same man was reckoned conclusive proof that Noël had this time ventured too far into the realms of stage degradation.

The shock-horror reaction of the press naturally ensured box office queues overnight, though in the following *Sunday Times* Agate provided a rather less heated appraisal of Coward at this stage in his career: 'He is a very young playwright of quite extraordinary gifts who at the moment can no more be trusted with his talent for playwriting than a schoolboy can be trusted who has stolen a piece of chalk and encounters a providentially blank wall ... he is too rapid, his tongue is too constantly in his cheek, and the circle of his characters is not wide enough.'

In the *Evening Standard* a few days later, Noël gleefully concurred: 'I really must say I have a frightfully depraved mind. I am never out of opium dens, cocaine dens and other evil places. My mind is a mass of corruption.'

Noël was also, as usual, his own best critic: 'When *Fallen Angels* was first produced at the Globe Theatre, London, in the Spring of 1925 it was described by a large section of the press as amoral, disgusting, vulgar, and an insult to British womanhood. It was, of course, none of these things. They might have said it was extremely slight and needed a stronger last act; they might, with equal truth and more kindness, have said that it had an amusing situation, some very funny lines, two excellent parts for two good actresses, and was vastly entertaining to the public ... I cannot honestly regard it as one of my very best comedies, but it is gay and light-hearted, and British womanhood has been cheerfully insulted by it on various occasions for almost a quarter of a century.'

Box office takings remained buoyant right through to the last night of the run, by which time a Mrs Hornibrook of the London Council for the Promotion of Public Morality was still in the stalls to voice her protest to the sordidness of the whole affair. An orchestra in the pit drowned out her shouting with a brisk rendering of 'I Want to Be Happy', though not before Mrs Hornibrook had given it as her opinion that the works of Eugene O'Neill were also deplorable and unsuitable for London audiences.

Noël was still denying that he had written the play in order to be daring or shocking ('neither of these exceedingly second-rate ambitions ever occurred to me') and the play went on to provide a considerable income for him around the world over the next forty years, though he was rather less than happy with the best-known of its London revivals in 1949. This was conceived as a vehicle for the two Hermiones (Gingold and Baddeley), then at the height of their revue fame, both of whom treated a tricky period piece as a kind of parody much to the author's fury:

'I have never yet in my long experience seen a more vulgar, silly, unfunny, disgraceful performance . . . Gingold at moments showed signs that she could be funny. Baddeley was disgusting. Afterwards I told them exactly what I thought'. Nevertheless the revival achieved over three hundred performances, and was followed in 1967 by another starring Joan Greenwood and Constance Cummings. *Fallen Angels* has never been filmed, nor has it achieved in America its frequent British and European success despite a number of productions there over the years.

For Noël, the abiding memory was of the furore the play first caused, one which overshadowed even that of *The Vortex*:

It had one disagreeable effect, which was to unleash on me a mass of insulting letters from all over the country. This was the first time I had ever experienced such a strange pathological avalanche, and I was quite startled. In the years that followed, of course, I have become completely accustomed to anonymous letters dropping into the letter box. They have come in their hundreds, crammed with abuse and frequently embellished with pornographic drawings. Then I was still ingenuous enough to be amazed to think that there were so many people in the world with so much time to waste.

The fourth and last play in this first volume, *Easy Virtue*, remains the least familiar and most seldom revived of the quartet: written in 1923, and first staged in New York two years later, then seen in London in 1926 and made into a silent film by Hitchcock a year after that, its origins were unusual, in that Noël was not here writing for any particular player, or to fulfil any very definite assignment. He merely found himself one day, as he himself later noted, 'in a mood of nostalgic regret' at the decline of social and theatrical conventions which had led, in the period from the 1880's to the beginning of World War One, to such plays as *The Second Mrs Tanqueray*, *The Notorious Mrs Ebbsmith* and *Lady Frederick*. What the writers of these plays had in common, and derived essentially from Oscar Wilde, was an interest in drawing-room dramas which would deal with the psychological and social problems of the upper-middle classes, and specifically of wealthy, well bred, articulate 'women with a past'.

Noël, as he said, 'worked hard on the play and thought it excellent. I fully realised its similarity of theme to *The Second Mrs Tanqueray*, but its construction and characterisation on the whole seemed to be more mature and balanced than anything I had written to date'.

What was happening in the meantime was his quadruple 1924/25 success with *The Vortex*, *Hay Fever*, *Fallen Angels* and the Cochran revue *On with the Dance*, all of which played simultaneously in the same West End season. Even so, it was decided to launch *Easy Virtue* in America during the time that Noël was there playing in *The Vortex*. Basil Dean directed a cast headed (as later in London) by Jane Cowl, with whom the author was never happy. 'Her performance was smooth and touching, but she always played the big scene at the end of the second act too dramatically, thereby jerking the play too far back into Pineroism ... my object in writing it had been primarily to adapt a story intrinsically Pinero in theme and structure to present-day behaviour; to compare the declassée women of the 1920s with the more flamboyant demi-mondaine of the 1890s.' Nevertheless, Miss Cowl scored a considerable personal success on both sides of the Atlantic. When, however, the play arrived in Manchester on a pre-London tour during the May of 1926, the local Watch Committee ruled the title altogether too scandalous to use on any posters; it was therefore solemnly billed as 'a new play in three acts by Noël Coward', while at the cinema next door, not subject to Watch Committee control or censorship, posters were shamelessly advertising *Flames of Passion*.

The London opening was on June 9, 1926 at the Duke of York's, where Miss Cowl took ecstatic curtain calls amid an orgy of flowers; critics next morning were however divided about the value of the piece. The *Daily Telegraph* thought it 'a good piece of theatrical mechanism, unworthy of Mr Coward's promise' and the *Daily Express* offered their usual opinion that it was 'a play from an author not yet grown up'. Box-office business remained good throughout that summer and autumn however, much helped by a royal visit from King George V and Queen Mary.

After its respectable runs in London and New York, *Easy Virtue* all but disappeared for over 60 years, then to reappear in a triumphant London revival in 1988 at the King's Head, transferring to the Garrick, with a cast headed by Jane How under the direction of Tim Luscombe.

*Easy Virtue* is essentially *The Second Mrs Tanqueray* brought up to date, but it has never really achieved the afterlife of its forerunners and remains of interest chiefly as Noël's elegant, laconic tribute to a lost world of drawing-room dramas. What is intriguing about the play, apart from the light it throws on Coward as a craftsman working from the models of his immediate theatrical and social past, is the way it mocks the conventions, prejudices and complacencies of its period while remaining well inside the drawing-room barricades. No writer of Noël's generation ever went more directly to the jugular of that moralistic, tight-lipped but fundamentally hypocritical Twenties society.

In the last decade, there have been no other notable revivals of *Easy Virtue* or *Fallen Angels*, though the Coward Centenary in 1999 may change all that; in the meantime *Hay Fever* has long been planned as a film and has turned up in frequent regional-repertory (and indeed one Broadway) revival, while *The Vortex* was radically restaged by Philip Prowse, first for the Glasgow Citizens and then the Garrick Theatre in 1989. The first truly contemporary play of its era, dealing with drugs and nympho-mania and perhaps even sub-textual homosexuality, *The Vortex* dragged the West End into the twentieth century; not since Wilde's *The Importance of Being Ernest* 30 years earlier had any play enjoyed so marked an effect on the social life of London, and 65 years further down the line Prowse's hothouse production starred Maria Aitken as the social-butterfly mother, Rupert Everett as the drug-addicted son and Prowse's own amazing settings, characterised by full-length mirrors and the sort of interior décor that made Marie Antoinette's Versailles look like a triumph of quiet good taste. This production focused strongly on the druggy aspects of the play, with Everett carefully injecting himself in the arm; but it confirmed Aitken as one of the greatest contemporary Coward players on either side of the Atlantic, and put the play back in the gossip columns it first occupied in the mid-1920s. It was electrifying in its sheer dramatic intensity, and almost operatic in its use of naked emotion.

SHERIDAN MORLEY
1998

1899　16 December, Noël Pierce Coward born in Teddington, Middlesex, eldest surviving son of Arthur Coward, piano salesman and Violet (*née* Veitch). A 'brazen, odious little prodigy', his early circumstances were of refined suburban poverty.

1907　First public appearances in school and community concerts.

1908　Family moved to Battersea and took in lodgers.

1911　First professional appearance as Prince Mussel in *The Goldfish*, produced by Lila Field at the Little Theatre, and revived in same year at Crystal Palace and Royal Court Theatre. Cannard, the page-boy, in *The Great Name* at the Prince of Wales Theatre, and William in *Where the Rainbow Ends* with Charles Hawtrey's Company at the Savoy Theatre.

1912　Directed *The Daisy Chain* and stage-managed *The Prince's Bride* at Savoy in series of matinees featuring the work of the children of the *Rainbow* cast. Mushroom in *An Autumn Idyll*, ballet, Savoy.

1913　An angel (Gertrude Lawrence was another) in Basil Dean's production of *Hannele*. Slightly in *Peter Pan*, Duke of York's.

1914　Toured in *Peter Pan*. Collaborated with fellow performer Esmé Wynne on songs, sketches, and short stories – 'beastly little whimsies'.

1915　Admitted to sanatorium for tuberculosis.

1916　Five-month tour as Charley in *Charley's Aunt*. Walk-on in *The Best of Luck*, Drury Lane. Wrote first full-length song, 'Forbidden Fruit'. Basil Pycroft in *The Light Blues*, produced by Robert Courtneidge, with daughter Cicely also in cast, Shaftesbury. Short spell as dancer at Elysée Restaurant (subsequently the Café de Paris). Jack Morrison in *The Happy Family*, Prince of Wales.

1917　'Boy pushing barrow' in D.W. Griffith's film *Hearts of the World*. Co-author with Esmé Wynne of one-acter *Ida Collaborates*, Theatre Royal, Aldershot. Ripley Guildford in *The Saving Grace*, with Charles Hawtrey, 'who . . . taught me many points of comedy acting', Garrick. Family moved to Pimlico and re-opened boarding house.

1918 Called-up for army. Medical discharge after nine months. Wrote unpublished novels *Cats and Dogs* (loosely based on Shaw's *You Never Can Tell*) and the unfinished *Cherry Pan* ('dealing in a whimsical vein with the adventures of a daughter of Pan'), and lyrics for Darewski and Joel, including 'When You Come Home on Leave' and 'Peter Pan'. Also composed 'Tamarisk Town'. Sold short stories to magazines. Wrote plays *The Rat Trap*, *The Last Trick* (unproduced) and *The Impossible Wife* (unproduced). Courtenay Borner in *Scandal*, Strand. *Woman and Whiskey* (co-author Esmé Wynne) produced at Wimbledon Theatre.

1919 Ralph in *The Knight of the Burning Pestle*, Birmingham. Repertory, played with 'a stubborn Mayfair distinction' demonstrating a 'total lack of understanding of the play'. Collaborated on *Crissa*, an opera, with Esmé Wynne and Max Darwski (unproduced). Wrote *I'll Leave It to You*.

1920 Bobbie Dermott in *I'll Leave It to You*, New Theatre. Wrote play *Barriers Down* (unproduced). *I'll Leave It to You* published, London.

1921 On holiday in Alassio, met Gladys Calthrop for the first time. Clay Collins in American farce *Polly with a Past*: during the run 'songs, sketches, and plays were bursting out of me'. Wrote *The Young Idea*, *Sirocco*, and *The Better Half*. First visit to New York, and sold parts of *A Withered Nosegay* to *Vanity Fair* and short-story adaptation of *I'll Leave It to You* to *Metropolitan*. House-guest of Laurette Taylor and Hartley Manners, whose family rows inspired the Bliss household in *Hay Fever*.

1922 *Bottles and Bones* (sketch) produced in benefit for Newspaper Press Fund, Drury Lane. *The Better Half* produced in 'grand guignol' season, Little Theatre. Started work on songs and sketches for *London Calling!* Adapted Louise Verneuil's *Pour avoir Adrienne* (unproduced). Wrote *The Queen Was in the Parlour* and *Mild Oats*.

1923 Sholto Brent in *The Young Idea*, Savoy. Juvenile lead in *London Calling!* Wrote *Weatherwise*, *Fallen Angels*, and *The Vortex*.

1924 Wrote *Hay Fever* (which Marie Tempest at first refused to do, feeling it was 'too light and plotless and generally lacking in action') and *Easy Virtue*. Nicky Lancaster in *The Vortex*, produced at Everyman by Norman MacDermott.

1925 Established as a social and theatrical celebrity. Wrote *On with the Dance* with London opening in spring followed by *Fallen*

*Angels* and *Hay Fever*. *Hay Fever* and *Easy Virtue* produced, New York. Wrote silent screen titles for Gainsborough Films.

1926 Toured USA in *The Vortex*. Wrote *This Was a Man*, refused a licence by Lord Chamberlain but produced in New York (1926), Berlin (1927), and Paris (1928). *Easy Virtue*, *The Queen Was in the Parlour*, and *The Rat Trap* produced, London. Played Lewis Dodd in *The Constant Nymph*, directed by Basil Dean. Wrote *Semi-Monde* and *The Marquise*. Bought Goldenhurst Farm, Kent, as country home. Sailed for Hong Kong on holiday but trip broken in Honolulu by nervous breakdown.

1927 *The Marquise* opened in London while Coward was still in Hawaii, and *The Marquise* and *Fallen Angels* produced, New York. Finished writing *Home Chat*. *Sirocco* revised after discussions with Basil Dean and produced, London.

1928 Clark Storey in Behrman's *The Second Man*, directed by Dean. Gainsborough Films productions of *The Queen Was in the Parlour*, *The Vortex* (starring Ivor Novello), and *Easy Virtue* (directed by Alfred Hitchcock) released – but only the latter, freely adapted, a success. *This Year of Grace!* produced, London, and with Coward directing and in cast, New York. Made first recording, featuring numbers from this show. Wrote *Concerto* for Gainsborough Films, intended for Ivor Novello, but never produced. Started writing *Bitter-Sweet*.

1929 Played in *This Year of Grace!* (USA) until spring. Directed *Bitter-Sweet*, London and New York. Set off on travelling holiday in Far East.

1930 On travels wrote *Private Lives* (1929) and song 'Mad Dogs and Englishmen', the latter on the road from Hanoi to Saigon. In Singapore joined the Quaints, company of strolling English players, as Stanhope for three performances of *Journey's End*. On voyage home wrote *Post-Mortem*, which was 'similar to my performance as Stanhope: confused, under-rehearsed and hysterical'. Directed and played Elyot Chase in *Private Lives*, London, and Fred in *Some Other Private Lives*. Started writing *Cavalcade* and unfinished novel *Julian Kane*.

1931 Elyot Chase in New York production of *Private Lives*. Directed *Cavalcade*, London. Film of *Private Lives* produced by MGM. Set off on trip to South America.

1932 On travels wrote *Design for Living* (hearing that Alfred Lung and Lynn Fontanne finally free to work with him) and material for new revue including songs 'Mad about the Boy', 'Children of the Ritz' and 'The Party's Over Now'. Produced in London as

*Words and Music*, with book, music, and lyrics exclusively by Coward and directed by him. The short-lived Noël Coward Company, independent company which enjoyed his support, toured UK with *Private Lives*, *Hay Fever*, *Fallen Angels*, and *The Vortex*.

1933    Directed *Design for Living*, New York, and played Leo. Films of *Cavalcade*, *To-Night Is Ours* (remake of *The Queen Was in the Parlour*), and *Bitter-Sweet* released. Directed London revival of *Hay Fever*. Wrote *Conversation Piece* as vehicle for Yvonne Printemps, and hit song 'Mrs Worthington'.

1934    Directed *Conversation Piece* in London and played Paul. Cut links with C. B. Cochran and formed own management in partnership with John C. Wilson. Appointed President of the Actors' Orphanage, in which he invested great personal commitment until resignation in 1956. Directed Kaufman and Ferber's *Theatre Royal*, Lyric, and Behrman's *Biography*, Globe. Film of *Design for Living* released, London. *Conversation Piece* opened, New York. Started writing autobiography, *Present Indicative*. Wrote *Point Valaine*.

1935    Directed *Point Valaine*, New York. Played lead in film *The Scoundrel* (Astoria Studios, New York). Wrote *To-Night at 8.30*.

1936    Directed and played in *To-Night at 8.30*, London and New York. Directed *Mademoiselle* by Jacques Deval, Wyndham's.

1937    Played in *To-Night at 8.30*, New York, until second breakdown in health in March. Directed (and subsequently disowned) Gerald Savory's *George and Margaret*, New York. Wrote *Operette*, with hit song 'The Stately Homes of England'. *Present Indicative* published, London and New York.

1938    Directed *Operette*, London. *Words and Music* revised for American production as *Set to Music*. Appointed adviser to newly-formed Royal Naval Film Corporation.

1939    Directed New York production of *Set to Music*. Visited Soviet Union and Scandinavia. Wrote *Present Laughter* and *This Happy Breed*: rehearsals stopped by declaration of war. Wrote for revue *All Clear*, London. Appointed to head Bureau of Propaganda in Paris, to liaise with French Ministry of Information, headed by Jean Giraudoux and André Maurois. This posting prompted speculative attacks in the press, prevented by wartime secrecy from getting a clear statement of the exact nature of his work (in fact unexceptional and routine). Troop concert in Arras with Maurice Chevalier. *To Step Aside* (short story collection) published.

1940    Increasingly 'oppressed and irritated by the Paris routine'. Visits USA to report on American isolationism and attitudes to war in Europe. Return to Paris prevented by German invasion. Returned to USA to do propaganda work for Ministry of Information. Propaganda tour of Australia and New Zealand, and fund-raising for war charities. Wrote play *Time Remembered* (unproduced).

1941    Mounting press attacks in England because of time spent allegedly avoiding danger and discomfort of Home Front. Wrote *Blithe Spirit*, produced in London (with Coward directing) and New York. MGM film of *Bitter-Sweet* (which Coward found 'vulgar' and 'lacking in taste') released, London. Wrote screenplay for *In Which We Serve*, based on the sinking of HMS Kelly. Wrote songs including 'London Pride', 'Could You Please Oblige Us with a Bren Gun?', and 'Imagine the Duchess's Feelings'.

1942    Produced and co-directed (with David Lean) *In Which We Serve*, and appeared as Captain Kinross (Coward considered the film 'an accurate and sincere tribute to the Royal Navy'). Played in countrywide tour of *Blithe Spirit*, *Present Laughter*, and *This Happy Breed*, and gave hospital and factory concerts. MGM film of *We Were Dancing* released.

1943    Played Garry Essendine in London production of *Present Laughter* and Frank Gibbons in *This Happy Breed*. Produced *This Happy Breed* for Two Cities Films. Wrote 'Don't Let's Be Beastly to the Germans', first sung on BBC Radio (then banned on grounds of lines 'that Geobbels might twist'). Four-month tour of Middle East to entertain troops.

1944    February–September, toured South Africa, Burma, India, and Ceylon. Troop concerts in France and 'Stage Door Canteen Concert' in London. Screenplay of *Still Life*, as *Brief Encounter*. *Middle East Diary*, an account of his 1943 tour, published, London and New York – where a reference to 'mournful little boys from Brooklyn' inspired formation of a lobby for the 'Prevention of Noël Coward Re-entering America'.

1945    *Sigh No More*, with hit song 'Matelot', completed and produced, London. Started work on *Pacific 1860*. Film of *Brief Encounter* released.

1946    Started writing 'Peace in Our Time'. Directed *Pacific 1860*, London.

1947    Gary Essendine in London revival of *Present Laughter*. Supervised production of 'Peace in Our Time'. *Point Valaine* produced,

London. Directed American revival of *To-Night at 8.30*. Wrote *Long Island Sound* (unproduced).

1948  Replaced Graham Payn briefly in American tour of *To-Night at 8.30*, his last stage appearance with Gertrude Lawrence. Wrote screenplay for Gainsborough film of *The Astonished Heart*. Max Aramont in *Joyeux Chagrins* (French production of *Present Laughter*). Built house at Blue Harbour, Jamaica.

1949  Christian Faber in film of *The Astonished Heart*. Wrote *Ace of Clubs* and *Home and Colonial* (produced as *Island Fling* in USA and *South Sea Bubble* in UK).

1950  Directed *Ace of Clubs*, London. Wrote *Star Quality* (short stories) and *Relative Values*.

1951  Deaths of Ivor Novello and C. B. Cochran. Paintings included in charity exhibition in London. Wrote *Quadrille*. One-night concert at Theatre Royal, Brighton, followed by season at Café de Paris, London, and beginning of new career as leading cabaret entertainer. Directed *Relative Values*, London, which restored his reputation as a playwright after run of post-war flops. *Island Fling* produced, USA.

1952  Charity cabaret with Mary Martin at Café de Paris for Actors' Orphanage. June cabaret season at Café de Paris. Directed *Quadrille*, London. 'Red Peppers', *Fumed Oak*, and *Ways and Means* (from *To-Night at 8.30*) filmed as *Meet Me To-Night*. September, death of Gertrude Lawrence: 'no one I have ever known, however brilliant . . . has contributed quite what she contributed to my work'.

1953  Completed second volume of autobiography, *Future Indefinite*. King Magnus in Shaw's *The Apple Cart*. Cabaret at Café de Paris, again 'a triumphant success'. Wrote *After the Ball*.

1954  *After the Ball* produced, UK. July, mother died. September, cabaret season at Café de Paris. November, Royal Command Performance, London Palladium. Wrote *Nude With Violin*.

1955  June, opened in cabaret for season at Desert Inn, Las Vegas, and enjoyed 'one of the most sensational successes of my career'. Played Hesketh-Baggott in film of *Around the World in Eighty Days*, for which he wrote own dialogue. October, directed and appeared with Mary Martin in TV spectacular *Together with Music* for CBS, New York. Revised *South Sea Bubble*.

1956  Charles Condomine in television production of *Blithe Spirit*, for CBS, Hollywood. For tax reasons took up Bermuda residency. Resigned from presidency of the Actors' Orphanage. *South Sea*

*Bubble* produced, London. Directed and played part of Frank Gibbons in television production of *This Happy Breed* for CBS, New York. Co-directed *Nude With Violin* with John Gielgud (Eire and UK), opening to press attacks on Coward's decision to live abroad. Wrote play *Volcano* (unproduced).

1957 Directed and played Sebastien in *Nude With Violin*, New York. *Nude With Violin* published, London.

1958 Played Gary Essendine in *Present Laughter* alternating with *Nude With Violin* on US West Coast tour. Wrote ballet *London Morning* for London Festival Ballet. Wrote *Look After Lulu!*

1959 *Look After Lulu!* produced, New York, and by English Stage Company at Royal Court, London. Film roles of Hawthorne in *Our Man in Havana* and ex-King of Anatolia in *Surprise Package*. *London Morning* produced by London Festival Ballet. Sold home in Bermuda and took up Swiss residency. Wrote *Waiting in the Wings*.

1960 *Waiting in the Wings* produced, Eire and UK. *Pomp and Circumstance* (novel) published, London and New York.

1961 Alec Harvey in television production of *Brief Encounter* for NBC, USA. Directed American production of *Sail Away*. *Waiting in the Wings* published, New York.

1962 Wrote music and lyrics for *The Girl Who Came to Supper* (adaptation of Rattigan's *The Sleeping Prince*, previously filmed as *The Prince and the Showgirl*). *Sail Away* produced, UK.

1963 *The Girl Who Came to Supper* produced, USA. Revival of *Private Lives* at Hampstead signals renewal of interest in his work.

1964 'Supervised' production of *High Spirits*, musical adaptation of *Blithe Spirit*, Savoy. Introduced Granada TV's 'A Choice of Coward' series, which included *Present Laughter*, *Blithe Spirit*, *The Vortex*, and *Design for Living*. Directed *Hay Fever* for National Theatre, first living playwright to direct his own work there. *Pretty Polly Barlow* (short story collection) published.

1965 Played the landlord in film, *Bunny Lake is Missing*. Wrote *Suite in Three Keys*. Badly weakened by attack of amoebic dysentry contracted in Seychelles.

1966 Played in *Suite in Three Keys*, London, which taxed his health further. Started adapting his short story *Star Quality* for the stage.

1967 Caesar in TV musical version of *Androcles and the Lion* (score by Richard Rodgers), New York. Witch of Capri in film *Boom*, adaptation of Tennessee Williams's play *The Milk Train Doesn't*

*Stop Here Any More*. Lorn Loraine, Coward's manager, and friend for many years, died, London. Worked on new volume of autobiography, *Past Conditional*. *Bon Voyage* (short story collection) published.

1968   Played Mr Bridger, the criminal mastermind, in *The Italian Job*.

1970   Awarded knighthood in New Year's Honours List.

1971   Tony Award, USA, for Distinguished Achievement in the Theatre.

1973   26 March, died peacefully at his home in Blue Harbour, Jamaica. Buried on Firefly Hill.

# HAY FEVER

## Characters

JUDITH BLISS            RICHARD GREATHAM
DAVID BLISS             JACKIE CORYTON
SOREL BLISS             SANDY TYRELL
SIMON BLISS             CLARA
MYRA ARUNDEL

---

ACT I
*Saturday afternoon*

ACT II
*Saturday evening*

ACT III
*Sunday morning*

*The action of the play takes place in the Hall of the Blisses' house at Cookham in June.*

# ACT I

SCENE: *The Hall of* DAVID BLISS's *house is very comfortable and extremely untidy. There are several of* SIMON's *cartoons scattered about the walls, masses of highly-coloured American and classical music strewn about the piano, and comfortable furniture. A staircase ascends to a small balcony leading to the bedrooms,* DAVID's *study and* SIMON's *room. There is a door leading to the library down L. A service door above it under the stairs. There are french windows at back and front door on the R.*

*When the curtain rises it is about three o'clock on a Saturday afternoon in June.*

SIMON, *in an extremely dirty tennis shirt and baggy grey flannel trousers, is kneeling in the middle of the floor, drawing on cartridge paper, of which there are two pieces by him.*

SOREL, *more neatly dressed, is stretched on L. end of the sofa, reading a very violently-bound volume of poems which have been sent to her by an aspiring friend.*

SOREL: Listen to this, Simon. (*She reads.*)
'Love's a Trollop stained with wine,
Clawing at the breasts of Adolescence,
Nuzzling, tearing, shrieking, beating—
God, why were we fashioned so!'

    *She laughs.*

SIMON (*looking up from his drawing*): The poor girl's potty!

SOREL: I wish she hadn't sent me the beastly book. I must say something nice about it.

SIMON: The binding's very dashing.

SOREL: She used to be such fun before she married that gloomy little man.

SIMON: She was always a fierce poseuse. It's so silly of people to try and cultivate the artistic temperament. *Au fond* she's just a normal, bouncing Englishwoman.

3

SOREL: You didn't shave this morning.

SIMON: I know I didn't, but I'm going to in a minute, when I've finished this. (*Pointing to drawing.*)

SOREL: I sometimes wish *we* were more normal and bouncing, Simon.

SIMON: Why? (*Starts to draw again.*)

SOREL: I should like to be a fresh, open-air girl with a passion for games.

SIMON: Thank God you're not.

SOREL: It would be so soothing.

SIMON: Not in this house.

SOREL: Where's mother?

SIMON: In the garden, practising.

SOREL: Practising?

SIMON (*stops drawing and looks at* SOREL): She's learning the names of the flowers by heart.

SOREL: What's she up to?

SIMON: I don't know. (*Looks down at drawing.*) Damn! That's crooked.

SOREL: I *always* distrust her when she becomes the Squire's lady.

SIMON: So do I. (*Starts drawing again.*)

SOREL: She's been at it hard all day – she tapped the barometer this morning.

SIMON: She's probably got a plan about impressing somebody.

SOREL (*taking a cigarette from table behind sofa*): I wonder who.

SIMON: Some dreary, infatuated young man will appear soon, I expect.

SOREL: Not to-day? (*Lights cigarette.*) You don't think she's asked anyone down to-day, do you?

SIMON (*stops drawing and looks up*): I don't know. Has father noticed anything?

SOREL: No; he's too immersed in work.

SIMON: Perhaps Clara will know.

SOREL: Yell for her.

SIMON (*rises and goes up C., calling off door below stairs*): Clara! Clara! . . .

SOREL (*moves to R. end of sofa*): Oh, Simon, I *do* hope she hasn't asked anyone down to-day.

SIMON (*coming down to R. end of sofa*)   Why? Have you?

SOREL: Yes.

SIMON (*crossly*): Why on earth didn't you tell me?

SOREL: I didn't think you'd care one way or another.

SIMON: Who is it?

SOREL: Richard Greatham.

SIMON (*goes back to drawing*): How exciting! I've never heard of him.

SOREL: I shouldn't flaunt your ignorance if I were you – it makes you look silly.

SIMON (*rising and picking up one sheet of cartridge paper and pencil*): Well, that's done. (*He rolls up the cartridge paper.*)

SOREL: Everybody's heard of Richard Greatham.

SIMON (*amiably*): How lovely for them! (*Going to piano.*)

SOREL: He's a frightfully well-known diplomatist – I met him at the Mainwarings' dance.

SIMON: He'll need all his diplomacy here. (*Puts pencil on piano.*)

SOREL: I warned him not to expect good manners, but I hope you'll be as pleasant to him as you can.

SIMON (*gently – moves to C.*): I've never met any diplomatists, Sorel, but as a class I'm extremely prejudiced against them. They're so suave and polished and debonair.

SOREL: You could be a little more polished without losing caste.

SIMON (*moves to* SOREL): Will he have the papers with him?

SOREL: What papers?

SIMON (*vaguely*): Oh, any papers. (*Goes up C. and puts paper on chair.*)

SOREL: I wish you'd confine your biting irony to your caricatures, Simon.

SIMON (*coming down to* SOREL): And I wish you'd confine your girlish infatuations to London, and not force them on your defenceless family.

SOREL: I shall keep him out of your way as much as possible.

SIMON: Do, darling. (*Goes to piano and lights cigarette.*)

> Enter CLARA *from door below stairs. She is a hot, round, untidy little woman. She stands L. by door.*

(*sits on form by piano*) Clara, has mother asked anyone down this week-end?

5

CLARA: I don't know, dear. There isn't much food in the house, and Amy's got toothache.

SOREL: I've got some oil of cloves somewhere.

CLARA: She tried that, but it only burnt her tongue. The poor girl's been writhing about in the scullery like one o'clock.

SOREL: You haven't forgotten to put those flowers in the Japanese room?

SIMON: The Japanese room is essentially feminine, and entirely unsuited to the Pet of the Foreign Office.

SOREL: Shut up, Simon!

CLARA: The room looks lovely, dear – you needn't worry. Just like your mother's dressing-room on a first night.

SIMON: How restful!

CLARA (moves to SOREL): Have you told her about your boy friend?

SOREL (pained): Not boy friend, Clara.

CLARA (picks up drawing that SIMON has left on floor C.): Oh, well, whatever he is. (Puts drawing on chair up C.)

SIMON: I think Sorel's beginning to be ashamed of us all, Clara – I don't altogether blame her; we are very slap-dash.

CLARA (coming down C. – speaking to SIMON): Are you going to leave that picture in the guests' bathroom, dear? I don't know if it's quite the thing – lots of pink, naked women rolling about in a field.

SIMON (severely): Nudity can be very beautiful, Clara.

CLARA: Oh, can it! Perhaps being a dresser for so long 'as spoilt me eye for it.

> CLARA goes out door below stairs.

SIMON: Clara's looking tired. We ought to have more servants and not depend on her so much.

SOREL: You know we can never keep them. You're right about us being slap-dash, Simon. I wish we weren't.

SIMON: Does it matter?

SOREL: It must, I think – to other people.

SIMON: It's not our fault – it's the way we've been brought up.

SOREL: Well, if we're clever enough to realise that, we ought to be clever enough to change ourselves.

SIMON: I'm not sure that I want to.

SOREL: We're so awfully bad-mannered.

SIMON: Not to people we like.

SOREL: The people we like put up with it because they like *us*.

SIMON: What do you mean, exactly, by bad manners? Lack of social tricks and small-talk?

SOREL: We never attempt to look after people when they come here.

SIMON: Why should we? It's loathsome being looked after.

SOREL: Yes, but people like little attentions. We've never once asked anyone if they've slept well.

SIMON: I consider *that* an impertinence, anyhow.

SOREL: I'm going to try to improve.

SIMON (*puts feet upon form*): You're only going on like this because you've got a mania for a diplomatist. You'll soon return to normal.

SOREL (*earnestly*): Abnormal, Simon – that's what we are. Abnormal. People stare in astonishment when we say what we consider perfectly ordinary things. I just remarked at Freda's lunch the other day how nice it would be if someone invented something to make all our faces go up like the Chinese, because I was so bored with them going down. And they all thought I was mad!

SIMON: It's no use worrying, darling; we see things differently, I suppose, and if people don't like it they must lump it.

> *Enter* JUDITH *from the garden. She is carrying an armful of flowers and wearing a tea-gown, a large garden hat, gauntlet gloves and galoshes.*

JUDITH (*coming down to behind sofa table*): You look awfully dirty, Simon. What have you been doing?

SIMON (*nonchalantly*): Not washing very much.

JUDITH (*puts basket on table, and starts to take off gloves*): You should, darling, really. It's so bad for your skin to leave things about on it.

SOREL: Clara says Amy's got toothache.

JUDITH: Poor dear! There's some oil of cloves in my medicine cupboard. Who is Amy?

SOREL: The scullery-maid, I think.

JUDITH (*puts gloves on table and comes C.*): How extraordinary! She

7

doesn't look Amy a bit, does she? Much more Flossie. Give me
a cigarette.

SIMON *gives her a cigarette from box on piano.*

Delphiniums are those stubby red flowers, aren't they?

SIMON (*lights cigarette for* JUDITH): No, darling; they're tall and
blue.

JUDITH: Yes, of course. The red ones are somebody's name –
Asters, that's it. I knew it was something opulent. (*Sits on stool
below piano.* SIMON *takes off her galoshes and puts them by the side of
the stool.*) I do hope Clara has remembered about the Japanese
room.

SOREL: Japanese room!

JUDITH: Yes; I told her to put some flowers in it and take
Simon's flannels out of the wardrobe drawer.

SOREL: So did I.

JUDITH (*ominously*): Why?

SOREL (*airily*): I've asked Richard Greatham down for the week-
end – I didn't think you'd mind.

JUDITH (*rises and crosses to* SOREL): Mind! How dared you do such
a thing?

SOREL: He's a diplomatist.

JUDITH (*goes behind table and starts to sort out flowers*): That makes
it much worse. We must wire and put him off at once.

SOREL: It's too late.

JUDITH: Well, we'll tell Clara to say we've been called away.

SOREL: That would be extremely rude, and, anyhow, I *want* to
see him.

JUDITH: You mean to sit there in cold blood and tell me you've
asked a complete stranger down for the week-end, and that
you *want* to see him!

SOREL: I've often done it before.

JUDITH: I fail to see how that helps matters. Where's he going to
sleep?

SOREL: The Japanese room.

JUDITH (*crosses with bunch of flowers to table below door R.*): Oh, no,
he isn't – Sandy Tyrell is sleeping there.

SIMON (*coming C.*): There now! What did I tell you?

SOREL: Sandy – what?

JUDITH: Tyrell, dear.

SIMON: Why didn't you tell us, mother?

JUDITH (*starting to arrange flowers in vase*): I did. I've talked of nothing but Sandy Tyrell for days – I adore Sandy Tyrell.

SIMON (*goes back to form and sits*): You've never mentioned him.

SOREL: Who is he, Mother?

JUDITH: He's a perfect darling, and madly in love with me – at least, it isn't me really, it's my Celebrated Actress glamour – but it gives me a divinely cosy feeling. I met him at Nora Trent's. (*Crosses to behind sofa table.*)

SOREL: Mother, I wish you'd give up this sort of thing.

JUDITH (*taking more flowers from basket*): What exactly do you mean by 'this sort of thing', Sorel?

SOREL: You know perfectly well what I mean.

JUDITH (*puts down flowers and goes to R. corner of sofa*): Are you attempting to criticise me?

SOREL: I should have thought you'd be above encouraging silly, callow young men who are infatuated by your name.

JUDITH (*goes back to table and picks up flowers*): That may be true, but I shall allow nobody but myself to say it. I hoped you'd grow up a good *daughter* to me, not a critical *aunt*.

SOREL (*moves to L. end of sofa*): It's so terribly cheap.

JUDITH: Cheap! Nonsense! How about your diplomatist?

SOREL: Surely that's a little different, dear?

JUDITH: If you mean that because you happen to be a vigorous *ingénue* of nineteen you have the complete monopoly of any amorous adventure there may be about, I feel it my firm duty to disillusion you.

SOREL: But, mother—

JUDITH (*crosses to top end of piano and picks up empty vase, which she gives SIMON to hold while she fills it with flowers*): Anyone would think I was eighty, the way you go on. It was a great mistake not sending you to boarding schools, and you coming back and me being your elder sister.

SIMON: It wouldn't have been any use, darling. Everyone knows we're your son and daughter.

JUDITH: Only because I was stupid enough to dandle you about

9

in front of cameras when you were little. I knew I should regret it.

SIMON: I don't see any point in trying to be younger than you are.

JUDITH: At your age, dear, it would be indecent if you did.

*Having finished arranging flowers, she puts vase back on piano, and crosses to R. corner of sofa.*

SOREL: But, mother darling, don't you see it's awfully undignified for you to go flaunting about with young men?

JUDITH: I don't flaunt about – I never have. I've been morally an extremely nice woman all my life – more or less – and if dabbling gives me pleasure, I don't see why I *shouldn't* dabble.

SOREL: But it *oughtn't* to give you pleasure any *more*.

JUDITH: You know, Sorel, you grow more damnably feminine every day. I wish I'd brought you up differently.

SOREL: I'm proud of being feminine.

JUDITH (*sits on sofa beside* SOREL – *kissing her*): You're a darling, and I adore you; and you're very pretty, and I'm madly jealous of you.

SOREL (*with her arms round her*): Are you really? How lovely!

JUDITH: You will be nice to Sandy, won't you?

SOREL (*sits up*): Can't he sleep in 'Little Hell'?

JUDITH: My dear, he's frightfully athletic and all those hot-water pipes will sap his vitality.

SOREL: They'll sap Richard's vitality too.

JUDITH: He won't notice them; he's probably used to scorching tropical Embassies with punkahs waving and everything.

SIMON: He's sure to be deadly, anyhow.

SOREL: You're getting far too blasé and exclusive, Simon.

SIMON: Nothing of the sort. Only I loathe being hearty with your men friends.

SOREL: You've never been even civil to any of my friends, men or women.

JUDITH: Don't bicker.

SIMON (*rises and crosses to C.*): Anyhow, the Japanese room's a woman's room, and a woman ought to have it.

JUDITH: I promised it to Sandy – he loves anything Japanese.

SIMON: So does Myra!

JUDITH: Myra!

SIMON: Myra Arundel. I've asked her down.

JUDITH: You've – what!

SIMON: I've asked Myra down for the week-end – she's awfully amusing.

SOREL: Well, all I can say is, it's beastly of you. You might have warned me. What on earth will Richard say?

SIMON: Something exquisitely non-committal, I expect.

JUDITH: This is too much! Do you mean to tell me, Simon—

SIMON (*goes to* JUDITH – *firmly*): Yes, mother, I do. I've asked Myra down and I have a perfect right to. You've always brought us up to be free about things.

JUDITH: Myra Arundel is straining freedom to its *utmost* limits.

SIMON: Don't you like her?

JUDITH: No, dear, I detest her. She's far too old for you, and she goes about using sex as a sort of shrimping-net.

SIMON: Really, mother—!

JUDITH: It's no use being cross. You know perfectly well I dislike her, and that's why you never told me she was coming until too late to stop her. It's intolerable of you.

SOREL (*grandly*): Whether she's here or not is a matter of extreme indifference to *me*, but I'm afraid Richard won't like her very much.

SIMON: You're afraid he'll like her *too* much!

SOREL: That was an offensive remark, Simon, and rather silly.

JUDITH (*plaintively*): Why on earth don't you fall in love with nice young girls, instead of self-conscious vampires?

SIMON: She's not a vampire, and I never said I was in love with her.

SOREL: He's crazy about her. She butters him up and admires his sketches.

SIMON (*leaning across* JUDITH *and shouting at* SOREL): What about you picking up old gentlemen at dances?

SOREL (*furiously – shouting back at him*): He's *not* old!

JUDITH (*stretches her arms up and parts them;* SIMON *goes C.*): You've both upset me thoroughly. I wanted a nice restful week-end, with moments of Sandy's ingenuous affection to warm the cockles of my heart when I felt in the mood, and now the house is going to be full of discord – not enough food, everyone fighting for the bath – perfect agony! I wish I were dead!

SIMON: You needn't worry about Myra and me. We shall keep out of everyone's way.

SOREL: I shall take Richard on the river all day to-morrow.

JUDITH: In what?

SOREL: The punt.

JUDITH: I absolutely forbid you to go near the punt.

SIMON: It's sure to rain, anyhow.

JUDITH: What your father will say I tremble to think. He needs complete quiet to finish off *The Sinful Woman*.

SOREL: I see no reason for there to be any noise, unless Sandy What's-his-name is given to shouting.

JUDITH: If you're rude to Sandy I shall be extremely angry.

*SIMON and SOREL bend over JUDITH and all talk loudly at once.*

SOREL: ⎫                    ⎧ Now, look here, mother—
SIMON: ⎬ (together) ⎨ Why you should expect—
JUDITH: ⎭                    ⎩ He's coming all the way down specially
                                      to be nice to me—

*Enter DAVID down stairs. He looks slightly irritable.*

DAVID (*coming down to C.*): Why are you all making such a noise?

*SIMON crosses to piano and picks up book.*

JUDITH: I think I'm going mad!

DAVID: Why hasn't Clara brought me my tea?

JUDITH: I don't know.

DAVID: Where is Clara?

JUDITH: Do stop firing questions at me, David.

DAVID: Why are you all so irritable? What's happened?

*Enter CLARA from below stairs, with a tray of tea for one, and thrusts it into DAVID's hands.*

CLARA: Here's your tea. I'm sorry I'm late with it. Amy forgot to put the kettle on – she's got terrible toothache.

DAVID: Poor girl! Give her some oil of cloves.

SOREL: If anyone else mentions oil of cloves, I shall do something desperate! (*Rises and moves a step L.*)

DAVID: It's wonderful stuff. Where's Zoe?

SIMON: She was in the garden this morning.

DAVID: I suppose no one thought of giving her any lunch?

CLARA: I put it down by the kitchen table as usual, but she never came in for it.

SOREL: She's probably mousing.

DAVID: She isn't old enough yet. She might have fallen into the river, for all you care. I think it's a shame!

CLARA: Don't you worry your head – Zoe won't come to any harm; she's too wily.

*Exit door below stairs.*

DAVID: I don't want to be disturbed. (*He takes his tray and goes upstairs; then he turns.*) Listen, Simon. There's a perfectly sweet flapper coming down by the four-thirty. Will you go and meet her and be nice to her? She's an abject fool, but a useful type, and I want to study her a little in domestic surroundings. She can sleep in the Japanese room.

*He goes off, leaving behind him a deathly silence.* SOREL *drops into chair down L.*

JUDITH (*pause*): I should like someone to play something very beautiful to me on the piano.

SIMON (*stamps up to french window C.*): Damn everything! Damn! Damn! Damn!

SOREL: Swearing doesn't help.

SIMON: It helps me a lot.

SOREL: What does father mean by going on like that?

JUDITH: In view of the imminent reception, you'd better go and shave, Simon.

SIMON *comes down and leans on piano.*

SOREL (*rising and bursting into tears of rage*): It's perfectly beastly! Whenever I make any sort of plan about anything, it's always done in by someone. I wish I were earning my own living somewhere   a free agent – able to do whatever I liked without being cluttered up and frustrated by the family—

JUDITH (*picturesquely*): It grieves me to hear you say that, Sorel.

SOREL: Don't be infuriating, mother!

JUDITH (*sadly*): A change has come over my children of late. I have tried to shut my eyes to it, but in vain. At my time of life one must face bitter facts!

SIMON: This is going to be the blackest Saturday-till-Monday we've ever spent!

JUDITH (*tenderly*): Sorel, you mustn't cry.

SOREL: Don't sympathise with me; it's only temper.

JUDITH (*pulling her down on to sofa beside her*): Put your head on my shoulder, dear.

SIMON (*bitterly*): Your head, like the golden fleece . . .

SOREL (*tearfully*): Richard'll have to have 'Little Hell' and that horrible flapper the Japanese room.

JUDITH: Over my dead body!

SIMON (*comes over to his mother*): Mother, what *are* we to do?

JUDITH (*pulls him down on his knees and places his head on her right shoulder. SOREL's head on her left. Makes a charming little motherly picture*): We must all be very, very kind to everyone!

SIMON: Now then, mother, none of that!

JUDITH (*aggrieved*): I don't know what you mean, Simon.

SIMON: You were being beautiful and sad.

JUDITH: But I am beautiful and sad.

SIMON: You're not particularly beautiful, darling, and you never were.

JUDITH: Never mind; I made thousands think I was.

SIMON: And as for being sad—

JUDITH (*pushes SIMON on the floor*): Now, Simon, I will not be dictated to like this! If I say I'm sad, I *am* sad. You don't understand, because you're precocious and tiresome. . . . There comes a time in all women's lives—

SOREL (*rises and stands at L. corner of sofa*): Oh dear! (*With pained expression.*)

JUDITH: What did you say, Sorel?

SOREL: I said, 'Oh dear!'

JUDITH: Well, please don't say it again, because it annoys me.

SOREL (*smiling*): You're such a lovely hypocrite!

JUDITH (*casting up her eyes*): I don't know what I've done to be cursed with such ungrateful children! It's very cruel at my time of life—

SIMON: There you go again!

JUDITH (*pause – inconsequently*): You're getting far too tall, Sorel.

SOREL: Sorry, mother!

JUDITH: Give me another of those disgusting cigarettes—

> SIMON *rises and goes to piano – quickly takes cigarette.*

JUDITH: I don't know where they came from. (*Rises and goes C.*)

SIMON (*moves C. and gives* JUDITH *cigarette*): Here! (*He lights it for her.*)

JUDITH: I'm going to forget entirely about all these dreadful people arriving. My mind henceforward shall be a blank on the subject.

SOREL: It's all very fine, mother, but—

JUDITH: I made a great decision this morning.

SIMON: What kind of decision?

JUDITH: It's a secret.

SOREL: Aren't you going to tell us?

JUDITH: Of course. I meant it was a secret from your father.

SIMON: What is it?

> JUDITH *goes up C. and looks off L. to make sure no one is listening, then returns to C.*

JUDITH: I'm going back to the stage.

SIMON: I knew it! (*Drops on to form below piano.*)

JUDITH. I'm stagnating here. I won't stagnate as long as there's breath left in my body.

SOREL: Do you think it's wise? You retired so very finally last year. What excuse will you give for returning so soon?

JUDITH: My public, dear – letters from my public!

SIMON: Have you had any?

JUDITH: One or two. That's what decided me, really – I ought to have had hundreds.

SOREL (*kneels on R. corner of sofa*): We'll write some lovely ones, and you can publish them in the papers.

JUDITH: Of course.

SOREL: You will be dignified about it all, won't you, darling?

JUDITH: I'm much more dignified on the stage than in the country – it's my *milieu*. I've tried terribly hard to be 'landed gentry', but without any real success. (*Moves up C. with outstretched arms.*) I long for excitement and glamour. (*Comes down to R. corner of sofa.*) Think of the thrill of a first night; all those ardent playgoers willing one to succeed; the critics all leaning forward with glowing faces, receptive and exultant – emitting queer little inarticulate noises as some witty line tickles their fancy. The satisfied grunt of the *Daily Mail*, the abandoned gurgle of the *Sunday Times*, and the shrill, enthusiastic scream of the *Daily Express!* I can distinguish them all—

SIMON: Have you got a play?

JUDITH: I think I shall revive *Love's Whirlwind*.

SOREL (*collapsing on to sofa*): Oh, mother! (*She gurgles with laughter.*)

SIMON (*weakly*): Father will be furious.

JUDITH: I can't help that.

SOREL: It's such a fearful play.

JUDITH: It's a marvellous part.

    SOREL *opens her mouth to speak.*

JUDITH: You mustn't say too much against it, Sorel. I'm willing to laugh at it a little myself, but, after all, it *was* one of my greatest successes.

SIMON: Oh, it's appalling – but I love it. It makes me laugh.

JUDITH: The public love it too, and it doesn't make them laugh – much. (*Moves to C. and very dramatically she recites.*) 'You are a fool, a blind pitiable fool. You think because you have bought my body that you have bought my soul!' (*Turning to* SOREL.) You must say that's dramatic – 'I've dreamed of love like this, but I never realised, I never knew how beautiful it could be in reality!' (*Wipes away imaginary tears.*) That line always brought a tear to my eye.

SIMON: The second act *is* the best, there's no doubt about that.

JUDITH (*turning to* SOREL): From the moment Victor comes in it's strong – tremendously strong. . . . Be Victor a minute, Sorel—

SOREL (*rising*): Do you mean when he comes in at the end of the act?

JUDITH: Yes. You know – 'Is this a game?'

SOREL (*going to* JUDITH *and speaking in a very dramatic voice*) 'Is this a game?'

JUDITH (*with spirit*): 'Yes – and a game that must be played to the finish.'

SIMON (*rising and moving to* JUDITH, *and speaking in deep dramatic voice*): 'Zara, what does this mean?'

JUDITH: 'So many illusions shattered – so many dreams trodden in the dust!'

SOREL (*runs behind* JUDITH *and in front of* SIMON *to down R.*): I'm George now – 'I don't understand! You and Victor – My God!' (*Strikes dramatic pose.*)

JUDITH (*moving a little to L. – listening*): 'Sssh! Isn't that little Pam crying?'

SIMON (*savagely*): 'She'll cry more, poor mite, when she realises her mother is a—'

*The front-door bell rings.*

JUDITH: Damn! There's the bell!

SOREL (*rushing to the glass – on piano*): I look hideous.

SIMON (*moves to R. side of piano*): Yes, dear!

CLARA *enters from door below stairs and crosses to door R.*

JUDITH: Clara – before you open the door – we shall be eight for dinner.

CLARA (*comes to R.C.*): My God!

SIMON: And for breakfast, lunch, tea, and dinner to-morrow.

JUDITH (*vaguely*): Will you get various rooms ready?

CLARA: I shall have to – they can't sleep in the passage!

SOREL: Now we've upset Clara!

JUDITH: It can't be helped – nothing can be helped. It's Fate – everything that happens is Fate. That's always a great comfort to me.

CLARA: More like arrant selfishness!

JUDITH: You mustn't be pert, Clara.

CLARA: Pert I may be, but I 'ave got some thought for others. Eight for dinner – Amy going home early! It's nothing more nor less than an imposition!

*The bell rings again.*

SIMON: Hadn't you better let them all in?

CLARA *goes to the front door and admits* SANDY TYRELL, *who is a fresh-looking young man; he has an unspoilt, youthful sense of honour and rather big hands, owing to a misplaced enthusiasm for amateur boxing.*

CLARA *goes out, door below stairs.*

SANDY (*crossing to* JUDITH *and shaking hands*): I say, it's perfectly
ripping of you to let me come down.

JUDITH: Are you alone?

SANDY (*surprised*): Yes.

JUDITH: I mean, didn't you meet anyone at the station?

SANDY: I motored down; my car's outside. Would you like me to
meet anybody?

JUDITH: Oh, no, I must introduce you. This is my daughter
Sorel, and my son Simon.

SANDY (*moves to* SOREL *and offers his hand, which she ignores*): How
do you do?

SOREL (*coldly*): I'm extremely well, thank you, and I hope you
are.

> *Brushes past him and exits upstairs.*

SIMON: So do I. (*Does the same.*)

> SANDY *looks shattered.*

JUDITH (*crosses in front of* SANDY *and glares after* SIMON *and*
SOREL): You must forgive me for having rather peculiar
children. Have you got a bag or anything?

SANDY: Yes; it's in the car.

JUDITH: We'd better leave it there for the moment, as Clara has
to get the tea. We'll find you a room afterwards.

SANDY: I've been looking forward to this most awfully.

JUDITH: It is nice, isn't it? (*Moves to window.*) You can see as far as
Marlow on a clear day, so they tell me.

SANDY (*goes up to her*): I meant I've been looking forward to
seeing you.

JUDITH: How perfectly sweet of you! (*Crosses to sofa and sits L.
corner.*) Would you like a drink?

SANDY: No, thanks. I'm in training.

JUDITH (*motioning him to sit beside her*): How lovely! What for?

SANDY: I'm boxing again in a couple of weeks.

JUDITH: I must come to your first night.

SANDY (*sits on sofa*): You look simply splendid.

JUDITH: I'm so glad. You know, you mustn't mind if Simon and
Sorel insult you a little – they've been very bad-tempered
lately.

SANDY: It's awfully funny you having a grown-up son and daughter at all. I can hardly believe it.

JUDITH (*quickly*): I was married very young.

SANDY: I don't wonder. You know, it's frightfully queer the way I've been planning to know you for ages, and I never did until last week.

JUDITH: I liked you from the first, really, because you're such a nice shape.

SANDY (*slightly embarrassed*): Oh, I see. . . .

JUDITH: Small hips and lovely broad shoulders – I wish Simon had smaller hips. (*Slight pause.*) Do you think you could teach him to box?

SANDY: Rather – if he likes!

JUDITH: That's just the trouble – I'm afraid he won't like. He's so dreadfully un – that sort of thing. You must use your influence subtly. I'm sure David would be pleased.

SANDY: Who's David?

JUDITH: My husband.

SANDY (*surprised*): Oh!

JUDITH: Why do you say 'Oh' like that? Didn't you know I had a husband?

SANDY: I thought he was dead.

JUDITH: No, he's not dead; he's upstairs. (*Pointing to stairs.*)

SANDY: You're quite different from what you were the other day.

JUDITH: It's this garden hat. I'll take it off. (*She does so and puts it on table behind sofa.*) There! I've been pruning the calceolarias.

SANDY (*puzzled*): Oh?—

JUDITH: I love my garden, you know – it's so peaceful and quaint. I spend long days dreaming away in it – you know how one dreams.

SANDY: Oh, yes.

JUDITH (*warming up*): I always longed to leave the brittle glamour of cities and theatres and find rest in some old-world nook. That's why we came to Cookham.

SANDY: Awfully nice place, Cookham.

JUDITH (*slight pause*): Have you ever seen me on the stage?

SANDY: Rather!

JUDITH: Oh, what in?

SANDY: That thing when you pretended to cheat at cards to save your husband's good name.

JUDITH: Oh, *The Bold Deceiver*. That play was never quite right.

SANDY: You were absolutely wonderful. That was when I first fell in love with you.

JUDITH (*delighted*): Was it, really?

SANDY: Yes; you were so frightfully pathetic and brave.

JUDITH (*basking*): Was I?

SANDY: Rather!

> *There is a pause.*

JUDITH: Well, go on. . . .

SANDY (*flustered*): I feel such a fool, telling you what I think, as though it mattered.

JUDITH: Of course it matters – to me, anyhow.

SANDY: Does it – honestly?

JUDITH: Certainly.

SANDY: It seems too good to be true – sitting here and talking as though we were old friends.

JUDITH: We *are* old friends – we probably met in another life. Reincarnation, you know – fascinating!

SANDY: You do say ripping things.

JUDITH: Do I? Give me a cigarette.

> *He takes cigarette from box on table and gives it to her.*

And let's put our feet up. (*She puts her feet up behind* SANDY, *and he lights her cigarette.*)

SANDY: All right.

> *They settle themselves comfortably at opposite ends of the sofa, smoking.*

JUDITH: Can you punt?

SANDY: Yes – a bit.

JUDITH: You must teach Simon – he always gets the pole stuck.

SANDY: I'd rather teach you.

JUDITH: You're so gallant and chivalrous – much more like an American than an Englishman.

SANDY: I should like to go on saying nice things to you for ever.

JUDITH (*giving him her hand*): Sandy!

*There comes a loud ring at the bell.*

There now! (*Takes her feet off sofa.*)

SANDY: Is anyone else coming to stay?

JUDITH: Anyone else! You don't know – you just don't know.

> CLARA *enters and crosses over to door R., opens it and lets it fall back in* MYRA's *face, then exits, L.*

SANDY: You said it would be quite quiet, with nobody at all.

JUDITH: I was wrong. It's going to be very noisy, with herds of angry people stamping about. Give me my hat.

> *He gives her her hat, which she puts on.*
>
> MYRA *pushes open door, and puts her suitcase and tennis racket just outside door, and enters, coming to C. and holding out her hand to* JUDITH.
>
> SANDY *rises.*

MYRA (*advancing*): Judith – my dear – this is divine!

JUDITH (*rises and meets* MYRA, C. – *emptily*): Too, too lovely! Where are the others?

MYRA: What others?

JUDITH: Did you come by the four-thirty?

MYRA: Yes.

JUDITH: Didn't you see anyone at the station?

MYRA: Yes, several people, but I didn't know they were coming here.

JUDITH: Well, they are.

MYRA: Sorel said it was going to be just ourselves this week-end.

JUDITH (*sharply*): Sorel?

MYRA: Yes – didn't she tell you she'd asked me? Weren't you expecting me?

JUDITH: Simon muttered something about your coming, but Sorel didn't mention it. (*Looks at* MYRA *and gives a chuckle.*) Wasn't that odd of her? (*Crosses to piano.*)

MYRA: You're a divinely mad family! (*To* SANDY.) How do you do? It's useless to wait for introductions, with the Blisses. My name's Myra Arundel.

JUDITH (*airily*): Sandy Tyrell, Myra Arundel; Myra Arundel, Sandy Tyrell. There!

MYRA: Is that your car outside?

SANDY: Yes.

MYRA (*moving to* JUDITH *again*): Well, Judith, I *do* think you might have told me someone was motoring down. A nice car would have been so much more comfortable than that beastly train.

JUDITH: I never knew you were coming until a little while ago.

MYRA: It's heavenly here – after London! The heat was terrible when I left. You look awfully well, Judith. Rusticating obviously agrees with you.

JUDITH: I'm glad you think so. Personally, I feel that a nervous breakdown is imminent.

MYRA: My dear, how ghastly! What's the matter?

JUDITH: Nothing's the matter yet, Myra, but I have presentiments. (*Crosses in front of* MYRA *and takes* SANDY'*s hand. She begins to go upstairs, followed by* SANDY. *Then she turns.*) Come upstairs, Sandy, and I'll show you your room. I'll send Simon down to you. He's shaving, I think, but you won't mind that, will you?

> *She goes off.* MYRA *makes a slight grimace after her, then she helps herself to a cigarette and wanders to piano.*
>
> SIMON *comes downstairs very fast, putting on his coat. He has apparently finished his toilet.*

SIMON (*runs over to* MYRA): Myra, this is marvellous! (*He tries to kiss her.*)

MYRA (*pushing him away*): No, Simon, dear; it's too hot.

SIMON: You look beautifully cool.

MYRA: I'm more than cool, really, but it's not climatic coolness. I've been mentally chilled to the marrow by Judith's attitude.

SIMON: Why, what did she say?

MYRA: Nothing very much. She was bouncing about on the sofa with a hearty young thing in flannels, and seemed to resent my appearance rather.

SIMON: You mustn't take any notice of Mother.

MYRA: I'll try not to, but it's difficult.

SIMON: She adores you, really.

MYRA: I'm sure she does.

SIMON: She's annoyed to-day because Father and Sorel have been asking people down without telling her.

MYRA: Poor dear! I quite see why.

SIMON: You look enchanting!

MYRA: Thank you, Simon.

SIMON: Are you pleased to see me?

MYRA: Of course. That's why I came.

SIMON (*shouts*): Darling!

MYRA: Sssh! Don't shout.

SIMON (*moving away to C.*): I feel most colossally temperamental –
I should like to kiss you and kiss you and break everything in
the house and then jump into the river.

MYRA: Dear Simon!

SIMON (*he takes her hand and studies her*): You're everything I want
you to be – absolutely everything! Marvellous clothes,
marvellous looks, marvellous brain – oh, God, it's terrible!
(*Drops her hand and moves L.*)

MYRA: I dined with Charlie Templeton last night.

SIMON: Well, you're a devil! You only did it to annoy me. He's
far too plump, and he can't do anything but dither about the
Embassy in badly-cut trousers. You loathe him really; you
know you do – you're too intelligent not to. You couldn't like
him and me at the same time – it's impossible!

MYRA: Don't be so conceited.

SIMON (*running to her and clasping her in his arms*): Darling – I adore
you!

MYRA: That's right.

SIMON (*releasing her*): But you're callous – that's what it is,
callous! You don't care a damn. You don't love me a bit, do
you?

MYRA: Love's a very big word, Simon.

SIMON: It isn't – it's tiny. What are we to do?

MYRA: What do you mean?

SIMON: We can't go on like this.

MYRA: I'm not going on like anything. (*Crosses over and sits in chair
down L.*)

SIMON: Yes, you are; you're going on like Medusa, and there are
awful snakes popping their heads out at me from under your
hat – I shall be turned to stone in a minute, and then you'll be
sorry.

MYRA (*laughing*): You're very sweet, and I'm *very* fond of you.

SIMON (*crosses over to her and takes her hand*): Tell me what you've
been doing – everything.

MYRA: Nothing.

SIMON: What did you do after you'd dined with Charlie Templeton?

MYRA: Supped with Charlie Templeton.

SIMON: Well! (*Throws her hand down and goes to R. corner of sofa and sits on arm.*) I don't mind a bit. I hope you ate a lot and enjoyed yourself – there!

MYRA: Generous boy! Come and kiss me.

SIMON: You're only playing up to me now; you don't really want to a bit.

MYRA: I'm aching for it.

SIMON (*runs to her and kisses her violently*): I love you!

MYRA: This week-end's going to be strenuous.

SIMON (*moves away to C.*): Hell upon earth – fifteen million people in the house. We'll get up at seven and rush away down the river.

MYRA: No, we won't.

SIMON: Well, don't let either of us agree to anything we say – we'll both be difficult. (*Flings himself on sofa with his feet up on L. end.*) I love being difficult.

MYRA: You certainly do.

SIMON: But I'm in the most lovely mood now. Just seeing you makes me feel grand—

MYRA: Is your father here?

SIMON: Yes; he's working on a new novel.

MYRA: He writes brilliantly.

SIMON: Doesn't he? He drinks too much tea, though.

MYRA: It can't do him much harm, surely?

SIMON: It tans the stomach.

MYRA: Who is Sandy Tyrell?

SIMON: Never heard of him.

MYRA: He's here, with Judith.

SIMON: Oh, *that* poor thing with hot hands! We'll ignore him.

MYRA: I thought he looked rather nice.

SIMON: You must be mad! He looked disgusting.

MYRA (*laughing*): Idiot!

SIMON: Smooth my hair with your soft white hands.

MYRA (*rises and goes to R. end of sofa – ruffling it*): It's got glue on it.

SIMON (*catching her hand and kissing it*): You smell heavenly! What is it?

MYRA: Borgia of Rosine.

SIMON: How appropriate! (*He tries to pull her down and kiss her.*)

MYRA (*breaking away*): You're too demonstrative to-day, Simon.

*The front-door bell rings.*

SIMON: Damn, damn! It's those drearies. (*Takes his feet off sofa.*)

CLARA *enters, crosses to door R., opens it and lets it fall back in* RICHARD'*s face, and starts to return to door L., but stops as he speaks.* RICHARD GREATHAM *and* JACKIE CORYTON *come in. There is, by this time, a good deal of luggage on the step.* RICHARD *is iron-grey and tall;* JACKIE *is small and shingled, with an ingenuous manner which will lose its charm as she grows older.*

RICHARD: Is this Mrs Bliss's house?

CLARA (*off-hand*): Oh, yes, this is it.

RICHARD: Is Miss Sorel Bliss in?

CLARA: I expect so. I'll see if I can find her.

*She goes upstairs.*

RICHARD *closes door.* JACKIE *goes down R.*

SIMON (*rises and crosses to* RICHARD, *carelessly shakes hands, then turns back to* MYRA, *ignoring* RICHARD): Hallo! Did you have a nice journey?

RICHARD: Yes thank you, very nice. I met Miss Coryton at the station. We introduced ourselves while we were waiting for the only taxi to come back.

MYRA (*taking a step down L.C.*): Oh, I took the only taxi. How maddening of me!

RICHARD (*crosses to her and shakes hands*): Mrs Arundel! How do you do? I never recognised you.

SIMON *goes behind* RICHARD *to R.C. and stares at* JACKIE *rudely.*

JACKIE: I did.

MYRA: Why? Have we met anywhere?

JACKIE: No; I mean I recognised you as the one who took the taxi.

RICHARD (*to* SIMON): You are Sorel's brother?

SIMON: Yes; she'll be down in a minute. Come out into the garden, Myra—

MYRA: But, Simon, we can't. . . .

SIMON (*reaching across* RICHARD, *grabbing her hand and dragging her off through window*): Yes, we can. I shall go mad if I stay in the house a moment longer. (*Over his shoulder to* RICHARD *and* JACKIE.) Tea will be here soon.

> *He and* MYRA *go off into garden R.*
> *There's a slight pause.*

JACKIE: Well!

RICHARD: A strange young man! (*Moving up to window, looking after them.*)

JACKIE: Very rude, *I* think.

RICHARD (*turning back into the room*): Have you ever met him before?

JACKIE: No; I don't know any of them except Mr Bliss – *he's* a wonderful person.

RICHARD (*puts his coat and hat on chair up L.C.*): I wonder if he knows you're here.

JACKIE: Perhaps that funny woman who opened the door will tell him.

RICHARD: Yes, allow me. (*Takes her coat and puts it on chair with his.*) It was fortunate that we met at the station.

JACKIE: I'm frightfully glad. I should have been terrified arriving all by myself.

RICHARD (*looks out of window again. Slight pause*): I do hope the weather will keep good over Sunday – the country round here is delightful.

JACKIE: Yes.

> *Another pause.*

RICHARD: There's nowhere like England in the spring and summer.

JACKIE: No, there isn't, is there?

> *Another pause.*

RICHARD: There's a sort of *quality* you find in no other countries.

> *Another pause, in which* JACKIE *moves over to sofa and sits.*

JACKIE: Have you travelled a lot?

RICHARD (*modestly*): A good deal.

JACKIE: How lovely!

RICHARD *comes down and sits on form below piano.*
*There is a pause.*

RICHARD: Spain is very beautiful.

JACKIE: Yes, I've always heard Spain was awfully nice.

*Pause.*

RICHARD: Except for the bull-fights. No one who ever really loved horses could enjoy a bull-fight.

JACKIE: Nor anyone who loved bulls either.

RICHARD: Exactly.

*Pause.*

JACKIE: Italy's awfully nice, isn't it?

RICHARD: Oh, yes, charming.

JACKIE: I've always wanted to go to Italy.

*Pause.*

RICHARD: Rome is a beautiful city.

JACKIE: Yes, I've always heard Rome was lovely.

RICHARD: And Naples and Capri – Capri's enchanting.

JACKIE: It must be.

*Pause.*

RICHARD: Have you ever been abroad at all?

JACKIE: Oh, yes: I went to Dieppe once – we had a house there for the summer.

RICHARD (*kindly*): Dear little place, Dieppe.

JACKIE: Yes, it was lovely.

JUDITH *comes downstairs, followed by* SANDY, *with his arms full of cushions. Sits down on form and puts on her galoshes beside* RICHARD, *who rises. Then exits into garden without looking at* RICHARD *or* JACKIE. SANDY *picks up cushions and her gloves from table and goes out after her.*

JACKIE: Well!

*Pause, and sitting again.*

RICHARD: *Russia* used to be a wonderful country before the war.

JACKIE: It must have been. . . . Was that her?

RICHARD: Who?

JACKIE: Judith Bliss.

RICHARD: Yes, I expect it was.

JACKIE (*nearly crying*): I wish I'd never come.

RICHARD: You mustn't worry. They're a very Bohemian family, I believe.

JACKIE: I wonder if Mr Bliss knows I'm here.

RICHARD: I wonder.

JACKIE: Couldn't we ring a bell, or anything?

RICHARD: Yes, perhaps we'd better. (*Rises and crosses to door down L. He finds bell and presses it.*)

JACKIE: I don't suppose it rings.

RICHARD (*comes to L. corner of sofa*): You mustn't be depressed.

JACKIE: I feel horrid.

RICHARD: It's always a little embarrassing coming to a strange house for the first time. You'll like Sorel – she's charming.

JACKIE (*desperately*): I wonder where she is.

RICHARD (*consolingly*): I expect tea will be here soon.

JACKIE: Do you think they *have* tea?

RICHARD (*alarmed*): Oh, yes – they must.

JACKIE: Oh, well, we'd better go on waiting, then.

RICHARD (*takes cigarette-case out of his pocket*): Do you mind if I smoke?

JACKIE: Not a bit.

RICHARD: Will you?

JACKIE: No, thank you.

RICHARD (*sitting down on L. end of sofa*): I got this case in Japan. It's pretty isn't it?

JACKIE (*takes case, turns it over and hands it back*): Awfully pretty.

> *They lapse into hopeless silence.*
>
> *Enter* SOREL *downstairs – comes to L.C.*

SOREL: Oh, Richard, I'm dreadfully sorry! I didn't know you were here. (*They shake hands.*)

RICHARD: We've been here a good while.

SOREL: How awful! Please forgive me. I was upstairs.

> JACKIE *bobs up under their hands and stands in front of* RICHARD.

RICHARD: This is Miss Coryton.

SOREL: Oh!

JACKIE: How do you do?

SOREL: Have you come to see father?

RICHARD *lights his cigarette.*

JACKIE: Yes.

SOREL: He's in his study. (*Moves away to C.*) You'd better go up.

JACKIE (*looks hopelessly at* RICHARD, *then goes to* SOREL *and clutches her arm*): I don't know the way.

SOREL (*irritably*): Oh, well – I'll take you. Come on! Wait a minute, Richard. (*She takes her to the bottom of the stairs.*) It's along that passage and the third door on the right.

JACKIE: Oh, thank you. (*She goes upstairs despondently.*)

SOREL (*coming down again – to* RICHARD): The poor girl looks half-witted.

RICHARD: She's shy, I think.

SOREL: I hope Father will find her a comfort. (*Sits on R. end of sofa.*)

RICHARD: Tell me one thing, Sorel, did your father and mother know I was coming? (*Sits beside her.*)

SOREL: Oh, yes; they were awfully pleased.

RICHARD: A rather nice-looking woman came down, in a big hat, and went into the garden with a young man, without saying a word.

SOREL: That was mother, I expect. We're an independent family – we entertain our friends sort of separately.

RICHARD: Oh, I see.

*Slight pause.*

SOREL: It was sweet of you to come.

RICHARD: I wanted to come – I've thought about you a lot.

SOREL: Have you really? That's thrilling!

RICHARD: I mean it. You're so alive and vital and different from other people.

SOREL: I'm so frightened that you'll be bored here.

RICHARD: Bored! Why should I be?

SOREL: Oh, I don't know. But you won't be, will you? – or if you are, tell me at once, and we'll do something quite different.

RICHARD: You're rather a dear, you know.

SOREL: I'm not. (*Rises and goes C.*) I'm devastating, entirely lacking in restraint. So's Simon. It's father's and mother's fault, really; you see, they're so vague – they've spent their lives cultivating their Arts and not devoting any time to ordinary conventions and manners and things. I'm the only one who sees that, so I'm trying to be better. I'd love to be beautifully poised and carry off difficult situations with a lift of the eyebrows—

RICHARD: I'm sure you could carry off anything.

SOREL (*moves to R. corner of sofa*): There you are, you see, saying the right thing! You *always* say the right thing, and no one knows a bit what you're really thinking. That's what I adore.

RICHARD: I'm afraid to say anything now, in case you think I'm only being correct.

SOREL: But you are correct. I wish you'd teach Simon to be correct too. (*Sits beside* RICHARD *again.*)

RICHARD: It would be uphill work, I'm afraid.

SOREL: Why, don't you like him?

RICHARD: I've only met him for a moment.

*There is an uncomfortable pause.*

SOREL: Would you like to see the garden?

RICHARD (*he half rises*): Very much indeed.

SOREL: No, as a matter of fact (RICHARD *sits again.*) we'd better wait until after tea. (*Another pause.*) Shall I sing you something?

RICHARD: Please – I should love it.

*They both rise.* SOREL *goes reluctantly to piano.*

SOREL (*comes slowly to sofa*): I don't want to really a bit – only I'm trying to entertain you. It's as easy as pie to talk in someone else's house, like at the dance the other night, but here on my own *ground* I'm finding it difficult.

RICHARD (*puzzled*): I'm sorry.

SOREL: Oh, it isn't your fault; honestly, it isn't – you're awfully kind and responsive. (*Sits on sofa.*) What shall we do?

RICHARD: I'm quite happy talking (*Sits beside her.*) to you.

*Pause.*

SOREL: Can you play Mah Jong?

RICHARD: No, I'm afraid I can't.

SOREL: I'm *so* glad – I *do* hate it so.

CLARA *enters, with a small stool for tea, and places it with a bang at* RICHARD's *feet.*

SOREL: Here's tea!

CLARA: Where's your mother, dear?

SOREL: Out in the garden, I think.

CLARA: It's starting to rain. (*Goes out L. and fetches tea-tray loaded with tea-things, which she puts on stool.*)

SOREL: Oh, everyone will come dashing in, then. How awful!

RICHARD (*rises and goes C.*): Won't the luggage get rather wet out there?

SOREL: What luggage?

CLARA: I'll bring it in when I've made the tea.

RICHARD (*goes out R. and returns with two suitcases, which he places down R.C.*): Oh, don't trouble; I'll do it now.

SOREL: We ought to have got William up from the village.

CLARA: It's Saturday.

SOREL: I know it is.

CLARA: He's playing cricket.

> SOREL *rushes to help* RICHARD.

SOREL: Do sit down and smoke. I can easily manage it.

RICHARD: Certainly not.

SOREL (*goes out*): How typical of Myra to have so many bags! ... Ooh!

> She staggers with a suitcase. RICHARD *goes to her assistance, and they both drop it.*

There now – we've probably broken something!

RICHARD: Well, it's not my bag, so it doesn't matter.

> RICHARD *goes out to get the last case while* SOREL *holds the door open.*

RICHARD: This is the last one. . . . (*He brings in a dressing-case, and wipes his hand on his handkerchief.*)

SOREL: Do you know where to wash if you want to?

RICHARD: No – but I'm all right. (*They both stand leaning on piano, talking.*)

> Re-enter CLARA *with teapot. She puts it on stool and exits again.* SIMON *and* MYRA *come in from the garden.*

MYRA (*goes to shake hands with* SOREL, *but* SIMON *pulls her towards sofa*): Hallo, Sorel! How are you?

SOREL: I'm splendid. Do you know Mr Greatham?

MYRA: Oh, yes; we've met several times.

SIMON: Come and sit down, Myra. (MYRA, *pulled by* SIMON, *sits L. side of sofa,* SIMON *R. side.*)

> DAVID *and* JACKIE *come downstairs,* DAVID *leading her by the elbow like a small child. They come C.* ·

DAVID: Is tea ready?

SOREL: Yes; just.

DAVID (*leaving* JACKIE *R.C. and crossing to* SIMON): Simon, come and be nice to Miss Coryton.

SIMON: We've met already.

DAVID (*drags him out of his seat, and sits there himself*): That's no reason for you not to be nice to her.

MYRA (*firmly*): How do you do?

DAVID: How do you do? Are you staying here?

MYRA: I hope so.

> SIMON *moves round to behind L. corner of sofa and sits on table.*

DAVID: You must forgive me for being rather frowsy, but I've been working hard.

SOREL: Father, this is Mr Greatham.

> RICHARD *takes a step down R.*

DAVID: How are you? When did you arrive?

RICHARD: This afternoon.

DAVID: Good. Have some tea. (*He begins to pour it out.*) Everyone had better put their own sugar and milk in, or we shall get muddled. Where's your mother, Simon?

SIMON (*moves round and takes a cup of tea and a piece of cake, then returns to his seat*): She was last seen in the punt.

DAVID: How extraordinary! She can't punt.

SOREL: Sandy Tyrell's with her.

DAVID: Oh, well, she'll be all right, then. (*A slight pause.*) Who is he?

SOREL: I don't know.

DAVID: Do sit down, everybody.

> JACKIE *sits on form below piano. Enter* JUDITH *and* SANDY *from the garden. She comes to C. and kicks off galoshes.*

JUDITH: There's going to be a thunderstorm. I felt sick this morning. This is Sandy Tyrell – everybody—

SOREL: Mother, I want you to meet Mr Greatham.

RICHARD *goes to her and shakes hands, then returns to piano.*

JUDITH: Oh, yes. You were here before, weren't you?

SOREL: Before *what*, darling?

*SOREL crosses and gets a cup of tea and returns with it to settee down R.*

JUDITH: Before I went out in the punt. There was somebody else here, too – a fair girl. (*She sees* JACKIE.) Oh, there you are! How do you do? Sit down, Sandy, and eat anything you want. Give Sandy some bread-and-butter, Simon.

*JUDITH crosses L. and helps herself to tea, then sits in chair down L. RICHARD and JACKIE sit on form below piano. SANDY remains standing C.*

SIMON (*rises, picks up plate of bread-and-butter, crosses to SANDY and ungraciously thrusts it into his hands, then returns to his seat*): Here you are!

SANDY: Thanks.

*There is a long pause; then MYRA and RICHARD speak together.*

RICHARD:  ⎧            ⎫ How far are you from Maidenhead,
          ⎨ (together) ⎬ exactly?
MYRA:     ⎩            ⎭ What a pity it's raining – we might
                         have had some tennis—

*They both stop, to let the other go on. There is another terrible silence.*

MYRA:     ⎧            ⎫ I adore the shape of this hall – it's so—
RICHARD:  ⎨ (together) ⎬ The train was awfully crowded coming
          ⎩            ⎭ down—

*They both stop again, and there is another dead silence, during which the curtain slowly falls.*

# ACT TWO

*It is after dinner on the Saturday evening.*

   DAVID *and* MYRA *are seated on the settee down* R. SANDY *and*
JACKIE *are seated on form below piano.* SOREL *is standing down*
C. *with her back to the audience.* SIMON *is seated on* R. *arm of*
*sofa.* RICHARD *is seated on sofa.* JUDITH *is seated in chair down*
L. *Everyone is talking and arguing.*

   *The following scene should be played with great speed.*

SIMON: Who'll go out?

SOREL: I don't mind.

SIMON: No; you always guess it too quickly.

JACKIE: What do we have to do?

JUDITH: Choose an adverb, and then—

SIMON: Someone goes out, you see, and comes in, and you've
   chosen a word among yourselves, and she or he, whoever it is,
   asks you some sort of question, and you have to—

SOREL (*moves up to* SIMON): Not an ordinary question, Simon;
   they have to ask them to do something in the manner of the
   word, and then—

SIMON: Then, you see, you act whatever it is—

SOREL: The answer to the question, you see?

RICHARD (*apprehensively*): What sort of thing is one expected to
   do?

JUDITH: Quite usual things, like reciting 'If', or playing the
   piano—

RICHARD: I can't play the piano.

SIMON: Never mind; you can fake it, as long as it conveys an idea
   of the word.

JACKIE: The word we've all thought of?

SOREL (*impatient*): Yes, the word we've chosen when whoever it
   is is out of the room.

JACKIE: I'm afraid I don't quite understand yet.

SIMON: Never mind; I'll explain. You see, someone goes out. . . .

SOREL: I'll go out the first time, just to show her.

JUDITH: It's quite simple – all you have to do is just act in the manner of the word.

SOREL: Look here, everybody, I'm going out.

SIMON: All right; go on.

> SOREL *moves to door down L. but stops in doorway as* MYRA *speaks.*

MYRA: The History game's awfully good – when two people go out, and come back as Mary Queen of Scots and Crippen or somebody.

SANDY (*despondently*): I'm no earthly good at this sort of thing.

SOREL: I'll show you, Sandy. You see . . .

JUDITH: There's always 'How, When, and Where?' We haven't played that for ages.

SIMON: We will afterwards. We'll do this one first. Go on, Sorel.

SOREL: Don't be too long. (*She goes out door down L.*)

SIMON (*rises and faces company*): Now then.

JUDITH: 'Bitterly'.

SIMON: No, we did that last week; she'll know.

DAVID: 'Intensely'.

JUDITH: Too difficult.

RICHARD: There was an amusing game I played once at the Harringtons' house. Everyone was blindfolded except—

SIMON (*goes back to corner of sofa*): This room's not big enough for that. What about 'winsomely'?

JACKIE: I wish I knew what we had to do.

JUDITH: You'll see when we start playing.

MYRA (*rises and crosses to table behind sofa, takes cigarette and lights it*): If we start playing.

SIMON: Mother's brilliant at this. Do you remember when we played it at the Mackenzies'?

JUDITH: Yes, and Blanche was so cross when I kissed Freddie's ear in the manner of the word.

RICHARD: What was the word?

JUDITH: I can't remember.

MYRA (*having lit cigarette she returns to her seat*): Perhaps it's as well.

DAVID: What about 'drearily'?

JUDITH: Not definite enough.

SIMON: 'Winsomely' is the best.

JUDITH: She's sure to guess it straight off.

SANDY (*confidentially to* JACKIE): These games are much too brainy for me.

DAVID: Young Norman Robertson used to be marvellous – do you remember?

SIMON: Yes, wonderful sense of humour.

MYRA: He's lost it all since his marriage.

JUDITH: I didn't know you knew him.

MYRA: Well, considering he married my cousin—

   *Pause.*

RICHARD: We don't seem to be getting on with the game.

JUDITH: We haven't thought of a word yet.

MYRA: 'Brightly'.

SIMON: Too obvious.

MYRA: Very well – don't snap at me!

JUDITH: 'Saucily'. I've got a lovely idea for 'saucily'.

MYRA (*to* SIMON): I should think 'rudely' would be the easiest.

SIMON: Don't be sour, Myra.

JUDITH: The great thing is to get an obscure word.

SIMON: What a pity Irene isn't here – she knows masses of obscure words.

MYRA: She's probably picked them up from her obscure friends.

SIMON: It's no use being catty about Irene; she's a perfect darling.

MYRA: I wasn't being catty at all.

SIMON: Yes, you were.

SOREL (*off*): Hurry up!

JUDITH: Quickly, now! We must think—

JACKIE (*rises and comes C. – helpfully*): 'Appendicitis'.

JUDITH (*witheringly*): That's not an adverb.

SIMON: You're thinking of Charades.

   JACKIE *returns to her seat.*

SANDY: Charades are damned good fun.

SIMON: Yes, but we don't happen to be doing them at the moment.

SANDY: Sorry.

JUDITH: 'Saucily'.

SIMON: No, 'winsomely' is better.

JUDITH: All right. Call her in.

SIMON (*calling*): Sorel – come on; we're ready.

SANDY (*hoarsely to* SIMON): Which is it – 'saucily' or 'winsomely'?

SIMON (*whispering*): 'Winsomely'.

> *Re-enter* SOREL. *She moves to* C.

SOREL (*to* JUDITH): Go and take a flower out of that vase and give it to Richard.

JUDITH: Very well.

> *She trips lightly over to the vase on the piano, gurgling with coy laughter, selects a flower, then goes over to* RICHARD; *pursing her lips into a mock smile, she gives him the flower with a little girlish gasp at her own daring and wags her finger archly at him, and returns to her seat.* RICHARD *puts flower on sofa table and sits again.*

SIMON: Marvellous, Mother!

SOREL (*laughing*): Oh, lovely! (*Looking round the company.*) Now, Myra, get up and say good-bye to everyone in the manner of the word.

MYRA (*rises and starts with* DAVID): Good-bye. It really has been most delightful—

JUDITH: No, no, no!

MYRA (*moves C.*): Why – what do you mean?

JUDITH: You haven't got the right intonation a bit.

SIMON: Oh, mother darling, do shut up!

MYRA (*acidly*): Remember what an advantage you have over we poor amateurs, Judith, having been a professional for so long. (*Returns to her seat.*)

JUDITH: I don't like 'so long' very much.

SOREL: Do you think we might go on now?

MYRA: Go to the next one; I'm not going to do any more.

SIMON: Oh, please do. You were simply splendid.

SOREL: It doesn't matter. (*To* RICHARD.) Light a cigarette in the manner of the word. (RICHARD *rises.*)

RICHARD (*takes cigarette from box on sofa table*): I've forgotten what it is.

JUDITH (*grimacing at him violently*): You remember . . .

RICHARD: Oh, yes.

> *He goes to* SOREL. C. *and proceeds to light a cigarette with great*

*abandon, winking his eye and chucking* SOREL *under the chin, then looks round panic-stricken.*

JUDITH: Oh, no, no, no!

MYRA: I can't think *what* that's meant to be.

RICHARD (*offended*): I was doing my best.

JUDITH: It's so *frightfully* easy, and nobody can do it right.

SIMON: I believe you've muddled it up.

RICHARD (*returns to his seat*): You'd better go on to the next one.

JUDITH: Which word were you doing? Whisper—

RICHARD (*leans over to her, whispering*): 'Saucily'.

JUDITH: I knew it! – he was doing the wrong word. (*She whispers to him.*)

RICHARD: Oh, I see. I'm so sorry.

JUDITH: Give him another chance.

SIMON: No, it's Jackie's turn now; it will come round to him again, I'm afraid.

SOREL (*moves to* JACKIE): Do a dance in the manner of the word.

JACKIE (*giggling*): I can't.

JUDITH: Nonsense! Of course you can.

JACKIE: I can't – honestly – I . . .

SIMON (*crosses and pulls her to her feet*): Go on; have a shot at it.

JACKIE: No, I'd much rather not. Count me out.

JUDITH: Really, the ridiculous fuss everyone makes—

JACKIE: I'm awfully stupid, at anything like this.

SOREL: It's only a game, after all.

DAVID: Come along – try.

JACKIE (*dragging back*): I couldn't – please don't ask me to. I simply couldn't. (*She sits again.*)

SIMON: Leave her alone if she doesn't want to.

SOREL (*irritably*): What's the use of playing at all, if people won't do it properly!

JUDITH: It's *so* simple.

SANDY: It's awfully difficult if you haven't done it before.

SIMON: Go on to the next one.

SOREL (*firmly*): Unless everyone's in it we won't play at all.

SIMON: Now, don't lose your temper.

SOREL: Lose my temper! I like that! No one's given me the

slightest indication of what the word is – you all argue and squabble—

DAVID: Talk, talk, talk! Everybody talks too much.

JUDITH: It's so surprising to me when people won't play up. After all—

JACKIE (*with spirit*): It's a hateful game, anyhow, and I don't want to play it again ever.

SOREL: You haven't played it at all yet.

SIMON: Don't be rude, Sorel.

SOREL: Really, Simon, the way you go on is infuriating!

SIMON: It's always the same; whenever Sorel goes out she gets quarrelsome.

SOREL: Quarrelsome!

SIMON (*patting her hand in a fatherly fashion*): Don't worry, Jackie; you needn't do anything you don't want to.

JUDITH: I think, for the future, we'd better confine our efforts to social conversation and not attempt anything in the least intelligent.

SIMON: How can you be so unkind, mother!

JUDITH (*sharply*): Don't speak to me like that!

JACKIE (*speaking winsomely*): It's all my fault – I know I'm awfully silly, but it embarrasses me so terribly doing anything in front of people.

SOREL (*with acidity*): I should think the word was 'winsomely'.

SIMON: You must have been listening outside the door, then.

SOREL: Not at all – Miss Coryton gave it away.

SIMON: Why 'Miss Coryton' all of a sudden? You've been calling her Jackie all the evening. You're far too grand, Sorel.

SOREL (*stamping her foot*): And you're absolutely maddening – I'll never play another game with you as long as I live!

SIMON: That won't break my heart.

JUDITH: Stop, stop, stop!

SIMON (*grabbing* JACKIE's *hand – he pulls her up to window*): Come out in the garden. I'm sick of this.

SOREL (*following them up and shouting after them*): Don't let him take you on the river; he isn't very good at it.

SIMON (*over his shoulder*): Ha, ha! – very funny!

*He drags* JACKIE *off.* SOREL *returns to* C.

JUDITH: Sorel, you're behaving disgracefully.

SOREL: Simon ought to go into the army, or something.

DAVID: You both ought to be in reformatories.

SOREL: This always happens whenever we play a game. We're a beastly family, and I hate us.

JUDITH: Speak for yourself, dear.

SOREL: I can't, without speaking for everyone else too – we're all exactly the same, and I'm ashamed of us. (*Grasps* SANDY's *hand and drags him off door L.*) Come into the library, Sandy.

MYRA (*rises and goes to table behind sofa*): Charming! It's all perfectly charming!

DAVID (*rising and standing R.C.*): I think it would be better, Judith, if you exercised a little more influence over the children.

JUDITH: That's right – blame it all on me.

DAVID: After all, dear, you started it, by snapping everybody up.

JUDITH (*rises and crosses to him*): You ought never to have married me, David; it was a great mistake.

DAVID: The atmosphere of this house is becoming more unbearable every day, and all because Simon and Sorel are allowed to do exactly what they like.

JUDITH: You sit upstairs all day, writing your novels.

DAVID: Novels which earn us our daily bread.

JUDITH: 'Daily bread' – nonsense! (*Crosses down R.*) We've got enough money to keep us in comfort until we die.

DAVID: That will be very soon, if we can't get a little peace. (*To* MYRA.) Come out into the garden—

*They both go up to window.*

JUDITH: I sincerely hope the night air will cool you.

DAVID (*coming down to* JUDITH): I don't know what's happened to you, lately, Judith.

JUDITH: Nothing's happened to me – nothing ever does. You're far too smug to allow it.

DAVID: Smug! Thank you.

JUDITH: Yes, smug, smug, smug! And pompous!

DAVID: I hope you haven't been drinking, dear?

JUDITH: Drinking! (*Laughs.*) Huh! that's very amusing!

DAVID: I think it's rather tragic, at your time of life.

*He goes out with* MYRA.

JUDITH *goes after them as if to speak, changes her mind, and comes down to L. corner of sofa.*

JUDITH: David's been a good husband to me, but he's wearing a bit thin now.

RICHARD (*rises*): Would you like me to go? To leave you alone for a little?

JUDITH: Why? Are you afraid I shall become violent?

RICHARD (*smiling*): No; I merely thought perhaps I was in the way.

JUDITH: I hope you're not embarrassed – I couldn't bear you to be embarrassed.

RICHARD: Not in the least.

JUDITH: Marriage is a hideous affair altogether, don't you think?

RICHARD: I'm really hardly qualified to judge, you see—

JUDITH: Do stop being non-committal, just for once; it's doubly annoying in the face of us all having lost control so lamentably.

RICHARD: I'm sorry.

JUDITH: There's nothing to be sorry for, really, because, after all, it's your particular 'thing', isn't it? – observing everything and not giving yourself away an inch.

RICHARD: I suppose it is.

JUDITH: You'll get used to us in time, and then you'll feel cosier. Why don't you sit down? (*She sits on sofa.*)

RICHARD (*sits beside her*): I'm enjoying myself very much.

JUDITH: It's very sweet of you to say so, but I don't see how you can be.

RICHARD (*laughing suddenly*): But I am!

JUDITH: There now, that was quite a genuine laugh! We're getting on. Are you in love with Sorel?

RICHARD (*surprised and embarrassed*): In love with Sorel?

JUDITH (*repentantly*): Now I've killed it – I've murdered the little tender feeling of comfort that was stealing over you, by sheer tactlessness! Will you teach me to be tactful?

RICHARD: Did you really think I was in love with Sorel?

JUDITH: It's so difficult to tell, isn't it? – I mean, you might not know yourself. She's very attractive.

RICHARD: Yes, she is – very.

JUDITH: Have you heard her sing?

RICHARD: No, not yet.

JUDITH: She sings beautifully. Are you susceptible to music?

RICHARD: I'm afraid I don't know very much about it.

JUDITH: You probably are, then. I'll sing you something.

RICHARD: Please do.

JUDITH (*rises and crosses to piano; he rises and stands C.*): It's awfully sad for a woman of my temperament to have a grown-up daughter, you know. I have to put my pride in my pocket and develop in her all the charming little feminine tricks which will eventually cut me out altogether.

RICHARD: That wouldn't be possible.

JUDITH: I do hope you meant that, because it was a sweet remark. (*She is at the piano, turning over music.*)

RICHARD (*crosses to piano*): Of course I meant it.

JUDITH: Will you lean on the piano in an attentive attitude? It's such a help.

RICHARD (*leaning on piano*): You're an extraordinary person.

JUDITH (*beginning to play*): In what way extraordinary?

RICHARD: When I first met Sorel, I guessed what you'd be like.

JUDITH: Did you, now? And am I?

RICHARD (*smiling*): Exactly.

JUDITH: Oh, well! . . . (*She plays and sings a little French song.*)

> There is a slight pause when it is finished.

RICHARD (*with feeling*): Thank you.

JUDITH (*rising from the piano*): It's pretty, isn't it?

RICHARD: Perfectly enchanting.

JUDITH (*crosses to sofa*): Shall we sit down again? (*She re-seats herself on sofa.*)

RICHARD (*moving over to her*): Won't you sing any more?

JUDITH: No, no more – I want you to talk to me and tell me all about yourself, and the things you've done.

RICHARD (*sits beside her*): I've done nothing.

JUDITH: What a shame! Why not?

RICHARD: I never realise how *dead* I am until I meet people like you. It's depressing, you know.

JUDITH: What nonsense! You're not a bit dead.

RICHARD: Do you always live here?

JUDITH: I'm going to, from now onwards. I intend to sink into a very beautiful old age. When the children marry, I shall wear a cap.

RICHARD (*smiling*): How absurd!

JUDITH: I don't mean a funny cap.

RICHARD: You're far too full of vitality to sink into anything.

JUDITH: It's entirely spurious vitality. If you troubled to look below the surface, you'd find a very wistful and weary spirit. I've been battling with life for a long time.

RICHARD: Surely such successful battles as yours have been are not wearying?

JUDITH: Yes, they are – frightfully. I've reached an age now when I just want to sit back and let things go on around me – and they do.

RICHARD: I should like to know exactly what you're thinking about – really.

JUDITH: I was thinking of calling you Richard. It's such a nice uncompromising name.

RICHARD: I should be very flattered if you would.

JUDITH: I won't suggest you calling me Judith until you feel really comfortable about me.

RICHARD: But I do – Judith.

JUDITH: I'm awfully glad. Will you give me a cigarette?

RICHARD (*producing case*): Certainly.

JUDITH (*taking one*): Oh, what a divine case!

RICHARD: It was given to me in Japan three years ago. All those little designs mean things.

JUDITH (*bending over it*): What sort of things?

*He lights her cigarette.*

RICHARD: Charms for happiness, luck, and – love.

JUDITH: Which is the charm for love?

RICHARD: That one.

JUDITH: What a dear!

RICHARD *kisses her gently on the neck.*

(*she sits upright, with a scream*): Richard!

RICHARD (*stammering*): I'm afraid I couldn't help it.

JUDITH (*dramatically*): What are we to do? What are we to do?

RICHARD: I don't know.

JUDITH (*rises, thrusts the case in his hand and crosses to R.C.*): David must be told – everything!

RICHARD (*alarmed*): Everything?

JUDITH (*enjoying herself*): Yes, yes. There come moments in life when it is necessary to be honest – absolutely honest. I've trained myself always to shun the underhand methods other women so often employ – the truth must be faced fair and square—

RICHARD (*extremely alarmed*): The truth? I don't quite understand. (*He rises.*)

JUDITH: Dear Richard, you want to spare me, I know – you're so chivalrous; but it's no use. After all, as I said before, David has been a good husband to me, according to his lights. This may, of course, break him up rather, but it can't be helped. I wonder – oh, I wonder how he'll take it! They say suffering's good for writers, it strengthens their psychology. Oh, my poor, poor David! Never mind. You'd better go out into the garden and wait—

RICHARD (*flustered*): Wait? What for? (*Moves to C.*)

JUDITH: For me, Richard, for me. I will come to you later. Wait in the summer-house. I had begun to think that Romance was dead, that I should never know it again. Before, of course, I had my work and my life in the theatre, but now, nothing – nothing! Everything is empty and hollow, like a broken shell. (*She sinks on to form below piano, and looks up at* RICHARD *with a tragic smile, then looks quickly away.*)

RICHARD: Look here, Judith, I apologise for what I did just now. I—

JUDITH (*ignoring all interruption, she rises and crosses to L.C.*): But now you have come, and it's all changed – it's magic! I'm under a spell that I never thought to recapture again. Go along—

*She pushes him towards the garden.*

RICHARD (*protesting*): But, Judith—

JUDITH (*pushing him firmly until he is off*): Don't – don't make it any harder for me. I am quite resolved – and it's the only possible way. Go, go!

*She pushes him into the garden and waves to him bravely with her*

*handkerchief; then she comes back into the room and powders her
nose before the glass and pats her hair into place. Then, assuming an
expression of restrained tragedy, she opens the library door, screams
and recoils genuinely shocked to C.*

*After a moment or two,* SOREL *and* SANDY *come out rather
sheepishly and stand L.C.*

SOREL: Look here, mother, I—

JUDITH: Sorel, what am I to say to you?

SOREL: I don't know, mother.

JUDITH: Neither do I.

SANDY: It was my fault, Mrs Bliss – Judith—

JUDITH: What a fool I've been! What a blind fool!

SOREL: Mother, are you *really* upset?

JUDITH (*with feeling*): I'm stunned!

SOREL: But, darling—

JUDITH (*gently*): Don't speak for a moment, Sorel; we must all
be very quiet, and think—

SOREL: It was nothing, really. For Heaven's sake—

JUDITH: Nothing! I open the library door casually, and what do I
see? I ask you, what do I see?

SANDY: I'm most awfully sorry. . . .

JUDITH: Ssshh! It has gone beyond superficial apologies.

SOREL: Mother, be natural for a minute.

JUDITH: I don't know what you mean, Sorel. I'm trying to
realise a very bitter truth as calmly as I can.

SOREL: There's nothing so very bitter about it.

JUDITH: My poor child!

SOREL (*suddenly*): Very well, then! I love Sandy, and he loves me!

JUDITH: That is the only possible excuse for your behaviour.

SOREL: Why shouldn't we love each other if we want to?

JUDITH: Sandy was in love with me this afternoon.

SOREL: Not real love – you know it wasn't.

JUDITH (*bitterly*): I know now.

SANDY (*crosses to L. of* JUDITH): I say – look here – I'm most
awfully sorry.

JUDITH: There's nothing to be sorry for, really; it's my fault for
having been so – so ridiculous.

SOREL: Mother!

JUDITH (*sadly*): Yes, ridiculous. (*Goes up to piano.*) I'm getting old,

old, and the sooner I face it the better. (*She picks up mirror, looks at herself, and puts it down again quickly.*)

SOREL (*hopelessly*): But, darling . . .

JUDITH (*splendidly – she goes to* SOREL): Youth will be served. You're so pretty, Sorel, far prettier than I ever was – I'm very glad you're pretty.

SANDY (*moving down R.*): I feel a fearful cad.

JUDITH: Why should you? You've answered the only call that really counts – the call of Love, and Romance, and Spring. I forgive you, Sandy, completely. There! (*She goes to him and pats his shoulder.*)

SOREL: Well, that's all right then. (*She sits on sofa.*)

JUDITH: I resent your tone, Sorel; you seem to be taking things too much for granted. Perhaps you don't realise that I am making a great sacrifice. (*Pointing to* SANDY.)

SOREL: Sorry, darling.

JUDITH (*starting to act*): It's far from easy, at my time of life, to—

SOREL (*playing up*): Mother – mother, say you understand and forgive!

JUDITH: Understand! You forget, dear, I am a woman.

SOREL: I know you are, mother. That's what makes it all so poignant.

JUDITH (*magnanimously, to* SANDY): If you want Sorel, truly, I give her to you – unconditionally.

SANDY (*dazed*): Thanks – awfully, Mrs Bliss.

JUDITH: You can still call me Judith, can't you? – it's not much to ask.

SANDY: Judith!

JUDITH (*bravely*): There, now. Away with melancholy. This is all tremendously exciting, and we must all be very happy.

SOREL: Don't tell father – yet.

JUDITH: We won't tell anybody; it shall be *our* little secret.

SOREL: You are splendid, mother!

JUDITH: Nonsense! I just believe in being honest with myself – it's awfully good for one, you know, so cleansing. I'm going upstairs now to have a little aspirin— (*She goes upstairs, and turns.*) Ah, Youth, Youth, what a strange, mad muddle you make of things! (*She goes off upstairs.*)

46

SOREL *heaves a slight sigh.*

SOREL: Well, that's that!

SANDY: Yes. (*Sits on form below piano, looking very gloomy.*)

SOREL: It's all right. Don't look so gloomy – I know you don't love me really.

SANDY (*startled*): I say, Sorel—

SOREL: Don't protest; you know you don't – any more than I love you.

SANDY: But you told Judith—

SOREL (*nonchalantly*): I was only playing up – one always plays up to Mother in this house; it's a sort of unwritten law.

SANDY: Didn't she mean all she said?

SOREL: No, not really; we none of us ever mean *anything.*

SANDY: She seemed awfully upset.

SOREL: It must have been a slight shock for her to discover us clasped tightly in each other's arms.

SANDY (*rising and moving to C.*): I believe I do love you, Sorel.

SOREL: A month ago I should have let you go on believing that, but now I can't – I'm bent on improving myself.

SANDY: I don't understand.

SOREL: Never mind – it doesn't matter. You just fell a victim to the atmosphere, that's all. There we were alone in the library, with the windows wide open, and probably a nightingale somewhere about—

SANDY: I only heard a cuckoo.

SOREL: Even a cuckoo has charm, in moderation. (*Rises and goes to him.*) You kissed me because you were awfully nice and I was awfully nice and we both liked kissing very much. It was inevitable. Then mother found us and got dramatic – her sense of the theatre is always fatal. She knows we shan't marry, the same as you and I do. You're under absolutely no obligation to me at all.

SANDY: I wish I understood you a bit better.

SOREL: Never mind about understanding me – let's go back into the library.

SANDY: All right.

> *They go off door down L.*
> *After a moment's pause,* DAVID *and* MYRA *enter from the garden.*

DAVID: . . . and, you see, he comes in and finds her there waiting for him.

*They come down C.*

MYRA: She hadn't been away at all?

DAVID: No; and that's psychologically right, I'm sure. No woman, under those circumstances, *would*.

MYRA (*sitting on L. end of sofa*): It's brilliant of you to see that. I do think the whole thing sounds most excellent.

DAVID: I got badly stuck in the middle of the book, when the boy comes down from Oxford – but it worked out all right eventually.

MYRA: When shall I be able to read it?

DAVID: I'll send you the proofs – you can help me correct them.

MYRA: How divine! I shall feel most important.

DAVID: Would you like a cigarette, or anything?

MYRA: No, thank you.

DAVID: I think I'll have a drink. (*He goes to table up by window, and pours out some plain soda-water.*)

MYRA: Very well; give me some plain soda-water, then.

DAVID: There isn't any ice – d'you mind?

MYRA: Not a bit.

DAVID (*bringing her drink*): Here you are. (*He goes back and pours himself a whisky-and-soda, and returns to sofa.*)

MYRA: Thank you. (*She sips it.*) I wonder where everybody is.

DAVID: Not here, thank God.

MYRA: It must be dreadfully worrying for you, having a houseful of people.

DAVID (*sits down by her side*): It depends on the people.

MYRA: I have a slight confession to make.

DAVID: Confession?

MYRA: Yes. Do you know why I came down here?

DAVID: Not in the least. I suppose one of us asked you, didn't they?

MYRA: Oh, yes, they asked me, but—

DAVID: Well?

MYRA: I was invited once before – last September.

DAVID: I was in America then.

MYRA: Exactly.

48

DAVID: How do you mean 'exactly'?

MYRA: I didn't come. I'm a very determined woman, you know, and I made up my mind to meet you ages ago.

DAVID: That was charming of you. I'm not much to meet really.

MYRA: You see, I'd read *Broken Reeds*.

DAVID: Did you like it?

MYRA: Like it! I think it's one of the finest novels I've ever read.

DAVID: There now!

MYRA: How do you manage to know so much about women?

DAVID: I'm afraid my knowledge of them is sadly superficial.

MYRA: Oh, no; you can't call Evelyn's character superficial – it's amazing.

DAVID: Why are you being so nice to me? Have you got a plan about something?

MYRA (*laughing*): How suspicious you are!

DAVID: I can't help it – you're very attractive, and I'm always suspicious of attractive people, on principle.

MYRA: Not a very good principle.

DAVID (*leaning towards her*): I'll tell you something – strictly between ourselves.

MYRA: Do!

DAVID: You're wrong about me.

MYRA: Wrong? In what way?

DAVID: I write very bad novels.

MYRA: Don't be so ridiculous!

DAVID: And you *know* I do, because you're an intelligent person.

MYRA: I don't know anything of the sort.

DAVID: Tell me why you're being nice to me.

MYRA: Because I want to be.

DAVID: Why?

MYRA: You're a very clever and amusing man.

DAVID: Splendid!

MYRA: And I think I've rather lost my heart to you.

DAVID: Shall we elope?

MYRA: David!

DAVID: There now, you've called me David!

MYRA: Do you mind?

DAVID: Not at all.

MYRA: I'm not sure that you're being very kind.

DAVID: What makes you think that?

MYRA: You being rather the cynical author laughing up his sleeve at a gushing admirer.

DAVID: I think you're a very interesting woman, and extremely nice-looking.

MYRA: Do you?

DAVID: Yes. Would you like me to make love to you?

MYRA (*rising*): Really – I wish you wouldn't say things like that.

DAVID: I've knocked you off your plate – I'll look away for a minute while you climb on to it again. (*He does so.*)

MYRA (*laughing affectedly. She puts her glass down on table*): This is wonderful! (*She sits down again.*)

DAVID (*turning*): That's right. Now then—

MYRA: Now then, what?

DAVID (*leaning very close to her*): You're adorable – you're magnificent – you're tawny—

MYRA: I'm not tawny.

DAVID: Don't argue.

MYRA: This is sheer affectation.

DAVID: Affectation's very nice.

MYRA: No, it isn't – it's odious.

DAVID: You mustn't get cross.

MYRA: I'm not in the least cross.

DAVID: Yes, you are – but you're very alluring.

MYRA (*perking up*): Alluring?

DAVID: Terribly.

MYRA: I can hear your brain clicking – it's very funny.

DAVID: That was rather rude.

MYRA: You've been consistently rude to me for hours.

DAVID: Never mind.

MYRA: Why have you?

DAVID: I'm always rude to people I like.

MYRA: Do you like me?

DAVID: Enormously.

MYRA: How sweet of you!

DAVID: But I don't like your methods.

MYRA: Methods? What methods?

DAVID: You're far too pleasant to occupy yourself with the commonplace.

MYRA: And you spoil yourself by trying to be clever.

DAVID: Thank you.

MYRA: Anyhow, I don't know what you mean by commonplace.

DAVID: You mean you want me to explain?

MYRA: Not at all.

DAVID: Very well; I will.

MYRA: I shan't listen. (*She stops up her ears.*)

DAVID: You'll pretend not to, but you'll hear every word really.

MYRA (*sarcastically*): You're so inscrutable and quizzical – just what a feminine psychologist should be.

DAVID: Yes, aren't I?

MYRA: You frighten me dreadfully.

DAVID: Darling!

MYRA: Don't call me darling.

DAVID: That's unreasonable. You've been trying to make me – all the evening.

MYRA: Your conceit is outrageous!

DAVID: It's not conceit at all. You've been firmly buttering me up because you want a nice little intrigue.

MYRA (*rising*): How dare you!

DAVID (*pulling her down again*): It's true, it's true. If it weren't, you wouldn't be so angry.

MYRA: I think you're insufferable!

DAVID (*taking her hand*): Myra – dear Myra—

MYRA (*snatching it away – she rises*): Don't touch me!

DAVID: Let's have that nice little intrigue. (*He rises.*) The only reason I've been so annoying is that I love to see things as they are first, and then pretend they're what they're not.

MYRA: Words. (*Moves over R.*) Masses and masses of words!

DAVID (*following her*): They're great fun to play with.

MYRA: I'm glad you think so. Personally, they bore me stiff.

DAVID (*catching her right hand again*): Myra – don't be statuesque.

MYRA: Let go my hand!

DAVID: You're charming.

MYRA (*furiously*): Let go my hand!

DAVID: I won't!

MYRA: You will!

> *She slaps his face hard, and he seizes her in his arms and kisses her.*

DAVID (*between kisses*): You're – perfectly – sweet.

MYRA (*giving in*): David!

DAVID: You must say it's an entrancing amusement. (*He kisses her again.*)

> JUDITH *appears at the top of the stairs and sees them. They break away, he still keeping hold of her hand.*

JUDITH (*coming down C.*): Forgive me for interrupting.

DAVID: Are there any chocolates in the house?

JUDITH: No, David.

DAVID: I should like a chocolate more than anything in the world, at the moment.

JUDITH: This is a very unpleasant situation, David.

DAVID (*agreeably*): Horrible!

JUDITH: We'd better talk it all over.

MYRA (*making a movement*): I shall do nothing of the sort!

JUDITH: Please – please don't be difficult.

DAVID: I apologise, Judith.

JUDITH: Don't apologise – I quite understand.

MYRA: Please let go of my hand, David; I should like to go to bed.

> *She pulls her hand away.*

JUDITH: I should stay if I were you – it would be more dignified.

DAVID (*moves a step towards* JUDITH): There isn't any real necessity for a scene.

JUDITH: I don't want a scene. I just want to straighten things out.

DAVID: Very well – go ahead.

JUDITH: June has always been an unlucky month for me.

MYRA: Look here, Judith – I'd like to explain one thing—

JUDITH (*austerely*): I don't wish to hear any explanations or excuses – they're so cheapening. This was bound to happen sooner or later – it always does, to everybody. The only thing is to keep calm.

DAVID: I am – perfectly.

JUDITH (*sharply*): There is such a thing as being too calm.

DAVID: Sorry, dear.

JUDITH: Life has dealt me another blow, but I don't mind.

DAVID: What did you say?

JUDITH (*crossly*): I said Life had dealt me another blow, but I didn't mind.

DAVID: Rubbish!

JUDITH (*gently*): You're probably irritable, dear, because you're in the wrong. It's quite usual.

DAVID: Now, Judith—

JUDITH: Ssshhh! Let me speak – it is my right.

MYRA: I don't see why.

JUDITH (*surprised*): I am the injured party, am I not?

MYRA: Injured?

JUDITH (*firmly*): Yes, extremely injured.

DAVID (*contemptuously*): Injured!

JUDITH: Your attitude, David, is nothing short of deplorable.

DAVID: It's all nonsense – sheer, unbridled nonsense!

JUDITH: No, David, you can't evade the real issues as calmly as that. I've known for a long time – I've realised subconsciously for years that you've stopped caring for me in 'that way'.

DAVID (*irritably*): What do you mean – 'that way'?

JUDITH (*with a wave of the hand*): Just that way. . . . It's rather tragic, but quite inevitable. I'm growing old now – men don't grow old like women, as you'll find to your cost, Myra, in a year or two. David has retained his youth astonishingly, perhaps because he has had fewer responsibilities and cares than I—

MYRA: This is all ridiculous hysteria.

DAVID (*goes to* MYRA): No, Myra – Judith is right. What are we to do?

MYRA (*furious*): Do? Nothing!

JUDITH (*ignoring her*): Do you love her truly, David?

DAVID (*looks* MYRA *up and down as if to make sure*): Madly!

MYRA (*astounded*): David!

DAVID (*intensely*): You thought just now that I was joking. Couldn't you see that all my flippancy was only a mask, hiding my real emotions – crushing them down desperately—?

MYRA (*scared*): But, David, I—

53

JUDITH: I knew it! The time has come for the dividing of the ways.

MYRA: What on earth do you mean?

JUDITH: I mean that I am not the sort of woman to hold a man against his will.

MYRA: You're both making a mountain out of a molehill. David doesn't love me madly, and I don't love him. It's—

JUDITH: Ssshhh! – you *do* love him. I can see it in your eyes – in your every gesture. David, I give you to her – freely and without rancour. We must all be good friends, always.

DAVID: Judith, do you mean this?

JUDITH (*with a melting look*): You know I do.

DAVID: How can we ever repay you?

JUDITH: Just by being happy. (*Sits on sofa.*) I may leave this house later on – I have a feeling that its associations may become painful, specially in the autumn—

MYRA: Look here, Judith—

JUDITH (*shouting her down*): October is such a mournful month in England. I think I shall probably go abroad – perhaps a *pension* somewhere in Italy, with cypresses in the garden. I've always loved cypresses, they are such sad, weary trees.

DAVID (*goes to her, speaking in a broken voice*): What about the children?

JUDITH: We must share them, dear.

DAVID: I'll pay you exactly half the royalties I receive from everything, Judith.

JUDITH (*bowing her head*): That's very generous of you.

DAVID: You have behaved magnificently. This is a crisis in our lives, and thanks to you—

MYRA (*almost shrieking – moves over to* JUDITH, *but is stopped by* DAVID): Judith – I *will* speak – I—

DAVID (*speaking in a very dramatic voice*): Ssshhh, Myra darling – we owe it to Judith to keep control of our emotions – a scene would be agonising for her now. She has been brave and absolutely splendid throughout. Let's not make things harder for her than we can help. Come, we'll go out into the garden.

MYRA: I will *not* go out into the garden.

JUDITH (*twisting her handkerchief*): Please go. (*Rises to L.C.*) I don't think I can bear any more just now.

DAVID: So this is the end, Judith?

JUDITH: Yes, my dear – the end.

> *They shake hands sadly.*
> SIMON *enters violently from the garden and breaks in between them.*

SIMON: Mother – mother, I've got something important to tell you.

JUDITH (*smiling bravely*): Very well, dear.

SIMON: Where's Sorel?

JUDITH: In the library, I'm afraid.

SIMON (*runs to library door and shouts off*): Sorel, come out – I've got something vital to tell you. (*Returns to C.*)

DAVID (*fatherly*): You seem excited, my boy! What has happened?

SOREL (*enters with* SANDY *and remains down L.*): What's the matter?

SIMON: I wish you wouldn't all look so depressed – it's good news!

DAVID: Good news! I thought perhaps Jackie had been drowned—

SIMON: No, Jackie hasn't been drowned – she's been something else.

JUDITH: Simon, what *do* you mean?

SIMON (*running up C., calling off*). Jackie – Jackie!

> JACKIE *enters coyly from the garden.* SIMON *takes her hand and leads her down C.*

She has become engaged – to me!

JUDITH (*in heartfelt tones*): Simon!

SOREL: Good heavens!

JUDITH: Simon, my dear! Oh, this is too much! (*She cries a little.*)

SIMON: What on earth are you crying about, mother?

JUDITH (*picturesquely*): All my chicks leaving the nest! Now I shall only have my memories left. Jackie, come and kiss me.

> JACKIE *goes to her.*
> SIMON *goes to his* FATHER, *who congratulates him.*

You must promise to make my son happy—

JACKIE (*worried*): But, Mrs Bliss—

JUDITH: Ssshhh! I understand. I have not been a mother for nothing.

JACKIE (*wildly*): But it's not true – we don't—

JUDITH: You're trying to spare my feelings – I know—

MYRA (*furiously*): Well, I'm not going to spare your feelings, or anyone else's. You're the most infuriating set of hypocrites I've ever seen. This house is a complete feather-bed of false emotions – you're posing, self-centred egotists, and I'm sick to death of you.

SIMON: Myra!

MYRA: Don't speak to me – I've been working up for this, only every time I opened my mouth I've been mowed down by theatrical effects. You haven't got one sincere or genuine feeling among the lot of you – you're artificial to the point of lunacy. It's a great pity you ever left the stage, Judith – it's your rightful home. You can rant and roar there as much as ever you like—

JUDITH: Rant and roar! May God forgive you!

MYRA: And let me tell you this—

SIMON (*interrupting*): I'm not going to allow you to say another word to mother—

*They all try to shout each other down.*

| | | |
|---|---|---|
| SOREL: | | You ought to be ashamed of yourself— |
| MYRA: | (*together*) | Let me speak – I will speak— |
| DAVID: | | Look here, Myra— |
| JUDITH: | | This is appalling – appalling! |

| | | |
|---|---|---|
| SOREL: | | You must be stark, staring mad— |
| MYRA: | | Never again – never as long as I live— |
| DAVID: | (*together*) | You don't seem to grasp one thing that— |
| SIMON: | | Why are you behaving like this, anyhow? |

*In the middle of the pandemonium of everyone talking at once,* RICHARD *comes in from the garden. He looks extremely apprehensive, imagining that the noise is the outcome of* JUDITH's *hysterical confession of their lukewarm passion. He goes to* JUDITH's *side, summoning all his diplomatic forces. As he speaks everyone stops talking.*

RICHARD (*with forced calm*): What's happened? Is this a game?

JUDITH's *face gives a slight twitch; then, with a meaning look at* SOREL *and* SIMON, *she answers him.*

JUDITH (*with spirit*): Yes, and a game that must be played to the finish! (*She flings back her arm and knocks* RICHARD *up stage.*)

SIMON (*grasping the situation*): Zara! What does this mean? (*Advancing to her.*)

JUDITH (*in bell-like tones*): So many illusions shattered – so many dreams trodden in the dust—

DAVID (*collapsing on to the form in hysterics*): *Love's Whirlwind*! Dear old *Love's Whirlwind*!

SOREL (*runs over to R., pushes* MYRA *up stage and poses*): I don't understand. You and Victor – My God!

JUDITH (*moves away L., listening*): Hush! Isn't that little Pam crying—?

SIMON (*savagely*): She'll cry more, poor mite, when she realises her mother is a – a—

JUDITH (*shrieking and turning to* SIMON): Don't say it! Don't say it!

SOREL: Spare her that.

JUDITH: I've given you all that makes life worth living – my youth, my womanhood, and now my child. Would you tear the very heart out of me? I tell you, it's infamous that men like you should be allowed to pollute Society. You have ruined my life. I have nothing left – nothing! God in heaven, where am I to turn for help? . . .

SOREL (*through clenched teeth – swings* SIMON *round*): Is this true? Answer me – is this true?

JUDITH (*wailing*): Yes, yes!

SOREL (*as if to strike* SIMON): You cur!!!

JUDITH: Don't strike! He is your father!!!!

*She totters and falls in a dead faint.*

MYRA, JACKIE, RICHARD *and* SANDY *look on, dazed and aghast.*

CURTAIN.

# ACT III

*It is Sunday morning, about ten o'clock. There are various breakfast dishes on a side table L., and a big table is laid down L.C.*

*SANDY appears at the top of the stairs. On seeing no one about, he comes down quickly and furtively helps himself to eggs and bacon and coffee, and seats himself at the table. He eats very hurriedly, casting occasional glances over his shoulder. A door bangs somewhere upstairs, which terrifies him; he chokes violently. When he has recovered he tears a bit of toast from a rack, butters it and marmalades it, and crams it into his mouth. Then, hearing somebody approaching, he darts into the library.*

*JACKIE comes downstairs timorously; her expression is dismal, to say the least of it. She looks miserably out of the window at the pouring rain, then assuming an air of spurious bravado, she helps herself to some breakfast and sits down and looks at it. After one or two attempts to eat it, she bursts into tears.*

*SANDY opens the library door a crack, and peeps out. JACKIE, seeing the door move, screams. SANDY re-enters.*

JACKIE: Oh, it's only you – you frightened me!

SANDY: What's the matter?

JACKIE (*sniffing*): Nothing.

SANDY: I say, don't cry. (*Sits down at the table, facing her.*)

JACKIE: I'm not crying.

SANDY: You were – I heard you.

JACKIE: It's this house. It gets on my nerves.

SANDY: I don't wonder – after last night.

JACKIE: What were you doing in the library just now?

SANDY: Hiding.

JACKIE: Hiding?

SANDY: Yes; I didn't want to run up against any of the family.

58

JACKIE: I wish I'd never come. I had horrible nightmares with all those fearful dragons crawling across the walls.

SANDY: Dragons?

JACKIE: Yes; I'm in a Japanese room – everything in it's Japanese, even the bed.

SANDY: How awful!

JACKIE (*looks up at stairs to see if anyone is coming*): I believe they're all mad, you know.

SANDY: The Blisses?

JACKIE: Yes – they must be.

SANDY: I've been thinking that too.

JACKIE: Do you suppose they know they're mad?

SANDY: No; people never do.

JACKIE: It was Mr Bliss asked me down and he hasn't paid any attention to me at all. I went into his study soon after I arrived yesterday, and he said, 'Who the hell are you?'

SANDY: Didn't he remember?

JACKIE: He did afterwards; then he brought me down to tea and left me.

SANDY: Are you really engaged to Simon?

JACKIE (*bursting into tears again*): Oh, no – I hope not!

SANDY: You were, last night.

JACKIE: So were you – to Sorel.

SANDY: Not properly. We talked it over.

JACKIE: I don't know what happened to me. I was in the garden with Simon, and he was being awfully sweet, and then he suddenly kissed me, and rushed into the house and said we were engaged – and that hateful Judith asked me to make him happy!

SANDY: That's exactly what happened to me and Sorel. Judith *gave* us to one another before we knew where we were.

JACKIE: How frightful!

SANDY: I like Sorel, though; she was jolly decent about it afterwards.

JACKIE: I think she's a cat.

SANDY: Why?

JACKIE: Look at the way she lost her temper over that beastly game.

SANDY: All the same, she's better than the others.

JACKIE: That wouldn't be very difficult.

SANDY (*hiccups loudly*): Hic!

JACKIE: I beg your pardon?

SANDY (*abashed*): I say – I've got hiccups.

JACKIE: Hold your breath.

SANDY: It was because I bolted my breakfast. (*He holds his breath.*)

JACKIE: Hold it as long as you can.

> JACKIE *counts aloud. There is a pause.*

SANDY (*letting his breath go with a gasp*): I can't any more – hic!

JACKIE (*rises and gets sugar basin from side table down L.*): Eat a lump of sugar.

SANDY (*taking one*): I'm awfully sorry.

JACKIE: I don't mind – but it's a horrid feeling, isn't it?

SANDY: Horrid – hic!

JACKIE (*puts sugar basin down in front of* SANDY *and sits again – conversationally*): People have died from hiccups you know.

SANDY (*gloomily*): Have they?

JACKIE: Yes. An aunt of mine once had them for three days without stopping.

SANDY: How beastly!

JACKIE (*with relish*): She had to have the doctor, and everything.

SANDY: I expect mine will *stop* soon.

JACKIE: I hope they will.

SANDY: Hic! Damn!

JACKIE: Drink some water the wrong way round.

SANDY: How do you mean – the wrong way round?

JACKIE (*rising*): The wrong side of the glass. I'll show you. (*She goes to side table L.*) There isn't any water.

SANDY (*rises and stands below table*): Perhaps coffee would do as well.

JACKIE: I've never tried coffee, but it might. (*Picks up his cup and hands it to him.*) There you are!

SANDY (*anxiously*): What do I do?

JACKIE: Tip it up and drink from the opposite side, sort of upside down.

SANDY (*trying*): I can't reach any—

60

JACKIE (*suddenly*): Look out – somebody's coming. Bring it into the library – quick.

SANDY: Bring the sugar.

> JACKIE *picks up sugar basin and runs into library, leaving* SANDY *to follow.*

I might need it again – hic! Oh, God!

> *He goes off into the library hurriedly.*
>
> RICHARD *comes downstairs. He glances round a trifle anxiously, goes to the window, looks out at the rain and shivers, then pulling himself together, he goes boldly to the barometer and taps it. It falls off the wall and breaks; he picks it up quickly and places it on the piano. Then he helps himself to some breakfast and sits down C. chair L. of table.*
>
> MYRA *appears on the stairs, very smart and bright.*

MYRA (*vivaciously*): Good morning.

RICHARD (*half rising*): Good morning.

MYRA: Are we the first down?

RICHARD: No, I don't think so.

MYRA (*looking out of the window*): Isn't this rain miserable?

RICHARD: Appalling! (*Starts to drink his coffee.*)

MYRA: Where's the barometer? (*Crosses to side table L.*)

RICHARD (*at the mention of barometer, he chokes*): On the piano.

MYRA: What a queer place for it to be!

RICHARD: I tapped it, and it fell down.

MYRA: Typical of this house. (*At side table.*) Are you having eggs and bacon, or haddock?

RICHARD: Haddock.

MYRA: I'll have haddock too. I simply couldn't strike out a line for myself this morning. (*She helps herself to haddock and coffee, and sits down opposite* RICHARD.) Have you seen anybody.

RICHARD: No.

MYRA: Good. We might have a little peace.

RICHARD: Have you ever stayed here before?

MYRA: No, and I never will again.

RICHARD: I feel far from well this morning.

MYRA: I'm so sorry, but not entirely surprised.

RICHARD: You see, I had the boiler room.

MYRA: How terrible!

RICHARD: The window stuck and I couldn't open it – I was nearly suffocated. The pipes made peculiar noises all night, as well.

MYRA (*looks round table*): There isn't any sugar.

RICHARD: Oh – we'd better ring.

MYRA: I doubt if it will be the slightest use, but we'll try.

RICHARD (*rising and ringing bell, above door L.*): Do the whole family have breakfast in bed?

MYRA: I neither know – nor care.

RICHARD (*returns to his seat*): They're strange people, aren't they?

MYRA: I think 'strange' is putting it mildly.

*Enter* CLARA. *She comes to top of table.*

CLARA: What's the matter?

MYRA: There isn't any sugar.

CLARA: There is – I put it 'ere myself.

MYRA: Perhaps you'd find it for us, then?

CLARA (*searching*): That's very funny. I could 'ave sworn on me Bible oath I brought it in.

MYRA: Well, it obviously isn't here now.

CLARA: Someone's taken it – that's what it is.

RICHARD: It seems a queer thing to do.

MYRA: Do you think you could get us some more?

CLARA: Oh, yes, I'll fetch you some. (*Looks suspiciously and shakes her finger at* RICHARD.) But mark my words, there's been some 'anky-panky somewhere. (*She goes out.*)

RICHARD *looks after her.*

MYRA: Clara is really more at home in a dressing-room than a house.

RICHARD: Was she Judith's dresser?

MYRA: Of course. What other excuse could there possibly be for her?

RICHARD: She seems good-natured, but quaint.

MYRA: This haddock's disgusting.

RICHARD: It isn't very nice, is it?

*Re-enter* CLARA, *with sugar. She plumps it down on the table.*

CLARA: There you are, dear!

MYRA: Thank you.

CLARA: It's a shame the weather's changed – you might 'ave 'ad such fun up the river.

> There comes the sound of a crash from the library, and a scream.

What's that? (*Crosses to door and flings it open.*) Come out! What are you doing?

> JACKIE *and* SANDY *enter, rather shamefaced.*

JACKIE: Good morning. I'm afraid we've broken a coffee-cup.

CLARA: Was there any coffee in it?

SANDY: Yes, a good deal.

CLARA (*rushing into the library*): Oh dear, all over the carpet!

SANDY: It was my fault. I'm most awfully sorry.

> JACKIE *moves up* L. *above table.*
> CLARA *reappears.*

CLARA: How did you come to do it?

JACKIE: Well, you see, he had the hiccups, and I was showing him how to drink upside down.

MYRA: How ridiculous!

CLARA: Well, thank 'Eaven it wasn't one of the Crown Derbys.

> She goes out.

SANDY: They've gone now, anyhow. (*Moves up to window and looks out.*)

JACKIE: It was the sudden shock, I expect.

SANDY (*observantly*): I say – it's raining!

MYRA: It's been raining for hours.

RICHARD: Mrs Arundel—

MYRA: Yes?

RICHARD: What are you going to do about – about to-day?

MYRA: Nothing, except go up to London by the first train possible.

RICHARD: Do you mind if I come too? I don't think I could face another day like yesterday.

JACKIE: Neither could I. (*Comes down to chair below* RICHARD *and sits.*)

SANDY (*comes eagerly to top of table and sits*): Let's all go away – quietly!

RICHARD: Won't it seem a little rude if we *all* go?

MYRA: Yes, it will. (*To* SANDY.) You and Miss Coryton must stay.

JACKIE: I don't see why.

SANDY: I don't think they'd mind *very* much.

MYRA: Yes, they would. You must let Mr Greatham and me get away first, anyhow. Ring for Clara. I want to find out about trains.

> SANDY *rings bell and returns to his seat.*

RICHARD: I hope they won't all come down now.

MYRA: You needn't worry about that; they're sure to roll about in bed for hours – they're such a slovenly family.

RICHARD: Have you got much packing to do?

MYRA: No; I did most of it before I came down.

> *Re-enter* CLARA – *comes to top of table.*

CLARA: What is it now?

MYRA: Can you tell me what trains there are up to London?

CLARA: When?

MYRA: This morning.

CLARA: Why? – you're not leaving, are you?

MYRA: Yes; Mr Greatham and I have to be up by lunch-time.

CLARA: Well, you've missed the 10.15.

MYRA: Obviously.

CLARA: There isn't another till 12.30.

RICHARD: Good heavens!

CLARA: And that's a slow one.

> *She goes out.*

SANDY (*to* JACKIE): Look here. I'll take you up in my car as soon as you like.

JACKIE: All right; lovely!

MYRA: Oh, you have got a car, haven't you?

SANDY: Yes.

MYRA: Will it hold all of us?

JACKIE: You said it would be rude for us all to go. Hadn't you and Mr Greatham better wait for the train?

MYRA: Certainly not.

RICHARD (*to* SANDY): If there is room, we should be very, very grateful.

SANDY: I think I can squeeze you in.

MYRA: Then that's settled.

JACKIE: When shall we start?

SANDY: As soon as you're ready. (*Rises.*)

JACKIE: Mrs Arundel, what are you going to do about tipping Clara?

MYRA: I don't know. (*To* RICHARD.) What do you think?

RICHARD: I've hardly seen her since I've been here.

JACKIE: Isn't there a housemaid or anything?

RICHARD: I don't think so.

SANDY: Is ten bob enough?

JACKIE: Each?

MYRA: Too much.

RICHARD: We'd better give her one pound ten between us.

MYRA: Very well, then. Will you do it, and we'll settle up in the car?

RICHARD: Must I?

MYRA: Yes. Ring for her.

RICHARD: You'd do it much better.

MYRA: Oh, no, I shouldn't. (*To* JACKIE.) Come on; we'll finish our packing. (*Rises and goes to stairs.*)

JACKIE: All right. (*She follows* MYRA.)

> *They begin to go upstairs.*

RICHARD (*rises and goes to C.*): Here – don't leave me.

SANDY (*crosses to door R.*): I'll just go and look at the car. Will you all be ready in ten minutes?

MYRA: Yes, ten minutes.

> *She goes off with* JACKIE.

SANDY: Righto! (*He rushes out.*)

> RICHARD *moves over to bell as* CLARA *re-enters with large tray.*

CLARA: 'Allo, where's everybody gone?

RICHARD (*sorts out thirty shillings from his note-case*): They've gone to get ready. We're leaving in Mr Tyrell's car.

CLARA: A bit sudden, isn't it?

RICHARD (*pressing the money into her hand*): This is from all of us, Clara. Thank you very much for all your trouble.

CLARA (*surprised*): Aren't you a dear, now! There wasn't any trouble.

RICHARD: There must have been a lot of extra work.

CLARA: One gets used to that 'ere.

RICHARD: Good morning, Clara.

CLARA: Good morning, hope you've been comfortable.

RICHARD: Com— Oh, yes. (*He goes upstairs.*)

> CLARA *proceeds to clear away the dirty breakfast things, which she takes out singing 'Tea for Two' in a very shrill voice. She returns with a fresh pot of coffee, and meets* JUDITH *coming downstairs.*

JUDITH (*goes to head of table and sits*): Good morning, Clara. Have the papers come?

CLARA: Yes – I'll fetch them. (*She goes out and re-enters with papers, which she gives to* JUDITH.)

JUDITH: Thank you. You've forgotten my orange-juice.

CLARA (*pours out a cup of coffee for* JUDITH): No, I 'aven't, dear; it's just outside. (*She goes out again.*)

> JUDITH *turns to the theatrical column of the* Sunday Times.
> SOREL *comes downstairs and kisses her.*

SOREL: Good morning, darling.

JUDITH: Listen to this. (*She reads.*) 'We saw Judith Bliss in a box at the Haymarket on Tuesday, looking as lovely as ever.' There now! I thought I looked hideous on Tuesday.

SOREL: You looked sweet. (*She goes to get herself some breakfast, and sits L. of* JUDITH.)

> CLARA *reappears, with a glass of orange-juice.*

CLARA: There you are, dear. (*Placing it in front of* JUDITH.) Did you see that nice bit in the *Referee*?

JUDITH: *No* – the *Times*.

CLARA: The *Referee*'s much better. (*She finds the place and hands it to* SOREL.)

SOREL (*reading*): 'I saw gay and colourful Judith Bliss at the Waifs and Strays Matinée last week. She was talking vivaciously to Producer Basil Dean. "'sooth," said I to myself, "where ignorance is Bliss, 'tis folly to be wise."'

JUDITH (*taking it from her*): Dear *Referee*! It's so unselfconscious.

CLARA: If you want any more coffee, ring for it. (*She goes out.*)

SOREL: I wish I were sitting on a lovely South Sea Island, with masses of palm-trees and coconuts and turtles—

JUDITH: It would be divine, wouldn't it?

SOREL: I wonder where everybody is.

JUDITH (*still reading*): I wonder ... Mary Saunders has got another failure.

SOREL: She must be used to it by now.

SIMON *comes downstairs with a rush.*

SIMON (*kissing* JUDITH): Good morning, darling. Look! (*He shows her a newly-completed sketch.*)

JUDITH: Simon! How lovely! When did you do it?

SIMON: This morning – I woke early.

SOREL: Let's see. (*Takes sketch from* SIMON.)

SIMON (*looking over her shoulder*): I'm going to alter Helen's face; it's too pink.

SOREL (*laughing*): It's exactly like her. (*Puts it on chair beside her.*)

JUDITH (*patting his cheek*): What a clever son I have!

SIMON: Now then, mother! (*He gets himself breakfast.*)

JUDITH: It's too wonderful – when I think of you both in your perambulators.... Oh dear, it makes me cry! (*She sniffs.*)

SOREL: I don't believe you ever saw us in our perambulators.

JUDITH: I don't believe I did.

SIMON, *having got his breakfast, sits at table R. of* JUDITH.
DAVID *comes downstairs.*

DAVID (*hilariously*): It's finished!

JUDITH: What, dear?

DAVID: The Sinful Woman. (*He kisses* JUDITH.)

JUDITH: How splendid! Read it to us now.

DAVID (*takes chair from table and sits L.C.*): I've got the last chapter here.

JUDITH: Go on, then.

SANDY *rushes in from the front door. On seeing everyone, he halts.*

SANDY: Good morning. (*He bolts upstairs, two at a time.*)

*There is a pause, they all look after him.*

JUDITH: I seem to know that boy's face.

DAVID (*preparing to read*): Listen! You remember that bit when Violet was taken ill in Paris?

JUDITH: Yes, dear. – Marmalade, Simon.

*He passes it to her.*

DAVID: Well, I'll go on from there.

JUDITH: Do, dear.

DAVID (*reading*): 'Paris in spring, with the Champs Elysées alive and dancing in the sunlight; lightly-dressed children like gay painted butterflies—'

SIMON (*shouting to* SOREL): What's happened to the barometer?

SOREL (*sibilantly*): I don't know.

DAVID: Damn the barometer!

JUDITH: Don't get cross, dear.

DAVID: Why can't you keep quiet, Simon, or go away.

SIMON: Sorry, father.

DAVID: Well, don't interrupt again . . . (*Reading.*) '. . . gay painted butterflies; the streets were thronged with hurrying vehicles, the thin peek-peek of taxi-hooters—'

SOREL: I love 'peek-peek'.

DAVID (*ignoring her*): '– seemed to merge in with the other vivid noises, weaving a vast pattern of sound which was Paris—'

JUDITH: What was Paris, dear?

DAVID: *Which* was Paris.

JUDITH: What was Paris?

DAVID: You can't say a vast pattern of sound *what* was Paris.

A *slight pause.*

JUDITH: Yes, but— What was Paris?

DAVID: A vast pattern of sound *which was Paris.*

JUDITH: Oh, I see.

DAVID: 'Jane Sefton, in her scarlet Hispano, swept out of the Rue St Honoré into the Place de la Concorde—'

JUDITH: She couldn't have.

DAVID: Why?

JUDITH: The Rue St Honoré doesn't lead into the Place de la Concorde.

DAVID: Yes, it does.

SOREL: You're thinking of the Rue Boissy d'Anglais, Father.

DAVID: I'm not thinking of anything of the sort.

JUDITH: David darling, don't be obstinate.

DAVID (*hotly*): Do you think I don't know Paris as well as you do?

SIMON: Never mind. Father's probably right.

SOREL: He isn't right – he's wrong!

DAVID: Go on with your food, Sorel.

JUDITH: Don't be testy, David; it's a sign of age.

DAVID (*firmly*): 'Jane Sefton, in her scarlet Hispano, swept out of the Rue St Honoré into the Place de la Concorde—'

JUDITH: That sounds absolutely ridiculous! Why don't you alter it?

DAVID: It isn't ridiculous; it's perfectly right.

JUDITH: Very well, then; get a map, and I'll show you.

SIMON: We haven't got a map.

DAVID (*putting his MS down*): Now, look here, Judith – here's the Rue Royale – (*He arranges the butter-dish and marmalade pot.*) – here's the Crillon Hotel, and *here's* the Rue St Honoré—

JUDITH: It isn't – it's the Boissy d'Anglais.

DAVID: That runs parallel with the Rue de Rivoli.

JUDITH: You've got it all muddled.

DAVID (*loudly – banging the table with his fist*): I have *not* got it all muddled.

JUDITH: Don't shout. You have.

SIMON: Why not let father get on with it?

JUDITH: It's so silly to get cross at criticism – it indicates a small mind.

DAVID: Small mind my foot!

JUDITH: That was very rude. I shall go to my room in a minute.

DAVID: I wish you would.

JUDITH (*outraged*): David!

SOREL: Look here, Father, Mother's right. (*Starts to draw map.*) Here's the Place de la Concorde—

SIMON (*shouting at her*): Oh, shut up, Sorel!

SOREL (*shouting back at him*): Shut up yourself, you pompous little beast!

SIMON: You think you know such a lot about everything, and you're as ignorant as a frog.

SOREL: Why a *frog*?

JUDITH: I give you my solemn promise, David, that you're wrong.

DAVID: I don't want your solemn promise, because I *know* I'm right.

SIMON: It's no use arguing with father, mother.

SOREL: Why isn't it any use arguing with father?

SIMON: Because you're both so pig-headed!

DAVID: Are you content to sit here, Judith, and let your son insult me?

JUDITH: He's your son as well as mine.

DAVID: I begin to doubt it.

JUDITH (*bursting into tears of rage*): David!

SIMON (*consoling her*): Father, how can you!

DAVID (*throwing his MS on floor*): I'll never attempt to read any of you anything again, as long as I live. You're not a bit interested in my work, and you don't give a damn whether I'm a success or a failure.

JUDITH: You're dead certain to be a failure if you cram your books with inaccuracies.

DAVID (*hammering the table with his fist*): I am not inaccurate!

JUDITH: Yes (*Rising.*) you are; and you're foul-tempered and spoilt.

DAVID: Spoilt! I like that! Nobody here spoils me – you're the most insufferable family to live with—

JUDITH: Well, why in Heaven's name don't you go and live somewhere else?

DAVID: There's gratitude!

JUDITH: Gratitude for what, I'd like to know?

SOREL: Mother, keep calm.

JUDITH: Calm! I'm furious.

DAVID: What have you got to be furious about? Everyone rushing round adoring you and saying how wonderful you are—

JUDITH: I am wonderful, Heaven knows, to have stood you for all these years!

SOREL: Mother, do sit down and be quiet. (*Rises.*)

SIMON (*rises and puts his arm round his mother*): How dare you speak to mother like that!

> During this scene, MYRA, JACKIE, RICHARD and SANDY creep downstairs with their bags, unperceived by the family. They make for the front door.

JUDITH (*wailing*): Oh, oh! To think that my daughter should turn against me!

DAVID: Don't be theatrical.

JUDITH: I'm not theatrical – I'm wounded to the heart.

DAVID: Rubbish – rubbish – rubbish!

JUDITH: Don't you say Rubbish to me!

DAVID: I *will* say Rubbish!

*They all shout at each other as loud as possible.*

| | | |
|---|---|---|
| SOREL: | | Ssshhh, father! |
| SIMON: | | That's right! Be the dutiful daughter and encourage your father— |
| | (*together*) | |
| DAVID: | | Listen to me, Judith— |
| JUDITH: | | Oh, this is dreadful – dreadful! |

| | | |
|---|---|---|
| SOREL: | | The whole thing doesn't really matter in the least— |
| SIMON: | | – to insult your mother— |
| DAVID: | (*together*) | The Place de la Concorde— |
| JUDITH: | | I never realised how small you were, David. You're tiny. |

*The universal pandemonium is suddenly broken by the front door slamming. There is dead silence for a moment, then the noise of a car is heard.* SOREL *runs and looks out of the window.*

SIMON (*flops in his chair again*): There now!

SOREL: They've all gone!

JUDITH (*sitting down*): How very rude!

DAVID (*also sitting down*): People really do behave in the most extraordinary manner these days—

JUDITH: Come back and finish your breakfast, Sorel.

SOREL: All right. (*She sits down.*)

*Pause.*

JUDITH: Go on, David darling; I'm dying to hear the end—

DAVID (*picks up his MS from the floor – reading*): 'Jane Sefton, in her scarlet Hispano, swept out of the Rue St Honoré into the Place de la Concorde—'

CURTAIN.

71

# THE VORTEX

# Characters

# ACT I

*The scene is the drawing-room of* MRS LANCASTER'S *flat in London. The colours and decoration are on the verge of being original. The furniture is simple but distinctly expensive.*

*Persons shown are* HELEN SAVILLE *and* PAUNCEFORT QUENTIN. HELEN SAVILLE *and* PAUNCEFORT QUENTIN *are shown in by* PRESTON. HELEN *is a smartly dressed woman of about thirty.* 'PAWNIE' *is an elderly maiden gentleman.*

PRESTON: I'm expecting Mrs Lancaster in at any moment now, ma'am.

HELEN: Thank you, Preston, we'll wait a little.

PRESTON: Shall I get you some tea?

HELEN: No thanks, we've already had some – give me a cigarette, Pawnie, they're in that box on the table.

> PAWNIE *hands her cigarette box.* PRESTON *goes out.*

PAWNIE: It may be tiresome of me, but I think all this colouring is oppressive.

HELEN: You make such a 'Fetish' of house decoration, Pawnie.

PAWNIE (*wandering round the room*): Not at all, but I do like things to be good and right.

HELEN: Well, I don't consider the new frieze in your bathroom either good or right.

PAWNIE: How can you, Helen! It's too marvellous for words. Parelli designed it specially for me.

HELEN: Personally, it would make me self-conscious to sit in a bath surrounded by frisky gods and goddesses all with such better figures than mine.

PAWNIE: I find it encouraging. This whole room is so typical of Florence.

HELEN: In what way?

PAWNIE: Every way. Look at the furniture.

HELEN: A little artificial perhaps, but quite harmless.

75

PAWNIE: Dear Helen, you're such a loyal friend.

HELEN: I'm very fond of Florence.

PAWNIE: We all are. Oh, my God, look at that lamp-shade!

HELEN: I gave it to her last Christmas.

PAWNIE: Wasn't that a little naughty of you?

HELEN: I don't see why, it's extremely pretty.

PAWNIE: Too unrestrained. Such a bad example for the servants. (*He takes up frame from desk.*) Who's this boy?

HELEN: Tom Veryan. You must have seen him.

PAWNIE: Florence's past, present or future?

HELEN: Present.

PAWNIE: He has that innocent look that never fails to attract elderly women.

HELEN: Don't be a cat.

PAWNIE: I wasn't meaning Florence, she's too divine to be in any marked category.

HELEN: I wonder.

PAWNIE: Oh, yes, Helen, deathless sort of magnetism, you know.

HELEN: I often wonder what will happen to Florence eventually.

PAWNIE: My dear, I'm far too occupied in wondering what's going to happen to me to worry about other people.

HELEN: I've always thought your course was quite clear, Pawnie.

PAWNIE: However offensive that remark was intended to be, Helen, I shall take it in the most complimentary spirit.

HELEN: I'm sure you will.

PAWNIE: I expect Florence will just go on and on, then suddenly become quite beautifully old, and go on and on still more.

HELEN: It's too late now for her to become beautifully old, I'm afraid. She'll have to be young indefinitely.

PAWNIE: I don't suppose she'll mind that, but it's trying for David.

HELEN: And fiendish for Nicky.

PAWNIE: Oh, no, my dear, you're quite wrong there. I'm sure Nicky doesn't care a damn.

HELEN: It's difficult to tell with Nicky.

PAWNIE: He's divinely selfish; all amusing people are.

HELEN: Did you hear him play in Paris?

PAWNIE: Yes.

HELEN: Well?

PAWNIE: Erratic – one or two things perfect, but he's slovenly.

HELEN: He only takes things seriously in spurts, but still he's very young.

PAWNIE: Do you really think that's a good excuse.

HELEN: No, I'm afraid not, especially when so much depends on it.

PAWNIE: What does depend on it?

HELEN: Everything – his life's happiness.

PAWNIE: Don't be so terribly intense, dear.

HELEN: It's true.

PAWNIE: I'm quite sure Nicky will be perfectly happy as long as he goes on attracting people; he loves being attractive.

HELEN: Naturally, he's Florence's son.

PAWNIE: Such an exciting thing to be.

HELEN: You don't believe Nicky's got anything in him at all, do you?

PAWNIE (lightly): I don't think it matters, anyway.

HELEN: I do.

PAWNIE: But you've got a loving nature, Helen. I always knew it.

HELEN: Nicky hasn't had a chance.

PAWNIE: Nonsense – he's had everything he wanted ever since the day he was born, and he'll go on wasting his opportunities until he dies.

HELEN: Quite possibly.

PAWNIE: Well, there you are then.

HELEN: He may have had everything he wanted, but he's had none of the things he really needs.

PAWNIE: Are you talking socially or spiritually.

HELEN: You're quite right, Pawnie, you wouldn't be so beautifully preserved if you'd wasted any of your valuable time or sincerity.

PAWNIE: I forgive you for that, Helen, freely.

HELEN: Thank you so much.

PAWNIE: You must realise one thing, everyone is sacrificed to Florence – it's as it should be – of course, she's a couple of hundred years too late – she ought to have been a flaunting, intriguing King's mistress, with black page boys and jade baths and things too divine —

*Enter* PRESTON.

PRESTON *(announcing)*: Miss Hibbert.

*Enter* CLARA HIBBERT – *she is affected, but quite well dressed.* PRESTON *goes out.*

CLARA: My *dears*. Isn't Florence back *yet*?

HELEN: No, we're waiting for her.

PAWNIE: You look harassed, Clara.

CLARA: I am harassed.

HELEN: Why?

CLARA: I'm singing to-night for Laura Tennant – she's giving a dreadful reception at her dreadful house for some dreadful Ambassador —

PAWNIE: How dreadful!

CLARA: No one will listen to me, of course – they'll all be far too busy avoiding the Cup and searching for the Champagne.

HELEN: What are you singing?

CLARA: One Gabriel Faure, two Reynaldo Hahn's and an Aria.

PAWNIE: Which Aria?

CLARA: I can't think, but my accompanist will know – I've got a frightful headache.

HELEN: Why don't you take off your hat?

CLARA: My dear, I daren't – I've just had my hair done – I suppose you haven't got a 'Cachet Faivre', either of you?

HELEN: No, but Florence has, I expect – Preston will know where they are – ring the bell, Pawnie.

PAWNIE *(ringing bell)*: My poor Clara – I do hope your singing to-night will justify the fuss you're making this afternoon.

CLARA: Don't be so *brutal*, Pawnie.

HELEN: Is Gregory going with you?

CLARA: Of *course* – I *never* sing unless he's there – he gives me such marvellous moral support.

PAWNIE: 'Moral' is hardly the word *I* should have chosen, dear.

*Enter* PRESTON.

78

HELEN: Do you know if Mrs Lancaster has any 'Cachet Faivre' anywhere?

PRESTON: Yes, ma'am – I think so.

CLARA: *Do* get me one, Preston, I'm suffering *tortures*.

PRESTON: Very well, miss.

> *She goes out.*

PAWNIE: Preston has such wonderful poise, hasn't she?

HELEN: She needs it in this house.

CLARA: I do wish Florence would hurry up. I want to borrow her green fan. I've got a new Patou frock that positively *demands* it.

HELEN: She can't be long now.

CLARA: I suppose I daren't ask Preston for the fan and creep away with it?

HELEN: I shouldn't, if I were you – Florence is very touchy over that sort of thing.

CLARA: She promised it to me ages ago.

PAWNIE: Surely there isn't such a desperate hurry? You won't be singing until about half-past eleven.

CLARA (*petulantly*): My *dear*, I've got to *rehearse* – I don't know a word —

> *Re-enter* PRESTON *with a 'Cachet Faivre' and a glass of water.*

CLARA: You're a *Saint*, Preston – thank you a *thousand* times —

PAWNIE: Soak it a little first, dear, or you'll choke, and I should *detest* that.

> CLARA *soaks 'Cachet' and then swallows it.* PRESTON *goes out.*

CLARA: Now I must lie down *flat* – get out of the way, Helen.

PAWNIE: Perhaps you'd like us *both* to go *right* out of the room and sit in the *hall?*

CLARA: No, Pawnie, I should never expect the least consideration from you.

> *She lies down flat on the divan,* HELEN *arranges cushions for her.*

CLARA: Thank you, Helen darling – I shall always come to you whenever I'm ill.

HELEN: That *will* be nice.

> *Enter* FLORENCE LANCASTER *followed by* TOM VERYAN. FLOR-
> ENCE *is brilliantly dressed almost to the point of being 'outre'. Her*

*face still retains the remnants of great beauty.* TOM *is athletic and good looking. One feels he is good at games and extremely bad at everything else.*

FLORENCE: Helen – Pawnie, have you been here long?

PAWNIE: No, only a few hours.

FLORENCE: My dear. I'm so frightfully sorry – we've been held up for ages in the traffic. Davis is a congenital idiot. Always manages to get to a turning just as the policeman puts out his hand. No initiative whatever. What's happened to Clara? Has she been run over?

CLARA: No, dear, I've got a frightful head.

FLORENCE: Pawnie, you know Tom, don't you? – Tom Veryan, Mr Quentin, I'm sure you'll adore one another.

TOM (*shaking hands*): How are you?

PAWNIE: Very well, thank you – how sweet of you to ask me?

FLORENCE: Is there anything I can do, Clara?

CLARA: Yes, dear, lend me your green fan for to-night.

FLORENCE: All right – but you *won't* get too carried away with it, will you, dear? I should hate the feathers to come out. Does anyone want any tea?

HELEN: No thanks, dear.

FLORENCE: Cocktails, then?

PAWNIE: It's too early.

FLORENCE (*ringing bell*): It's never too early for a cocktail.

CLARA: I should like to go quite quietly into a Convent, and never see anybody again ever —

PAWNIE: Gregory would be bored stiff in a Convent.

FLORENCE: We've just been to a most frightful Charity *matinée*. Nothing but inaudible speeches from dreary old actors, and leading ladies nudging one another all over the stage. (PRESTON *enters.*) Cocktails, Preston, and ask Barker to wrap up my green fan for Miss Hibbert to take away with her.

PRESTON: Very good, ma'am.

    *She goes out.*

CLARA: You're an angel, Florence – I think I'll sit up now.

FLORENCE: Do, dear, then Tom will be able to sit down.

CLARA (*sitting up*): I really do feel most peculiar.

PAWNIE: You look far from normal, dear.

CLARA: If Pawnie's rude to me any more I shall burst into tears.

FLORENCE: Tom, give me a cigarette.

PAWNIE: Here are some.

FLORENCE: No, Tom has a special rather hearty kind that I adore.

CLARA: Lend me your lip stick, Helen, mine has sunk down into itself.

HELEN: Here you are.

CLARA: What a lovely colour! I look far prettier than I feel.

FLORENCE (to TOM): Thank you, angel.

CLARA: I shan't be able to get down to the house until Saturday evening, Florence – I'm seeing Gregory off to Newcastle.

PAWNIE: Why Newcastle?

CLARA: His home's just near there – isn't it too awful for him?

FLORENCE: Well, wire me the time of your train, won't you?

CLARA: Of course, dear.

HELEN: You're smelling divinely, Florence. What is it?

FLORENCE (flicking her handkerchief): It is good, isn't it?

PAWNIE: 'Narcisse Noir' of Caron, I use it.

FLORENCE: Yes, you would, Pawnie.

*Re-enter* PRESTON *with parcel.*

PRESTON: Here is the fan, miss.

CLARA (taking it): Thank you so much – you are sweet, Florence. A fan gives me such a feeling of security when I'm singing modern stuff (PRESTON goes out.) I must rush now —

FLORENCE: Don't you want a cocktail before you go?

CLARA: No, darling – I should only hiccup all the evening. Good-bye, you've been such a comfort – good-bye, Helen – Pawnie, you will be nicer to me over the week-end, won't you? I shall be so depressed, what with Gregory going away and every-thing – Good-bye, Tom – I shall dine in bed and give way at every pore —

*She goes out.*

PAWNIE: Poor Clara – she eternally labours under the delusion that she really matters.

HELEN: We all do that a little.

FLORENCE (laughing): You're awfully cruel to her, Pawnie.

PAWNIE: She upsets my vibrations.

FLORENCE (*before glass*): I've taken a sudden hatred to this hat. (*She takes it off.*) That's better – are you going to *The New Elaine* to-night, either of you?

HELEN: I'm not – but Pawnie is, of course.

PAWNIE: It's going to be *amazing* – what a cast, my dear! Marvellous Selwyn Steele, Nora Dean, and that perfect woman, Lily Burfield —

HELEN: I can't stand her, she always over-acts.

PAWNIE (*incensed*): How *can* you, Helen! Did you see her in *Simple Faith*?

HELEN: Yes, unfortunately.

PAWNIE: Oh, you really are too tiresome for words!

HELEN: Her technique creaks like machinery.

PAWNIE: It's sacrilege – she's too, too marvellous.

*Enter* PRESTON *with a tray of cocktails. Everyone helps themselves.*

FLORENCE: What do you think about it, Tom?

TOM: I've never seen her.

FLORENCE: Yes, you have. About three months ago, at the *Comedy*.

TOM: Oh. . . . I don't remember.

PAWNIE: Don't remember! An artist like that! Good God, it's agony!

HELEN: You'll look awfully tired at dinner-time, Pawnie, if you don't calm down a little.

FLORENCE: This is special – my own invention.

HELEN: Absolutely delicious.

TOM: A bit too sweet.

FLORENCE: Tom, *darling,* don't be so taciturn – he's always taciturn after a *matinée*.

PAWNIE: When's Nicky coming back?

FLORENCE: To-morrow, isn't it too divine? He's been away for a whole year, but I saw him for a moment on my way through Paris last month.

PAWNIE: Has he been working hard?

FLORENCE: I suppose so, but you know what Nicky is – bless his heart!

PAWNIE: I heard him play at Yvonne Mirabeau's.

FLORENCE: She's a loathsome woman, isn't she?

HELEN: Not as bad as that.

PAWNIE: She's a half-wit. I can't bear half-wits.

FLORENCE: She goes on so dreadfully about things – devastating.

PAWNIE: Funny Nicky liking her so much.

FLORENCE: Only because she keeps on saying how wonderful he is – that always appeals to Nicky.

PAWNIE: How old is he now?

FLORENCE: Twenty-four. Isn't it absurd to think I have such a grown-up son – old General Fenwick said last Thursday that — (*The telephone rings, she goes to it.*) Hallo – hallo – yes, my dear, how are you? – Yes, so am I, simply worn out. No, when? How perfectly marvellous.... No, dear, it's a prescription: but I can let you have a little in a jar.... Quite easy, all you do is just rub it on at night.... Don't be so silly ... not in the least, if you send the car round that will be all right.... Very well.... Good-bye, darling. (*She hangs up receiver.*) I give Clara Hibbert ten for stupidity, don't you, Helen?

HELEN: A hundred and ten.

PAWNIE: Ten's the limit.

TOM: I say, Florence – I think I'd better be getting along if I've got to be dressed and back here by half-past seven —

FLORENCE: You've got half an hour.

TOM: That's not very much.

FLORENCE: The car's outside ... take it and send it straight back.

PAWNIE: Can it drop me, Florence dear? I always feel so much richer in your car than anyone else's.

FLORENCE: Of course, Pawnie.

    *The telephone rings again.*

FLORENCE (*at telephone*): Hallo ... yes ... speaking.... How do you do —?

PAWNIE: Good-bye, Helen, it's been divine —

HELEN: Ring me up at tea-time to-morow.

FLORENCE: ... How perfectly sweet of you ... now, now really ... well, naturally, if you persist in saying such charming things ... (*laughing gaily*) ... what nonsense....

PAWNIE: Good-bye, Florence —

FLORENCE (*she puts her hand over mouthpiece*): It's that awful

General Fenwick. . . . Good-bye, Pawnie dear, you're coming down to the house on Friday?

PAWNIE: Yes, too lovely —

FLORENCE: Helen's coming by the five o'clock – you'd better travel together.

PAWNIE: Perfect. (*To* TOM.) Are you ready?

TOM: Quite.

PAWNIE (*as they go out*): You *can* drop me first, can't you? I'm not as young as I was —

FLORENCE (*at telephone*): Please forgive me – people rushing in and out, this house grows more like a railway station every day . . . now, General, that was a deliberate compliment. (*She laughs.*) Ridiculous man . . . very well. . . . good-bye. (*She hangs up receiver.*) My God, ten for dreariness!

HELEN: He's not a bad old thing.

FLORENCE: No, but he tries to be, and that's what's so frightful. (*Arranging her hair before glass.*) I look like Death. . . . Isn't Tom a darling?

HELEN: Yes, dear, without being aggressively brilliant.

FLORENCE: I'm afraid, Helen, you're getting rather bitter.

HELEN: Nonsense.

FLORENCE: It's silly to be sarcastic about Tom.

HELEN: It's better than being maudlin about him.

FLORENCE: I don't know what you mean, dear. I'm not in the least maudlin, and never have been about anybody. I sometimes wish I could be – I'm too hard.

HELEN (*taking a cigarette*): Tom will let you down.

FLORENCE: Let me down? Why . . . how . . . I don't understand —

HELEN: You're more in love with him than he is with you.

FLORENCE: Don't be so *absurd*, Helen.

HELEN: It's true.

FLORENCE (*complacently*): He adores me – worships me – he's never seen anyone like me before in his life. I'm something strange . . . exotic —

HELEN: You're more in love with him than he is with you.

FLORENCE: You're getting on my nerves to-day, Helen.

HELEN: You do see that I'm right, don't you?

84

FLORENCE: If you knew some of the things he's said to me.

HELEN: I can guess them.

FLORENCE: That boy was utterly unawakened until he met me.

HELEN: He's very young.

FLORENCE: I've taught him – everything.

HELEN: Or nothing.

FLORENCE: Helen, I believe you're jealous.

HELEN: Don't be a fool.

FLORENCE: I wish I hadn't this fatal knack of seeing through people.

HELEN: How's David?

FLORENCE: I don't know – he ought to be home soon.

HELEN: Doesn't he ever suspect anything?

FLORENCE: Of course not – he adores me.

HELEN: It seems so strange not to see —

FLORENCE: I'm devoted to David – I'd do anything for him, anything in the world – but he's grown old and I've kept young – it does muddle things up so. I can't help having a temperament, can I?

HELEN: Temperament. . . . No.

FLORENCE: David's always loved me and never understood me – you see, I'm such an extraordinary *mixture*. I have so many *sides* to my character. I adore being at home and running the house and looking after David and Nicky —

HELEN. You don't exactly overdo it.

FLORENCE: Well, Nicky's been away for such ages. Also, one must be in London for the season. You can't expect me to bury myself in the country indefinitely – I shall be there practically all through the spring and summer.

HELEN: Lovely tennis parties and cricket weeks and things —

FLORENCE: Certainly.

HELEN (*kissing her*): You're a divine creature, Florence.

FLORENCE (*basking*): Am I? (*The telephone rings.*) Hallo – yes – speaking. (*To* HELEN *in a whisper.*) It's Inez Zulieta, I never went to her recital. . . . Inez, *darling*, I never recognised your voice . . . didn't you get my note? . . . it was absolutely true, I was in agony. . . . Inez, don't be angry, if you only knew how I longed for the sound of your wonderful, wonderful voice . . .

darling ... Inez, don't be so cruel ... to-morrow, then. (*She
hangs up receiver.*) I do wish Inez wasn't so persistent.

HELEN: You never stop encouraging her.

FLORENCE: Oh, Helen, I'm so tired of everyone.

HELEN: Except Tom?

FLORENCE: Yes, except Tom; he's such a darling.

HELEN: How do you think he and Nicky will get on?

FLORENCE: Marvellously – Tom loves music.

HELEN: He says he does.

FLORENCE: My dear, I took him to that Russian thing the other
day and he sat entranced from beginning to end.

HELEN: Poor Nicky!

FLORENCE: Why do you say that?

HELEN: Because I sometimes feel it.

FLORENCE (*suddenly furious*): Oh, I wonder why we're such
friends – we're so opposite – you don't understand me a bit. I
used to think you did, but you've been different lately –
unsympathetic.

HELEN: No, I haven't.

FLORENCE: Yes, you have – over Tom – I believe you're in love
with him yourself.

HELEN (*smiling*): No – it isn't that.

FLORENCE: Anyhow, you can't bear him being in love with me.

HELEN: I don't think he is – really. I quite realise that he *was*
very violently infatuated, but that is wearing off a bit now. I'm
beginning to see him as he is. . . .

FLORENCE: No, no, it's not true – you don't understand —

HELEN: We *are* friends, Florence, though we're so 'opposite'.
Do you really know the truth – inside you? Or is all this shrill
vanity real?

FLORENCE: What's the matter with you?

HELEN: You're ten years older than I am, but when I'm your age
I shall be twenty years older than you.

FLORENCE: *Darling*, how deliciously involved – what *can* you
mean by that?

HELEN: I mean, I think it's silly not to grow old when the time
comes.

*She rises and goes towards door.*

FLORENCE (*outraged*): Helen! (*There is suddenly heard a violent knocking at the front door.*) What on earth is that?

> *There is a noise outside, then the door bursts open and* NICKY *enters. He is extremely well dressed in travelling clothes. He is tall and pale, with thin, nervous hands.*

FLORENCE: Nicky.

NICKY: Mother.

> *He embraces her.*

FLORENCE: But I'd no idea – I thought you were coming to-morrow.

NICKY: No, to-day – I wrote to you.

FLORENCE: I'm terribly, terribly excited.

NICKY: Helen, dear, how are you?

> *He kisses her.*

HELEN: Splendid, Nicky.

FLORENCE: I can't get over your arriving like this. . . . I never realized —

NICKY: Silly . . . you're looking awfully well.

FLORENCE: Am I?

NICKY: Wonderful, as usual.

FLORENCE: I was talking to George Morrison only last Thursday —

NICKY: The man who wrote that fearful book?

FLORENCE: It isn't a fearful book, it's brilliant – anyhow, he absolutely refused to believe that I had a grown-up son.

HELEN: My dears, I must fly.

NICKY: Don't go yet.

HELEN: I must – I'm hours late as it is.

NICKY: Be a little later, then.

FLORENCE: Remember, five o'clock train on Friday.

NICKY: Oh, is she coming down to the house – divine?

HELEN: Yes, if Florence is still speaking to me – good-bye.

> *She goes out.*

NICKY: Have you been having a scene?

FLORENCE: No, dear.

NICKY: She's a darling – Helen —

FLORENCE: Extremely stupid and tactless sometimes.

NICKY: It doesn't feel as though I'd been away at all.

FLORENCE: I've missed you appallingly – we had such a short time together in Paris – did you enjoy all my letters?

NICKY: I adored them – so did John Bagot. I used to read most of them aloud to him. He's mad on you, saw your pictures in the *Tatler*, or something, and fell in love with it.

FLORENCE: Is he nice?

NICKY: He's grand.

FLORENCE: We must all dine at the Embassy. When is he coming to England?

NICKY: Not until after Christmas.

FLORENCE: You must see my new photographs, they're wonderful.

> *She takes large packet from desk.*

NICKY: It's heavenly – being back.

FLORENCE: Look.

NICKY: I don't like that one.

FLORENCE: How can you, Nicky! – Tom likes that one best of all.

NICKY: Who's Tom?

FLORENCE: Tom Veryan – he's a dear, you'll like him frightfully – you know – the very nicest type of Englishman.

NICKY: I hate the very nicest type of Englishman.

FLORENCE: Don't be tiresome, Nicky, he's only twenty-four, and they all think *so* well of him —

NICKY: All who?

FLORENCE: All his officers and people, he's in the Brigade.

NICKY (*holding photograph away from him and scrutinising it through half-closed eyes*): Now that one really is *enchanting* – they've got your hair *beautifully* – Oh, yes, my dear, it's perfect.

FLORENCE (*complacently*): It *is* good – she's sweet – Madame Henderson, she simply won't hear of my paying for these – she says it's quite sufficient to be allowed to exhibit them in the window.

NICKY: Is anyone dining this evening?

FLORENCE: No – Oh, dear, I'd forgotten – I'm dining out with Tom.

NICKY: Oh – I see.

FLORENCE: Your first night home, too – how perfectly fiendish. What a fool I am to have muddled it up.

NICKY: It doesn't matter, darling.

FLORENCE: Oh, but it *does*. I wonder if we could get another seat —

NICKY: Seat, what for?

FLORENCE: We're going to the first night of *The New Elaine*, it's going to be marvellous.

NICKY: Who's in it?

FLORENCE: Nora Dean and Selwyn Steele —

NICKY: Oh, God!

FLORENCE: It's silly of you *always* to jeer at Selwyn Steele. He's a brilliant actor, if only he could get away from his wife. . . .

NICKY: I couldn't bear him to-night, anyway, I'm tired. Is father home yet?

FLORENCE: No, I don't think so. Oh, I do feel such a beast —

NICKY: Don't be silly – honestly, I don't mind a bit.

FLORENCE: I know – you have a nice quiet dinner here and join us at the Embassy afterwards.

NICKY: Is it a late night?

FLORENCE: Yes, they play the most heavenly tune there now – Tom always makes them do it over and over again – I'll put it on —

*She goes to the gramophone.*

NICKY: How's Iris?

FLORENCE: My dear, don't speak of her.

NICKY: Why – what's she done?

FLORENCE: She's been absolutely foul.

NICKY: In what way?

FLORENCE: Every way – I never trusted her, luckily – Thank God I've got instincts about people – listen, isn't this marvellous – She said the most filthy things to Gloria Craig about me – I always knew she was insanely jealous, but there are limits. I loathe being at people's beck and call. . . . Come and dance.

NICKY (*as they dance*): I'm sorry you've rowed – I rather liked her —

FLORENCE: Only because she kept on saying how wonderful you were. . . . She doesn't know a thing about music really.

NICKY: Oh, yes, she does.

FLORENCE: It's merely bluff – all that appreciation – *Darling*, how oddly you're dancing.

NICKY: It's probably because we haven't danced together for so long. . . .

FLORENCE: Anyhow, now she's gone off to Monte Carlo with Violet Fenchurch – silly fool —

> *Enter* DAVID LANCASTER. *He is an elderly grey-haired pleasant man.*

DAVID (*delighted*): Nicky – my boy —

NICKY (*kissing him*): Hallo, father —

DAVID: I thought – Florence said – to-morrow —

NICKY: Mother muddled it up.

DAVID: You look rather tired.

NICKY: I'm splendid – how's everything?

DAVID: The same as usual. I've made lots of improvements down at the house.

FLORENCE: David thinks and talks of nothing but the farm —

DAVID: It's beginning to pay a bit – Peterson's an awfully good man.

NICKY: We'll make a grand tour of it on Sunday.

DAVID: Have you enjoyed yourself in Paris?

NICKY: Oh, yes, rather – it's a splendid place to work.

DAVID: It never struck me that way quite, but still —

FLORENCE: Sophie de Molignac said Nicky's playing had improved wonderfully.

DAVID: I'm so glad, Nicky.

NICKY: I've been doing some Spanish stuff lately.

DAVID: I wish I knew more about it.

NICKY: Never mind, father.

DAVID: Come to my room and talk, I can't bear that thing —

FLORENCE: Father's such a beast, he never will dance with me.

DAVID: Is the *Evening News* anywhere about?

NICKY: Yes, here.

> *He gives it to him.*

DAVID: I'm so glad you're home again, Nicky – don't forget – come and talk. . . .

*He goes out.*

FLORENCE: David's so much happier in the country.

NICKY: Why on earth doesn't he retire and live at the house for good?

FLORENCE: Work has become such a habit with him – he's always hated giving up habits.

NICKY: Mother – I've got something rather important to tell you.

FLORENCE: Darling, how thrilling! What is it?

NICKY: I am engaged to be married.

FLORENCE: What!

NICKY: Practically – as much as one can be these days.

FLORENCE: Nicky!

NICKY: Don't look so stricken.

FLORENCE: But, Nicky – I never sort of visualised you being engaged, or married, or anything.

NICKY: Why not?

FLORENCE: You're not old enough.

NICKY: I'm twenty-four.

FLORENCE: You don't look it. . . . Thank God!

NICKY: What do you really feel about it, mother?

FLORENCE: *Darling* – I hardly know what to say – you've sprung it on me so suddenly – who is she?

NICKY: A girl called Bunty Mainwaring.

FLORENCE: What a silly name!

NICKY: It isn't at all – it's very attractive.

FLORENCE: Is she an actress, or a student, or what?

NICKY: Neither – she is what is technically termed a 'lady'.

FLORENCE: Do you think she'll like me?

NICKY: She went mad over your photograph.

FLORENCE: Which one?

NICKY: The 'looking out of the window' one.

FLORENCE: That really is one of the best I've ever had done.

NICKY: She said you had the face of an heroic little boy.

FLORENCE: What a *divine* thing to say!

*She glances at herself in the glass.*

NICKY: She does say divine things – she's supremely intelligent.

FLORENCE: Is she in Paris?

NICKY: No, she came over with me to-day.

FLORENCE: Where does she live?

NICKY: Just round the corner in Carbury Square.

FLORENCE: Near the Churchingtons?

NICKY: It's her mother's house, but her mother's away just now, so I asked her to change quickly and come on here.

FLORENCE: Nicky!

NICKY: Why not? I wanted you to see her as soon as possible.

FLORENCE (*realising parental responsibility*): It's an awful shock, you know.

NICKY: Nonsense, mother – you're quite excited about it, really.

FLORENCE (*with determination*): I shall be charming to her.

NICKY: Then she'll adore you at once – probably too much, and I shall be jealous.

FLORENCE: You'd better both dine here together and come on to the Embassy – how old is she?

NICKY: Twenty-three.

FLORENCE: What does she do?

NICKY: Nothing much – she writes things occasionally.

FLORENCE: Where did you meet her?

NICKY: First of all at a party at Olive Lloyd-Kennedy's.

FLORENCE: I can't bear Olive Lloyd-Kennedy – she's a cat.

NICKY: Then I met her again at Marion Fawcett's – a frightful sort of reception affair – she was staying with her.

FLORENCE: She seems to move exclusively among my worst enemies – is she pretty?

NICKY: I don't know – I haven't really noticed.

FLORENCE (*with a touch of real feeling*): Nicky, darling, I do feel so extraordinary about it.

NICKY: Why extraordinary?

FLORENCE: It's a milestone, isn't it – you being engaged? A definite milestone? (*She catches sight of herself.*) Look at my nose. (*She powders it.*) I do hope she'll like me – I must go and dress now, Tom is fetching me at half-past seven – bring her to my room when she comes.

NICKY: Don't go for a minute.

FLORENCE: I must, really – Tom will be furious.

NICKY: Oh, damn Tom!

FLORENCE: Oh, Nicky, *don't* go and take one of your tiresome prejudices against him.

NICKY (*smiling*): All right, I'll try not to.

FLORENCE: He's frightfully good-looking.

NICKY: Oh!

FLORENCE: And he adores music.

NICKY: Now, then, mother —

FLORENCE: He does, honestly.

NICKY: Good.

FLORENCE: And he dances beautifully.

NICKY: I shall never stop dancing with him.

FLORENCE: And he's so good at games.

NICKY: He sounds adorable.

FLORENCE: Of course, he needs knowing.

NICKY: So do I.

FLORENCE: You will make an effort though, darling, won't you? For my sake?

NICKY: Yes, mother.

FLORENCE: And we'll all have a divine time together, Tom and me and you and what's her name —

NICKY: Bunty.

FLORENCE: Oh, yes, of course, Bunty.

> *Front door bell rings.*

NICKY: This is her, I expect.

FLORENCE: Do you feel wonderful about her?

NICKY: Yes.

FLORENCE: It is thrilling, isn't it – being in love?

NICKY (*frowning a little*): Yes.

FLORENCE: Your father was right – you look awfully tired, Nicky.

NICKY: What nonsense! I feel grand.

> *Enter* PRESTON.

PRESTON (*announcing*): Miss Mainwaring.

> BUNTY *comes in, very self-assured and well dressed. She is more attractive than pretty in a boyish sort of way.*
> PRESTON *goes out.*

NICKY: Bunty. You have been quick.

BUNTY: I've simply flown.

NICKY: Bunty ... here is mother. ...

BUNTY: Oh!

FLORENCE (*taking both her hands*): This is frightfully exciting, isn't it?

> *She kisses her.*

NICKY: I've told her.

BUNTY: Are you furious?

FLORENCE: Of course not – why should I be? 'Specially now.

BUNTY: It's absolutely incredible, you being Nicky's mother.

FLORENCE: Am I anything like you thought I'd be?

BUNTY: Yes, exactly – but I couldn't believe it until I saw you.

FLORENCE: Take off that perfectly divine cloak and have a cigarette – I've got to rush and dress now, because I'm *terribly* late, but you're dining here with Nicky and joining Tom Veryan and me at the Embassy afterwards.

BUNTY: Tom Veryan ... ?

FLORENCE: Yes, do you know him?

BUNTY: I did when I was a child – if it's the same one.

> *She takes off her cloak.*

FLORENCE (*effusively*): Nicky – I don't feel extraordinary about it any more – I'm *delighted*.

NICKY: Angel.

FLORENCE: Perhaps Bunty would like to come down to the house on Friday for the week-end?

NICKY: Oh, yes, marvellous.

BUNTY: It's awfully sweet of you, Mrs Lancaster.

FLORENCE: You must call me Florence – I can't bear Mrs Lancaster. I must fly, Tom will be here at any moment – that's him on the desk.

BUNTY (*going over to photograph*): Yes – it is the same one.

FLORENCE: How too divine ...

> *Telephone rings.*

'Hallo – yes, speaking – Elsa, darling, how are you ... What? ... to-night ... how perfectly heavenly, of course, I'd adore it ... listen, Nicky's just back from Paris, can he come too with

Bunty Mainwaring – yes, he's here. – See you to-night, dear. . . .

Here, Nicky, talk to Elsa. . . .

*She snatches up her hand-bag and fur coat and kisses* BUNTY *effusively.*

I'm so glad about you and Nicky – it's too wonderful.

*She rushes out.*

NICKY (*at telephone*): Hallo, Elsa . . . I'd no idea you were in London. I'm terribly thrilled – my dear, you haven't . . . all those lovely tunes you played to me in Paris? . . . *how amazing,* I *am* glad . . . have you done anything with that Tango? . . . You must play it to-night, I want Bunty to hear it. . . . It is perfect, isn't it? . . . Good-bye, dear. (*He hangs up the receiver.*) Bunty.

BUNTY: What?

NICKY: I'm terribly happy.

BUNTY: So am I.

NICKY: Do you remember how we planned all this – coming home together – and breaking it to mother – and everything?

BUNTY: Rather.

NICKY: Do you really like her?

BUNTY: I adore her – she's a perfect angel.

NICKY: I told her your 'heroic little boy' line – she loved it.

BUNTY: It's true, you know – rather defiant too – laughing at Fate.

NICKY: Doesn't Paris seem ages away now?

BUNTY: A different life altogether.

NICKY: That nasty little bit of channel is such an enormous gulf, really. Did you put that dress on on purpose?

BUNTY (*smiling*): Perhaps.

NICKY: You are a devil.

BUNTY: It's such fun being reminded of things.

NICKY: And such agony, too.

BUNTY: Nicky, darling – why agony?

NICKY: It's always agony being in love, and I started loving you in that dress.

BUNTY: Did you?

NICKY: Don't pretend you didn't know.

BUNTY: I suppose one always knows – really.

NICKY: From the very first moment.

BUNTY: Yes.

NICKY: A sort of spark.

BUNTY: Your playing helped a lot.

NICKY: I meant it to.

BUNTY: Calculating pig.

NICKY: Have a cigarette?

BUNTY: All right.

*He hands her box, and she takes one.*

NICKY (*lighting her cigarette*): I wish we weren't so free.

BUNTY: Why? What do you mean?

NICKY: I feel I should like to elope, or something violently romantic like that.

BUNTY (*laughing*): There wouldn't be much point in it now, would there?

NICKY: Perhaps not. How much do you love me?

BUNTY: I don't know.

NICKY: It's fun analysing one's emotions.

BUNTY: Marvellous fun.

NICKY: And a comfort, too, when things go wrong – but it kills sentiment stone dead.

BUNTY: A good job too.

NICKY: You're frightfully hard, Bunty.

BUNTY: Am I?

NICKY: Much harder than me – really.

BUNTY: You've got so much hysteria.

NICKY: I can't help it.

BUNTY: Of course not, it's your temperament. You burst out suddenly.

NICKY: Not so badly as I used to.

BUNTY: You're growing older.

NICKY: God, yes; isn't it foul?

BUNTY: Hell, my dear.

NICKY: It's funny how mother's generation always longed to be old when they were young, and we strain every nerve to keep young.

BUNTY: That's because we see what's coming so much more clearly.

NICKY: Wouldn't it be terrible to know *exactly* – I feel frightened sometimes.

BUNTY: Why?

NICKY: We're all so hectic and nervy....

BUNTY: It doesn't matter – it probably only means we shan't live so long. . . .

NICKY (*suddenly*): Shut up – shut up. . . .

> *Enter* PRESTON.

PRESTON (*announcing*): Mr Veryan.

> *Enter* TOM. NICKY *greets him and shakes hands. Exit* PRESTON.

NICKY: How are you? – I'm Nicky – I came over to-day instead of to-morrow. . . .

TOM: Oh!

NICKY: Do you know Bunty Mainwaring?

TOM: Bunty – I say – I am glad.

> *They shake hands warmly.*

NICKY: We'd better have some cocktails.

> *He goes to the door and shouts.*

Preston . . . bring us some cocktails. . . .

TOM: This *is* jolly – I didn't know what had become of you.

BUNTY: I've been living in Paris a good deal.

TOM: How many years ago is it since we . . .

BUNTY: During the War – the last time I saw you, you were at Sandhurst.

NICKY: Such a pretty place.

TOM: You've hardly altered a bit – more grown up, of course.

NICKY: All this is most affecting.

TOM: Bunty and I used to know one another awfully well.

NICKY: What fun!

BUNTY (*warningly*): Nicky . . .

NICKY: But it is – it's thrilling – there's nothing so charming as a reunion.

BUNTY: Nicky and I have been travelling all day. . . . Boats and trains get on his nerves. . . .

NICKY: When the cocktails come, tell Preston to bring mine to me in father's room.

BUNTY: Nicky, don't be so silly.

NICKY: Surely it's not silly to want to talk to my aged father after a year's debauch in Paris? I fail to see why you should have the monopoly of reunions.

BUNTY: Well, don't be long.

TOM: Cheerio!

NICKY (crossly): Oh, God!

>    *He goes out.*

TOM: What's up?

BUNTY: These temperamental musicians.

TOM: Silly ass.

BUNTY: He isn't really – he's only jealous.

TOM: Why ... is he ...?

BUNTY: We're by way of being engaged.

TOM: What?

BUNTY: Why not?

TOM: Are you ... are you in love with him?

BUNTY (lightly): Yes – isn't it damnable?

TOM: Good Lord!

>    *He laughs.*

BUNTY: What are you laughing at?

TOM: It seems so funny you being in love with that sort of chap.

BUNTY: What do you mean by 'that sort of chap'?

TOM: Oh – I don't know, that type seems so unlike you.

BUNTY: Type?

TOM: Yes, you know – up in the air – effeminate.

BUNTY: You're more bucolic than you used to be, Tom.

TOM: Here, I say ...

>    *Enter* PRESTON *with cocktails.*

BUNTY: Will you please take Mr Nicky's in to him in his father's room?

PRESTON: Yes, miss.

TOM: Is Mrs Lancaster nearly ready?

PRESTON: I think so, sir.

TOM: Ask her to hurry – we shall be late.

PRESTON: Yes, sir.

*He goes out.*

BUNTY: I can laugh now.

*She does so.*

TOM: Why?

BUNTY: I've just realised something.

TOM: What?

BUNTY: We shall meet again – over the week-end.

TOM: Are you coming down to the house?

BUNTY: Yes.

TOM: That's splendid – come for a tramp Sunday morning and we'll talk.

BUNTY: What about?

TOM: Oh, lots of things – old times.

BUNTY (*lifting her cocktail*): Old times, Tom.

TOM (*doing the same*): Cheerio!


CURTAIN

# ACT II

*The scene is the hall of* MRS LANCASTER'S *house, about forty miles from London.*

*When the curtain rises it is just after dinner on the Sunday of the week-end party – the gramophone is going, and there is a continual buzz of conversation.* CLARA HIBBERT, *an emaciated soprano, is dancing with* TOM VERYAN, HELEN *with* PAWNIE, *and* NICKY *with* BUNTY. FLORENCE *is seated on the club fender talking intellectually with* BRUCE FAIRLIGHT, *an earnest dramatist, the squalor of whose plays is much appreciated by those who live in comparative luxury.*

*There must be a feeling of hectic amusement and noise, and the air black with cigarette smoke and superlatives. During the first part of the scene everyone must appear to be talking at once, but the actual lines spoken while dancing must be timed to reach the audience as the speakers pass near the footlights. This scene will probably be exceedingly difficult to produce, but is absolutely indispensable.*

HELEN: It's much too fast, Nicky.

TOM: Do slow down a bit.

NICKY: It's the place that's marked on the record.

PAWNIE: I've never danced well since the War, I don't know why.

FLORENCE: But your last act was so strong, when she came in half mad with fright and described everything minutely.

BRUCE: I try to write as *honestly* as possible.

CLARA: I gave her three for manners, but seven for charm, because I had to be a *little* nice!

TOM: I thought she was rather a decent sort.

BUNTY: No, but really, Nicky, his technique completely annihilated his inspiration.

NICKY: Not with Debussy and Ravel, with the older Masters, yes; but he's probably tired of them.

BUNTY: That's so stupid, I think.

HELEN: My dear, it was the most 'Chic' thing you've ever seen, but unfortunately the wrong colour.

PAWNIE: Marion Ferris had that Poiret model copied in the most frightful blue!

CLARA: I believe my shoe's coming off.

TOM: Shall we stop?

CLARA: No, it's all right.

FLORENCE: I wonder if you could gouge this cigarette-end out of the holder for me?

BRUCE: I'll try (*He does so.*) I always smoke a pipe when I'm working.

FLORENCE: How soothing!

BUNTY: I suppose one can never really judge properly from a recital.

NICKY: Not with him, because he's not dramatic enough.

BUNTY: Dramatic pianists make me uncomfortable.

HELEN: Pawnie, your tongue grows more venomous every day.

PAWNIE (*giggling*): Well, I had to say something – anyhow, it was true.

HELEN: Especially about her ankles.

PAWNIE: My dear, yes!

> *They both laugh.*
> *The record comes to an end, and* NICKY *begins to change it. Everyone talks and laughs.*

CLARA: You must come next Sunday week.

TOM: Thanks awfully, I'd love to.

CLARA: I'm only singing ballads, but you know what Sunday concerts are.

TOM: Oh, yes, rather.

CLARA (*to* NICKY): What's on the other side?

NICKY: 'You've got the cutest ears and eyes and nose'.

PAWNIE: Do put on 'Spoony Moon in Upper Carolina'.

HELEN: No, don't put it on, Nicky, play it yourself; you always make a gramophone go too quickly.

BUNTY: Yes, go on, Nicky.

FLORENCE (*refusing* BRUCE'S *offer of a cigarette*): No, thanks, not another – I'm dancing with Tom.

BUNTY (*gaily*): Missing one, Tom.

TOM: Righto!

> NICKY *commences to play a foxtrot.*

BUNTY (*dragging* BRUCE *to his feet*): Come on, Mr Fairlight, don't overdo the serious dramatist stunt!

BRUCE: I warn you I'm no good.

> *He dances with her, and confirms the truth of his warning.* CLARA
> HIBBERT *squashes down on the piano-seat next to* NICKY *and
> endeavours with one finger in the treble to follow the tune he is
> playing.* HELEN *and* PAWNIE *stand right down close to the
> footlights, smoking and talking, their backs are half-turned to the
> audience, but their remarks must be perfectly audible.*

HELEN: Tom Veryan doesn't dance as well as he thinks he does.

PAWNIE: With that figure he ought to be marvellous.

HELEN: He's too athletic.

PAWNIE: Anyhow, I'm sure he's a success at the Bath Club.

HELEN: Doesn't Florence look astounding?

PAWNIE: Absolutely. She knows exactly what suits her.

HELEN: Where's David?

PAWNIE: He went off to his study to smoke.

HELEN: I do wish Florence wouldn't be irritable with him in front of everybody. I felt acutely uncomfortable at dinner.

PAWNIE: It makes Nicky furious as a rule, but to-night he was too occupied with that stupid little fool Bunty Mainwaring to take any notice.

HELEN: She's an excellent type.

PAWNIE: Very average; I only hope nothing will come of Nicky's mania for her.

HELEN: I don't think we need worry.

PAWNIE: Why?

HELEN: Wait and see, my dear.

CLARA (*leaving* NICKY *at the piano and advancing on* PAWNIE): Come and dance, Pawnie, and tell me how divinely I sang on Tuesday.

PAWNIE (*agreeably*): You didn't.

CLARA: Ten for cruelty.

*They start to dance.* HELEN *moves over to the mantelpiece for a cigarette.*

HELEN: Have you a match, Nicky?

NICKY: Isn't this a marvellous tune?

HELEN: Fascinating! (*She goes over and sits next to him. Gently slipping her hand into his coat pocket.*) Darling, I *do* want a match. (*She brings out a little box.*) What a divine little box!

> NICKY *stops playing and jumps up.*

NICKY (*violently*): Helen, give that to me —

> *Everyone stops dancing.*

CLARA: Nicky, dear, *don't* be tiresome.

NICKY (*recovering himself*): I'm sick of playing, let's have the gramophone again. (*To* HELEN.) Here's a light, dearie.

> *He takes match-box out of another pocket and lights* HELEN'S *cigarette. She looks at him queerly for a moment, then he restarts the gramophone and everyone begins to dance again except* HELEN *and* BRUCE FAIRLIGHT. HELEN *goes over to the fireplace and takes a coffee cup from the mantelpiece.*

HELEN: Whose coffee is this? Someone drank mine, and I'd hardly touched it.

BRUCE: If it has no sugar in it, it's mine.

HELEN (*draining it*): It had no sugar in it.

FLORENCE: You're dancing abominably, Tom.

TOM: Oh, am I?

FLORENCE: What's the matter with you?

TOM: I don't know, I suppose I'm tired.

FLORENCE: You're not usually tired when you're dancing with me.

TOM: Oh, Florence, don't nag!

FLORENCE: How dare you speak to me like that?

> *She stops dancing and goes over to the fireplace.*

TOM (*following her*): I say, Florence – I'm sorry —

PAWNIE: Let's stop the music for a moment and think of something really marvellous to do.

BUNTY: No, let's go on dancing.

CLARA: I'm exhausted.

PAWNIE (*stopping the gramophone*): What was that divine game we played coming back from Paris, Helen?

HELEN: Just ordinary 'Clumps', wasn't it?

BUNTY: I loathe 'Clumps'.

NICKY: What about the History game?

BRUCE: What's that?

BUNTY: Oh, no, Nicky, it's too intellectual.

FLORENCE: There's a Mah-jong set in the drawing-room.

PAWNIE: How divine – let's make up a table immediately.

CLARA: I won't be happy until someone gives me a set made entirely of jade.

NICKY: Come on, Bunty.

BUNTY (*looking at* TOM): I can't play it.

NICKY: You can; you used to play it in Paris with Yvonne.

BUNTY: I've forgotten it.

NICKY: You'll soon remember again.

　　　*He drags her off.*

PAWNIE: Come along, Clara.

CLARA: I insist on Mr Fairlight learning.

BRUCE: I'm afraid I'm no good at that sort of thing.

CLARA: You'll be able to put it in one of your plays.

PAWNIE: Come and watch, it's too thrilling for words.

　　　CLARA, BRUCE *and* PAWNIE *go off.*

HELEN: Have you only one set, Florence?

FLORENCE: Yes, isn't it maddening? Clara promised to bring hers down but forgot.

HELEN: Does Bruce Fairlight play Bridge?

FLORENCE: No, I don't think so.

HELEN: Dramatists are such a comfort in a house-party, aren't they?

　　　*She goes off.*

TOM: Aren't you coming, Florence?

FLORENCE: No.

TOM (*nonplussed*): Oh!

FLORENCE: But please don't let me stop *you* going, I'm sure you're *dying* to be with the others.

TOM: I say, Florence, I wish you wouldn't go on like that.

FLORENCE: I don't know what is the matter with you, you've never behaved like this before.

TOM: I haven't behaved like anything.

FLORENCE: You've been exceedingly rude to me, both at dinner and afterwards.

TOM: I wasn't at dinner.

FLORENCE: Yes, you were; you snapped me up when I said I didn't like Elsie Saunders.

TOM: You know perfectly well she's a friend of mine.

FLORENCE: Well, she oughtn't to be, after the things she's said about me.

TOM: You will go on imagining.

FLORENCE: Nothing of the sort – I *know!* If you weren't so dense you'd see, too – the jealousy I have to put up with. I get so tired of it all, so desperately tired.

   *She becomes a little pathetic.*

TOM: Talk about being different, you're different too —

FLORENCE: I'm unhappy.

TOM: Why?

FLORENCE: Because I hate to see you being put against me.

TOM: Florence!

FLORENCE: You'll understand one day. They're all very subtle, but I can see.

TOM: Nobody's said a word to me about you, they'd better not try.

FLORENCE: Why, what would you do?

TOM: I'd – I'd be furious.

FLORENCE: Oh!

TOM: And I'd let them see it, too.

FLORENCE (*holding out her hands*): Tom —

TOM: Yes?

FLORENCE: I forgive you.

TOM: I can't bear you being angry with me.

FLORENCE: Can't you, really?

TOM: It makes me feel beastly.

FLORENCE: Come and sit here.

TOM (*sitting next to her on the club fender*): That's a lovely dress.

FLORENCE: It is sweet, isn't it?

TOM: You always wear wonderful clothes.

FLORENCE: Do I, Tom?

TOM: You know you do.

FLORENCE: Do you remember the very first time we met?

TOM: Rather.

FLORENCE: Oxford's so full of romance, isn't it?

TOM: It was when you came down.

FLORENCE: Thank you, Tom, dear.

TOM: We did have fun.

FLORENCE: You used to come up to *matinées*, and I'd motor you back afterwards.

TOM: Ripping!

FLORENCE: That reminds me, I've got seats for *Rolling Stones* on Tuesday – don't forget.

TOM: You never said you were going to get them.

FLORENCE: It doesn't matter, I thought I did. We'd better dine at Claridges.

TOM: But, Florence, I – I can't come!

FLORENCE: Why not?

TOM: I promised to go out.

FLORENCE: Who with?

TOM: Mother.

FLORENCE: Can't you put her off, it will be such a good first night?

TOM: Well – you see, as a matter of fact – it's rather awkward – I put her off the other day —

*There is a slight pause.*

FLORENCE (*a trifle coldly*): Oh, well, never mind, we'll go some other night.

*Enter* DAVID.

DAVID: Hallo, Florence, I thought you were in the drawing-room.

FLORENCE: They're playing Mah-jong, and there's only one set. I shall break in presently.

TOM: I'll just go and see how they're getting on.

*This obvious excuse for getting out of the room is not lost upon* FLORENCE.

FLORENCE: Yes, do.

TOM: Come and play soon.

*He goes out quietly.*

FLORENCE: Don't you think this is a divine frock?

DAVID: Very pretty.

FLORENCE: You and Helen seemed to be very thick at dinner. What were you talking about?

DAVID: Nothing much – I like Helen.

FLORENCE: Only because she flatters you and listens to everything you say.

DAVID: She doesn't flatter me.

FLORENCE: I suppose she was talking about the farm, and giving her opinions.

DAVID: We did discuss the farm a little.

FLORENCE: She doesn't know a thing about it, really.

DAVID: Perhaps not, but it passed the time.

*He goes out.*

*FLORENCE sits still for a moment, then she wearily buries her face in her hands. Enter NICKY.*

NICKY (*going to her*): What's the matter, darling?

FLORENCE: Nothing, I've got a slight headache.

NICKY: Why don't you go Byes?

FLORENCE: I can't, it's much too early.

NICKY: I'm sick of Mah-jong.

FLORENCE: Who's playing now?

NICKY: Pawnie and Helen and Clara are trying to teach Bruce Fairlight, he's an awful fool at it.

*He sits down at the piano and plays absently.*

FLORENCE: You must get Bunty out of that habit of contradicting everything people say.

NICKY: I don't see why.

FLORENCE: It's bad breeding.

NICKY (*striking a note viciously*): Who cares nowadays? We've all got a right to our opinions.

FLORENCE: She seems to forget that I'm much older than she is.

NICKY: That's no argument, mother; it's silly only to remember your age when someone says something you don't like.

FLORENCE: She's having a bad effect on you.

NICKY: Nonsense!

FLORENCE: You've changed since Paris.

NICKY: Naturally.

FLORENCE: You never used to be rude to me.

NICKY: Oh, damn, I'm not rude.

FLORENCE: Yes, you are.

NICKY: Well, don't start running down Bunty.

FLORENCE: Stop playing – stop playing!

NICKY (*getting up angrily*): Oh, God!

    *He goes towards door and collides with* HELEN.

HELEN: What's happening?

FLORENCE: Nothing, Bunty's just putting Nicky against me. I knew she'd try to.

    *She goes out.*

HELEN: You must be having a delightful evening! You leave the drawing-room having rowed with Bunty, and come here and row with Florence.

NICKY: Mother's impossible.

HELEN: She's no different from what she's always been.

NICKY: Well, I haven't realised it before.

HELEN (*taking a cigarette and lighting it*): You haven't been engaged before.

NICKY: I'm hating this house-party.

HELEN (*lightly*): Don't say that, dear, it's not kind.

NICKY: You know I don't mean you.

HELEN: Are you very much in love?

NICKY: Yes. – No. – I don't know.

HELEN: I wonder.

NICKY: It's utterly devastating, anyhow.

HELEN: When did you meet her?

NICKY: About five months ago.

HELEN: What was she doing in Paris?

NICKY: Oh, I don't know – fooling about.

HELEN: Splendid.

NICKY: She's been studying French literature.

HELEN: Why?

NICKY: She's going to write – herself – some day.

HELEN: Oh, I see!

NICKY: Helen, do you like her?

HELEN: I can't tell yet – yesterday was the first time I'd ever set eyes on her.

NICKY: She's wonderfully intelligent.

HELEN: Yes – I'm sure she is.

NICKY: You *don't* like her?

HELEN: I tell you – I'm not sure yet.

NICKY: It's generally the way – one's friends always hate one another.

HELEN (*smiling*): It *is* difficult for you, isn't it?

NICKY: I should so like you to like her.

HELEN: Very well – I'll try.

NICKY: She's utterly opposite to me in every way.

HELEN: Yes, I see that.

NICKY: But that's as it ought to be, isn't it?

HELEN: It depends.

NICKY: I need a sort of restraining influence terribly.

HELEN: Yes, Nicky.

NICKY: She's awfully good for me.

HELEN: Is she?

NICKY: Yes – she curbs me when I get temperamental and silly.

HELEN: I always felt you needed encouraging more than curbing.

NICKY (*laughing*): Oh, Helen   aren't you a darling!

HELEN: I mean it.

NICKY: You're wrong, though – I'm all over the place.

HELEN: Anyhow, I do hope you'll be very happy with her.

NICKY: I don't suppose I shall ever be that – I haven't got the knack.

HELEN: Do you work hard?

NICKY: Yes.

HELEN: Really hard?

NICKY: Frightfully.

HELEN: Liar!

NICKY: If you'd seen me in Paris – studying, studying – all night long until the grey dawn put the guttering candle to shame – and my nerveless hands dropped from the keys —

HELEN: Candles gutter awfully quickly when they're burnt at both ends.

NICKY: Meaning that I look a debauched wreck of my former self?

HELEN: Exactly.

NICKY: If you go on encouraging me at this rate I shall commit suicide.

HELEN: You do resent anyone taking a real interest in you, don't you?

NICKY: I distrust it.

HELEN: Why?

NICKY: I don't know – I'm not worth it.

HELEN: You seem to be suffering from a slight inferiority complex.

NICKY: Not a bit of it – I'm gay and witty and handsome.

HELEN: Oh, Nicky, you're so maddening.

NICKY: Don't be cross, Helen.

HELEN: I'm one of the few people who know what you're really like, and you won't give me the credit for it.

NICKY: Do you think you do, honestly?

HELEN: Yes – and I'm exceedingly worried about you.

NICKY: You needn't be.

HELEN: You're sensitive and reserved and utterly foolish.

NICKY: Thank you – I'm beginning to feel beautifully picturesque.

HELEN: And you're scared.

NICKY: Why! What have I to be scared about?

HELEN: Would you like me to tell you?

NICKY: No.

HELEN: Why not?

NICKY: Because you're a sentimentalist, and you see things that aren't there at all.

HELEN: You're far more sentimental than I.

NICKY: Darling Helen – you've got such a lovely mind – like a Christmas card – with frosted robins and sheep wandering about in the snow – bleating.

HELEN: All the same, I should give up drugs if I were you.

NICKY: Helen!

HELEN: Well?

NICKY: I don't know what you mean.

HELEN: Do you think I can't see?

NICKY (*forcing a laugh*): You're being terribly funny, aren't you?

HELEN: You fool! You unutterable little fool!

NICKY: Don't be dramatic, dear.

HELEN: I thought you had common sense; I credited you with more intelligence than that.

NICKY: If you persist in being absurd.

HELEN (*suddenly with intense feeling*): Nicky, don't resist me, don't fight me, I'm your friend, I wouldn't have said a word if I weren't. You've got to stop it; you haven't gone very far yet, there's still time – for God's sake listen to reason.

NICKY: Shut up, shut up, don't speak so loudly.

HELEN: Nicky, throw it away.

NICKY: When did you find out?

HELEN: To-night, you know, when you were playing, but I've guessed for ages.

NICKY: You needn't be frightened, Helen, I only take just the tiniest little bit, once in a blue moon!

HELEN: If anything goes wrong, you'll take a lot – throw it away.

NICKY: What could go wrong?

HELEN: Never mind, throw it away!

NICKY: I can't – look out, somebody's coming.

*Enter* DAVID.

DAVID: Hallo!

NICKY: Hallo, father!

DAVID: What's the matter?

NICKY: The matter – why?

DAVID: You look very worried.

NICKY: Helen and I have just had a grand heart-to-heart talk; we've undone our back hair, loosened our stays and wallowed in it.

DAVID: Oh, I see!

HELEN: We haven't seen one another for so long – it was inevitable.

DAVID: You never came and looked at the Farm this morning – I waited for you.

NICKY: I'm awfully sorry, father – I just went on sleeping.

HELEN: I'll see you later, Nicky.

NICKY: All right.

HELEN *goes out.*

DAVID: How do you think your mother's looking?

NICKY: Splendid – the same as ever.

DAVID: Would you like a cigar?

NICKY: No thanks, father – I'm not very good at them.

DAVID: I was just on my way to bed – there are far too many people in the house.

NICKY (*smiling*): You must be used to that by now.

DAVID: You ought to stay down here, you know – during the week and get some fresh air.

NICKY: I've got such millions of things to do in London.

DAVID: Worth doing?

NICKY: Yes, of course.

DAVID: You look as though you needed a rest.

NICKY: You needn't worry about me – I feel splendid.

DAVID: She seems a nice girl.

NICKY: Who – Bunty?

DAVID: Yes. Quiet and untiresome.

NICKY: She's a darling!

DAVID: When do you propose to get married?

NICKY: I don't know – the engagement's only a sort of try-out, you know.

DAVID: Oh, I see – I didn't realise that – I'm so unversed in modern technicalities.

NICKY: It's her idea really – just to tread water for a bit.

DAVID: It sounds an excellent plan.

NICKY: I'm awfully glad you like her.

DAVID: Is she musical?

NICKY: Oh, yes – frightfully!

DAVID: Good!

NICKY: Father, I think I will come down here for a few days – and work quietly.

DAVID: If you do that I'll only go up to London every other day – I see so little of you when you're at the flat.

NICKY: That's settled then. I wonder what mother will say!

DAVID: I'll talk to her.

NICKY: All right – she won't bother about us much.

DAVID: No – I don't suppose she will – I think I'll be getting along to bed now. Good night, my boy!

NICKY: Good night, father!

> *They shake hands, and* DAVID *pats* NICKY's *shoulder rather tentatively. He goes upstairs and* NICKY *wanders to the piano. He plays absently, and* BUNTY *enters.*

BUNTY: I want to talk to you.

NICKY (*still playing*): All right.

BUNTY: Perhaps you'd stop playing for a minute.

NICKY: Won't you let me woo you with a little Scriabin?

BUNTY: Please stop.

NICKY (*rising*): I'm unappreciated – that's what it is.

> *There is a slight pause – he goes over to her.*

I say, Bunty —

BUNTY: What?

NICKY: Before you say anything awful to me, I *am* sorry for being rude just now.

BUNTY: So you ought to be.

NICKY: Will you forgive me?

BUNTY: Yes, I forgive you.

NICKY: I've been irritable all the evening.

BUNTY: Give me a cigarette, Nicky.

NICKY: Here.

> *They both smoke.*

BUNTY: Thanks.

NICKY: What did you want to talk to me about?

BUNTY: Lots of things – Us!

NICKY (*hardening*): Oh, I see!

BUNTY: Don't you think it's rather silly – being engaged?

NICKY: No, not at all.

BUNTY: I do.

NICKY: Just because we bickered a bit to-night?

BUNTY: No, not only because of that.

NICKY: Why then?

BUNTY: Can't you see?

NICKY: No.

BUNTY: Well, we're not very suited to one another are we?

NICKY: Why do you suddenly say that?

BUNTY: Because I've only just realised it.

NICKY: I'm sorry.

BUNTY: It's not your fault particularly. .

NICKY: I'm glad.

BUNTY: It's circumstances and surroundings.

NICKY: Oh, that can be altered quite easily. We'll change the shape of the house – we'll take all that wall away and turn that into a studio – you love studios, don't you? – then we'll transform the drawing-room into an enormous aviary.

BUNTY: It's practically that now!

NICKY: And then we'll —

BUNTY: Shut up, Nicky!

NICKY: I'm only trying to be amenable.

BUNTY: Are you, really?

NICKY: Yes, I'm putting up a sort of defence, Bunty. I have a feeling that you're going to be unpleasant, and I want to establish myself comfortably before you start.

BUNTY: I don't want to be unpleasant – only honest.

NICKY: You won't let the two run together, will you?

BUNTY (*with vehemence*): You're hopeless, hopeless, hopeless!

NICKY: Yes – I think I am rather.

BUNTY: In a way I'm glad – it makes it easier.

NICKY: Does it?

BUNTY: You're not in love with me, really – you couldn't be!

NICKY: Please, don't say that.

BUNTY: Why don't you face things properly?

NICKY: One generally has to in the end – I like to put it off for as long as possible.

BUNTY: That's cowardly.

NICKY: Don't be pompous, darling.

BUNTY: You're a great help, I must say.

NICKY: Why should I help to destroy my own happiness?

BUNTY: That's self-pity and self-deception.

NICKY: Why are you going on like this?

BUNTY: Because I tell you – I've realised the truth.

NICKY: I suppose you've taken a hatred to mother!

BUNTY: No, not a hatred.

NICKY: You don't like her.

BUNTY: Not very much.

NICKY: Why not? She likes you.

BUNTY: She detests me.

NICKY: Nonsense, why should she?

BUNTY: Because I'm young.

NICKY: What a filthy thing to say!

BUNTY: It's true.

NICKY: It's nothing of the sort.

BUNTY: You're so stupid sometimes.

NICKY: Thank you.

BUNTY: Don't let's start bickering again.

NICKY: We won't discuss mother any more then.

BUNTY: You started it.

NICKY: I wish I could make you understand her like I do – I mean she's awfully irritating, I know – but deep down she's marvellous in spite of everything.

BUNTY (*coldly*): Everything?

NICKY (*vehemently*): Yes, *everything!* Don't be a beast, Bunty, just try to see her point a little, even if you do dislike her. She is terribly silly about being 'young', I know, but she's been used to so much admiration and flattery and everything always, she feels she sort of can't give it up – you do see that, don't you? And she hasn't really anything in the least comforting to fall back upon, she's not clever – real kind of brain cleverness – and father's no good, and I'm no good, and all the time she's wanting life to be as it was instead of as it is. There's no harm in her anywhere – she's just young inside. Can't you imagine the utter foulness of growing old? 'Specially if you've been lovely and attractive like she was. The beautiful Flo Lancaster! She used to be known as that – I can remember her when I was quite small, coming up to say good night to me, looking too perfectly radiant for words – and she used to come to the school, too, sometimes, and everyone used to go mad over her, and I used to get frightfully proud and excited —

BUNTY: I've never heard you talk like this before.

NICKY: I don't think I ever have.

BUNTY: I like you better clear cut, not blurred by sentiment.

> NICKY *looks at her for a moment in amazement.*

NICKY: To describe you as hard would be inadequate – you're metallic!

BUNTY: I can see straight.

NICKY (*politely*): Can you?

BUNTY: Yes. We could never be happy together.

NICKY: Perhaps not.

BUNTY: Shall we just – finish – then?

NICKY: Certainly, I'm sorry we were too modern to have an engagement ring, you'd have been able to give it back to me so beautifully.

BUNTY: Don't be ridiculous!

NICKY: Better than being blurred by sentiment.

> BUNTY *lights another cigarette and, kicking off her shoes, perches on the club fender and proceeds to warm her feet at the fire.*
> *Enter* CLARA HIBBERT.

CLARA: My dear, I'm *shattered* – and I'm going straight to bed – probably for several weeks.

BUNTY: Why?

CLARA: Shshsh! He's coming.

BUNTY: Who's coming!

CLARA: Bruce Fairlight – I've been teaching him Mah-jong – these master brains – agony, dear —

> *Enter* BRUCE FAIRLIGHT.

BRUCE: Very interesting, that game.

CLARA (*weakly*): I thought you'd like it.

BRUCE: It's interesting *psychologically!* The concentration and suspense —

> *Enter* FLORENCE, HELEN, PAWNIE *and* TOM. TOM *is grasping a whisky and soda* – PAWNIE *is eating a biscuit.*

PAWNIE: I'm quite exhausted – it must be the country air —

FLORENCE: – it was too lovely, because I started with two red dragons in my hand —

HELEN: I wondered who had them —

PAWNIE: One more tune, Nicky, before we go to bed —

FLORENCE: Yes, just one —

NICKY (*looking at* BUNTY): I'll play 'I love you!' – such a romantic tune.

>   *He puts on the gramophone.*

BUNTY: Do.

HELEN: What time's everyone going up in the morning?

FLORENCE: The ten o'clock's the best – we'll have breakfast at nine downstairs.

PAWNIE (*confidentially*): Do you know that in London I can never do more than nibble a piece of thin toast, and whenever I'm away I eat *enormously!*

NICKY: How very peculiar!

PAWNIE: Your tone revolts me, Nicky – you must never be irascible with your old friends.

NICKY: I haven't got any.

HELEN: Nicky!

NICKY: Sorry, Helen.

FLORENCE: I don't know what's the matter with Nicky – he's been in a vile temper all the evening – his first week-end home, too.

NICKY: Such a pity, when so much trouble has been taken to make me happy and cosy.

TOM: Come and dance, Bunty.

BUNTY: No, not now.

NICKY: Dance with him, Bunty – chaps must have exercise.

FLORENCE: You dance with Bunty, Pawnie – I'll dance with Tom – come on.

>   *She and* TOM *dance.*

HELEN: The great thing in this world is not to be obvious, Nicky – over *anything!*

>   FLORENCE *and* TOM *dance, also* HELEN *and* PAWNIE. *Everyone talks at once, as in the beginning of the act.*

PAWNIE: You are infuriating, Helen – it's a wonderful book.

HELEN: Thoroughly second-rate.

PAWNIE: What do you think about *Mischievous Passion*, Fairlight?

BRUCE: I never read novels on principle.

PAWNIE: Well, you must read this – it's colossal.

HELEN: Don't be led away by Pawnie, Mr Fairlight, he has no discrimination.

PAWNIE: But I tell you it's brilliant! Absolutely *brilliant!*

HELEN: Nonsense.

PAWNIE: There are times, Helen, when I could willingly see you dead at my feet.

FLORENCE: A little slower, for Heaven's sake!

NICKY: How's that?

> *He makes it far too slow.*

FLORENCE: I think you'd better go to bed, Nicky.

HELEN: We're all going, anyhow.

NICKY: Not yet, please, mummy dear – I'm having such a lovely time!

> *He slams off in a rage.*

PAWNIE: I always knew the Continent was fatal for the young.

BUNTY: Nicky's upset – it's my fault – we're not engaged any more.

FLORENCE: Why – what's happened?

BUNTY: Nothing happened – it was never very serious, really.

HELEN: I had a feeling that it was.

BUNTY: You were wrong.

FLORENCE: Well, I must say it's all been rather abrupt.

BUNTY: It's better to finish things off at once – cleanly – if you're not quite sure, don't you think?

FLORENCE: Well, I'm sorry, Bunty – if you feel like that about it there's nothing more to be said.

BUNTY: I wouldn't have mentioned it at all – only you all seemed to be blaming him for being irritable —

HELEN: Poor Nicky!

CLARA: I really must go up to bed now. I'm so tired. Good night, Florence dear.

FLORENCE: Good night, Clara. Breakfast at nine. Have you got books and everything you want?

CLARA: Yes, thanks. Good night, everyone.

> *Everyone murmurs good night politely.*

FLORENCE: Tom, be an angel and fetch me a glass of milk – it's in the drawing-room.

TOM: All right.

*He goes off.*

HELEN: Come on up, Florence, I'm dead.

FLORENCE: So am I. Will you turn out the lights when you come?

PAWNIE: With beautiful precision, dear.

FLORENCE (*as she and* HELEN *go upstairs*): Tell Tom to bring my milk up to me, somebody.

PAWNIE: All right.

FLORENCE: Good night, Mr Fairlight.

BRUCE: Good night.

PAWNIE: Good night, Florence.

FLORENCE *and* HELEN *go off.*

BRUCE: I suppose we'd all better go up.

BUNTY: I don't feel I could sleep yet.

*Re-enter* TOM *with a glass of milk.*

TOM: Hallo! where's Florence!

BUNTY: Gone up to bed – will you take her milk to her?

PAWNIE: What's become of Nicky?

TOM: In the smoking-room, I think.

BRUCE: Good night, Miss Mainwaring.

BUNTY: Good night.

*They shake hands.*

PAWNIE: I shall come, too – good night.

TOM: Good night.

PAWNIE (*to* BRUCE *as they go upstairs*): When you're writing, do your characters grow as you go along?

BRUCE: No, I think each one out minutely beforehand.

PAWNIE: How too intriguing!

*They go off.*

TOM: So you've broken it off already?

BUNTY: Yes.

TOM: I didn't know you were going to do it so soon.

BUNTY: It's better to get things over.

TOM: What did he say?

BUNTY: Nothing much.

TOM: Was he furious?

BUNTY: Oh! what does it matter? Don't let's go on about it.

TOM: It's all damned awkward.

BUNTY: What?

TOM: The whole thing.

BUNTY: You're rather scared, aren't you?

TOM: No, not exactly – now that I've got you to back me up.

BUNTY: I shall be glad when we're out of this house.

TOM: So shall I.

BUNTY: I hate the atmosphere.

TOM: I don't know how I've stood it for so long.

BUNTY: You didn't notice it until I came, any more than I noticed Nicky's atmosphere until you came.

TOM: It's queer, isn't it?

BUNTY: We're reverting to type, don't you see?

TOM: How d'you mean?

BUNTY: Never mind, it's true.

TOM: Do you think I'm being a cad to Florence?

BUNTY: Yes, I do rather.

TOM: But, Bunty! You said this morning —

BUNTY: That I didn't see how you could help yourself, neither I do – it's frightfully difficult, but it's not altogether your fault, any more than it would have been mine if I'd married Nicky. One gets carried away by glamour, and personality, and magnetism – they're beastly treacherous things.

TOM: You are wonderful.

BUNTY: Don't be silly.

TOM: You're so cool and clear, and you see everything.

BUNTY: I'm sorry – for Nicky.

TOM: Oh, damn Nicky!

BUNTY (*laughing*): Oh, Tom!

TOM: Why, what's up?

BUNTY: You're so dead set.

TOM: You're worth ten of him any day. What's the use of a chap like that? He *doesn't do* anything except play the piano – he can't play any games, he's always trying to be funny —

BUNTY: Shut up, Tom, you're being rather cheap; I haven't reverted to type so quickly that I can't see some of the things I'm missing.

TOM: I wish I knew what you were talking about.

BUNTY: Oh, God! I feel so miserable!

*She bursts into tears.*

TOM (*flummoxed*): I say – Bunty – for Heaven's sake —

*He puts his arms round her.*

BUNTY (*shaking him off*): Don't, don't – give me my shoes —

*He picks up her shoes; she puts them on. She is half sobbing all the time.*

TOM: I say, old girl, hadn't you better go to bed? You're all wrought up!

BUNTY: He said beastly things.

TOM: I'll wring his neck.

BUNTY (*with a fresh burst of tears*): Shut up, Tom, shut up —

TOM: Bunty, stop crying – there's a dear – please, please stop crying —

*He takes her in his arms and kisses her, she is groping for her handkerchief.* FLORENCE *comes quietly downstairs.*

BUNTY: I can't find my hanky!

TOM: Here's mine.

FLORENCE (*like a pistol shot*): Tom!

*TOM and BUNTY break away.*

TOM: Yes, Florence?

FLORENCE (*ominously*): What does this mean?

TOM: I'm sorry, Florence – I —

FLORENCE: You utter cad!

BUNTY: Look here – I should like to say —

FLORENCE: Be quiet – mind your own business.

*NICKY enters.*

NICKY (*seeing tears on* BUNTY'S *face*): What's the matter – is anybody hurt?

FLORENCE (*ominously*): No, not hurt!

BUNTY: I banged my hand, that's all.

FLORENCE: Liar!

121

NICKY: Mother – don't be so stupid —

TOM: Florence – I —

FLORENCE: Don't *speak* to me —

NICKY (*quietly*): Mother – not now – not now – it's all wrong – control yourself! Bunty – Bunty – do go to bed – please.

> *He goes to the piano and begins to play jazz.*

BUNTY: All right – Tom —

> FLORENCE *goes to the fireplace, trembling with rage.* NICKY *goes on playing.* TOM *and* BUNTY *go towards the stairs.*

FLORENCE: Stop – I want an explanation, please!

BUNTY: How dare you speak to me like that?

FLORENCE: Get out of my house! Get out of my house!

BUNTY: This is disgusting!

TOM: I say, Florence —

FLORENCE: Get out of my house!

BUNTY: I shall leave the first thing in the morning, it's much too late to-night.

> *She goes off.*
> > NICKY *never stops playing for a moment.*

FLORENCE: Tom. (*He goes towards her absolutely silent.*) You kissed her – you kissed her – I saw you —!

TOM: Yes.

FLORENCE: In this house!

TOM: Yes, Florence, I apologise.

FLORENCE: Apologise! You're beneath contempt – never speak to me again, never touch me again – I hate you!

TOM: Look here, Florence – I'm desperately sorry – you see, I'm afraid I love her.

FLORENCE (*hysterically*): You dare to stand there and say that to me? It's incredible – after all I've done for you – after all we've been to one another. Love! You don't know what it means. You've lied to me – all these months. It's contemptible – humiliating. Get out of my sight!

TOM (*turning and going upstairs*): Very well.

FLORENCE (*suddenly realising that he is gone*): Tom – Tom – come back – come back —!

*She runs upstairs after him.* NICKY *at last stops playing and lets his hands drop from the keys.*


CURTAIN

# ACT III

*The scene is* FLORENCE'S *bedroom the same night – about two hours have elapsed. When the curtain rises* FLORENCE *is lying face downwards on the bed, she is dressed in a very beautiful but slightly exotic négligé.*

HELEN *is standing by the window fully dressed, she is holding the curtain aside, and a bar of moonlight comes in to mingle with the amber of the dressing-table lights.* FLORENCE *is obviously extremely hysterical.*

HELEN: Florence, what *is* the use of going on like that?

FLORENCE: I wish I were dead!

HELEN: It's so cowardly to give way utterly – as you're doing.

FLORENCE: I don't care – I don't care!

HELEN: If you don't face things in this world, they only hit you much harder in the end.

FLORENCE: He loved me – he adored me!

HELEN: Never! He hadn't got it in him.

FLORENCE: After all I've done for him, to go to – to Bunty!

HELEN (*leaving the window*): If it hadn't been Bunty it would have been someone else – don't you see how inevitable it was?

FLORENCE: How dared they! – Here! – In this house!

HELEN: That's a little thing, it doesn't matter at all.

FLORENCE: It does – it does —

HELEN: Florence, sit up and pull yourself together.

FLORENCE (*sitting up slowly*): I think I'm going mad.

HELEN: Not a bit of it, you're just thoroughly hysterical.

FLORENCE: Give me some water.

    HELEN *goes to the bathroom and returns with a glass of water.*

FLORENCE (*taking it*): What time is it?

HELEN (*looking at her watch*): Ten-past one.

FLORENCE: Don't go to London by the early train, Helen; stay and come up with me in the car.

HELEN: Very well.

FLORENCE: Thank God, you were here!

HELEN: I wish I'd known what was happening, I might have done something.

FLORENCE: What can I do to get him back?

HELEN: Don't be silly.

FLORENCE: What can I do – what can I do —?

HELEN: Do you mean to say you'd *take* him back after to-night?

FLORENCE: No, never. Not if he crawled to me – never —

HELEN: Well, then, make up your mind definitely never to see him again whatever happens.

FLORENCE: Yes – I will.

HELEN: Why don't you go to bed now?

FLORENCE: I couldn't sleep.

HELEN: Put it all out of your mind – make an effort.

FLORENCE: I can't – I'm too unhappy.

HELEN: Think of Nicky.

FLORENCE: Nicky's young.

HELEN: That doesn't make it any better for him.

FLORENCE: He'll get over it in the long run.

HELEN: The long run never counts at the moment.

FLORENCE: He wasn't in love – really?

HELEN: As much as either you or he are capable of it.

FLORENCE: He's well rid of her – she'd never have appreciated him properly – she hasn't the intelligence.

HELEN: I don't agree with you there – she's got intelligence right enough.

FLORENCE: Treacherous little beast!

HELEN: Yes, but far-seeing.

FLORENCE: Are you standing up for her? Do you think it was *right* of her to get Tom away from me?

HELEN: Yes, quite right.

FLORENCE: Helen!

HELEN: To do her justice, she didn't deliberately set herself out to get him away from you at all. She discovered that in spite of the somewhat decadent years Tom was still her type, and likely to remain so. So with common sense she decided to shelve Nicky forthwith and go for him.

125

FLORENCE: Her type indeed!

HELEN: Yes, she'd have been quite a nice girl really if she'd been left alone and not allowed to go to Paris and get into the wrong set.

FLORENCE: You are extraordinary, Helen. Do you realise that you're making excuses for the girl who's betrayed your best friend?

HELEN: Don't be so utterly absurd – I'm not making excuses, and anyhow she hasn't betrayed you. She hardly knows you in the first place, and she's just followed her instincts regardless of anyone else's feelings – as you've done thousands of times.

FLORENCE: Helen – you're being horrible to me!

HELEN: I'm not, I'm trying to make you see! You're battering your head against silly cast-iron delusions, and I want to dislodge them.

FLORENCE: Helen, I'm so unhappy – so desperately unhappy.

HELEN: Yes, but not because you've lost Tom, it's something far deeper than that.

FLORENCE: What then?

HELEN: You're on the wrong tack, and have been for years.

FLORENCE: I don't understand.

HELEN: You *won't* understand!

> FLORENCE *gets off the bed and goes over to the dressing-table. She sits and stares at herself in the glass for a moment without speaking.*

FLORENCE: My eyes are sore. (*She powders her face and sprays a little scent on her hair.*) It's so lovely this – and so refreshing.

HELEN: I think I'll go to bed now.

FLORENCE: No, wait a little longer with me – please, Helen – just a few minutes.

HELEN: It's so hot in here.

FLORENCE: Open the window, then.

HELEN: All right.

> *She goes to the window and opens it.* FLORENCE *takes a cigarette out of a box and then shakes a scent-bottle and rubs the cigarette lightly with the stopper.*

FLORENCE: Do you ever do this? It's divine.

HELEN: What a wonderfully clear night – you can see the hills right across the valley – the moon's quite strong.

FLORENCE *goes to the window and stands next to* HELEN *looking out – she is puffing her cigarette.*

FLORENCE: I chose this room in the first place because the view was so lovely.

HELEN: Do you ever look at it?

FLORENCE (*listlessly*): Of course I do, often!

HELEN: It's been raining – I wish you'd throw away that cigarette – it spoils the freshness.

FLORENCE (*turning away*): It's soothing me – calming my nerves.

HELEN: I do wish I could help you – really.

FLORENCE: You are helping me, darling – you're being an angel.

HELEN (*suddenly angry*): Don't talk so emptily, Florence, I'm worth more than that.

FLORENCE: I don't know what you mean.

HELEN: It sickens me to see you getting back so soon.

FLORENCE: Getting back?

HELEN: Yes, to your usual worthless attitude of mind.

FLORENCE: Helen!

HELEN: A little while ago you were really suffering for once, and in a way I was glad because it showed you were capable of a genuine emotion. Now you're glossing it over – smarming it down with your returning vanity, soon you won't be unhappy any more – just vindictive.

FLORENCE: Don't go on at me like that – I'm too wretched.

HELEN (*going to her*): Florence dear, forgive me, but it's true and I don't want it to be.

*The door opens and* NICKY *enters. He is in dressing-gown and pyjamas. His face looks strained and white.*

FLORENCE: Nicky!

NICKY: Helen, I want to talk to mother, please.

HELEN: All right, Nicky.

FLORENCE: What is it?

NICKY: I couldn't sleep.

HELEN: Florence dear – good night.

FLORENCE: No – no, Helen – don't go yet —

HELEN: I must.

FLORENCE: Helen – stay with me.

NICKY: Please go.

HELEN: I can't stay, Florence – it's quite impossible.

> *She goes out.*

FLORENCE: I don't know what you mean – by coming here and ordering Helen out of my room.

NICKY: I'm sorry, mother. I felt I had to talk to you alone.

FLORENCE: At this hour of the night – you're mad!

NICKY: No, I'm not, I think I'm probably more unhappy than I've ever been in my life.

FLORENCE: You're young – you'll get over it.

NICKY: I hope so.

FLORENCE: I knew the first moment I saw her – what sort of a girl she was.

NICKY: Oh, mother!

FLORENCE: It's true. I had an *instinct* about her.

NICKY: It's all been rather a shock, you know —

FLORENCE (*becoming motherly*): Yes, dear – I know – I know – but you mustn't be miserable about her – she isn't worth it. (*She goes to kiss him.*)

NICKY (*gently pushing her away*): Don't, mother!

FLORENCE: Listen, Nicky – go back to bed now – there's a dear – my head's splitting.

NICKY: I can't yet.

FLORENCE: Take some aspirin – that'll calm your nerves.

NICKY: I'm afraid I'm a little beyond aspirin.

FLORENCE: I don't want you to think I don't sympathise with you, darling – my heart *aches* for you – I know so well what you're going through.

NICKY: Do you?

FLORENCE: It's agony – absolute agony – but, you see – it will wear off – it always does in time. (NICKY *doesn't answer.*) Nicky, please go now!

NICKY: I want to talk to you.

FLORENCE: To-morrow – we'll talk to-morrow.

NICKY: No, now – *now!*

FLORENCE: You're inconsiderate and cruel – I've told you my head's bursting.

NICKY: I want to sympathise with you, too – and try to understand everything – as well as I can —

FLORENCE: Understand everything?

NICKY: Yes, please.

FLORENCE: I don't know what you mean —

NICKY: Will you tell me things – as though I were somebody quite different?

FLORENCE: What kind of things?

NICKY: Things about you – your life.

FLORENCE: Really, Nicky – you're ridiculous – asking me to tell you stories at this hour!

NICKY (*with dead vehemence*): Mother – sit down quietly. I'm not going out of this room until I've got everything straight in my mind.

FLORENCE (*sinking down – almost hypnotised*): Nicky – please – I —

NICKY: Tom Veryan has been your lover, hasn't he?

FLORENCE (*almost shrieking*): Nicky – how dare you!

NICKY: Keep calm – it's our only chance – keep calm.

FLORENCE (*bursting into tears*): How dare you speak to me like that – suggest such a thing – I —

NICKY: It's true, isn't it?

FLORENCE: Go away – go away!

NICKY: It's true, isn't it?

FLORENCE: No – no!

NICKY: It's true, isn't it?

FLORENCE: No – I tell you – no – no – no!

NICKY: You're lying to me, mother. What's the use of that?

FLORENCE: You're mad – mad —

NICKY: Does father know?

FLORENCE: Go away!

NICKY: Does father know?

FLORENCE: Your father knows nothing – he doesn't understand me any more than you do.

NICKY: Then it's between us alone.

FLORENCE: I tell you I don't know what you're talking about.

NICKY: Mother – don't go on like that, it's useless – we've arrived at a crisis, wherever we go – whatever we do we can't escape from it. I know we're neither of us very strong-minded or capable, and we haven't much hope of coming through successfully – but let's try – it's no good pretending any more

– our lives are built up of pretences all the time. For years –
ever since I began to think at all, I've been bolstering up my
illusions about you. People have made remarks not realising
that I was your son, and I've pretended that they were inspired
by cattiness and jealousy. I've noticed things – trivial
incriminating little incidents, and I've brushed them aside and
not thought any more about them because you were my
mother – clever and beautiful and successful – and naturally
people *would* slander you *because* you were so beautiful – and
now I *know* – they were right!

FLORENCE: Nicky – I implore you – go away now – leave me
alone.

NICKY: No, I can't.

FLORENCE: You're cruel – cruel to torment me —

NICKY: I don't want to be cruel —

FLORENCE: Go to bed then, and we'll talk everything over
quietly another time.

NICKY: It is true about Tom Veryan, isn't it?

FLORENCE: No. No —

NICKY: We're on awfully dangerous ground – I'm straining every
nerve to keep myself under control. If you lie to me and try to
evade me any more – I won't be answerable for what might
happen.

FLORENCE (*dropping her voice – terrified*): What do you mean?

NICKY: I don't know – I'm frightened.

FLORENCE: Nicky – darling Nicky – I —

　　*She approaches him.*

NICKY: Don't touch me, please.

FLORENCE: Have a little pity for me.

NICKY: Was Tom Veryan your lover?

FLORENCE (*in a whisper*): Yes.

NICKY: I want to understand why —

FLORENCE: He loved me.

NICKY: But you – did you love him?

FLORENCE: Yes.

NICKY: It was something you couldn't help, wasn't it – something that's always been the same in you since you were quite,
quite young —?

FLORENCE: Yes, Nicky – yes —

NICKY: And there have been others, too, haven't there?

FLORENCE (*with her face in her hands*): I won't be cross-questioned any more – I won't – I won't —

NICKY: I wish you'd understand I'm not blaming you – I'm trying to help you – to help us both —

FLORENCE: What good can all this possibly do?

NICKY: Clear things up, of course. I can't go on any more half knowing —

FLORENCE: Why should that side of my life be any concern of yours?

NICKY: But, mother!

FLORENCE: I'm different from other women – completely different – and you expect me to be the same – why can't you realise that with a temperament like mine it's impossible to live an ordinary humdrum life – you're not a boy any longer – you're a man – and —

NICKY: I'm nothing – I've grown up all wrong.

FLORENCE: It's not my fault.

NICKY: Of course it's your fault, mother – who else's fault *could* it be?

FLORENCE: Your friends – the people you mix with —

NICKY: It wouldn't matter *who* I mixed with if only I had a background.

FLORENCE: You've got as much money as you want – you've got your home —

NICKY (*bitterly*): Home! That's almost funny – there's no peace anywhere – nothing but the ceaseless din of trying to be amused —

FLORENCE: David never complains.

NICKY: I don't suppose you've looked at father during the last few years – or you wouldn't say that.

FLORENCE: He's perfectly happy because he's sensible – he lives his own life and doesn't try to interfere with mine.

NICKY: It must be your vanity that makes you so dreadfully blind – and foolish.

FLORENCE: Understand once and for all, I *won't* be spoken to like this —

NICKY: You've had other lovers besides Tom Veryan – haven't you?

FLORENCE: Yes, I have – I have. Now then!

NICKY: Well, anyhow – that's the truth – at last —

*He rises, turns his back on her and stands looking out of the window.*

FLORENCE (*after a pause – going to him*): Nicky – don't be angry – please don't be angry with me.

NICKY: I'm not angry a bit – I realise that I'm living in a world where things like this happen – and they've got to be faced and given the right value. If only I'd had the courage to realise everything before – it wouldn't be so bad now – it's the sudden shock that's thrown the whole thing out of focus for me – but I mean to get it right – please help me!

FLORENCE (*dully*): I don't know what to do.

NICKY: It's your life, and you've lived it as you've wanted to live it – that's fair —

FLORENCE: Yes – yes.

NICKY: You've wanted love always – passionate love, because you were made like that – it's not your fault – it's the fault of circumstances and civilisation – civilisation makes rottenness so much easier – we're utterly rotten – both of us —

FLORENCE: Nicky – don't – don't —

NICKY: How can we help ourselves? – We swirl about in a vortex of beastliness – this is a chance – don't you see – to realise the truth – our only chance.

FLORENCE: Oh, Nicky, do stop – go away!

NICKY: Don't keep on telling me to stop when our only hope is to hammer it out.

FLORENCE: You're overwrought – it isn't as bad as you think.

NICKY: Isn't it?

FLORENCE: No, no. Of course it isn't. To-morrow morning you'll see things quite differently.

NICKY: You haven't understood.

FLORENCE: Yes, I have – I have.

NICKY: You haven't understood. Oh, my God, you haven't understood! You're building up silly defences in your mind. I'm overwrought. To-morrow morning I shall see things quite differently. That's true – that's the tragedy of it, and you won't

see – To-morrow morning I *shall* see things differently. All this
will seem unreal – a nightmare – the machinery of our lives
will go on again and gloss over the truth as it always does –
and our chance will be gone for ever.

FLORENCE: Chance – chance? What are you talking about – what
chance?

NICKY: I must make you see somehow.

FLORENCE: You're driving me mad.

NICKY: Have patience with me – please – please —

FLORENCE (*wildly*): How can I have patience with you? – You
exaggerate everything.

NICKY: No I don't – I wish I did.

FLORENCE: Listen – let me explain something to you.

NICKY: Very well – go on.

FLORENCE: You're setting yourself up in judgment on me – your
own mother.

NICKY: No, I'm not.

FLORENCE: You are – you are – let me speak – you don't
understand my temperament in the least – nobody does – I —

NICKY: You're deceiving yourself – your temperament's no
different from thousands of other women, but you've been
weak and selfish and given way all along the line —

FLORENCE: Let me speak, I tell you —!

NICKY: What's the use – you're still pretending – you're building
up barriers between us instead of helping me to break them
down.

FLORENCE: What are you accusing me of having done?

NICKY: Can't you see yet?

FLORENCE: No, I can't. If you're preaching morality you've no
right to – that's my affair – I've never done any harm to
anyone.

NICKY: Look at me.

FLORENCE: Why – what do you mean?

NICKY: You've given me *nothing* all my life – nothing that counts.

FLORENCE: Now you're pitying yourself.

NICKY: Yes, with every reason.

FLORENCE: You're neurotic and ridiculous – just because Bunty broke off your engagement you come and say wicked, cruel things to me —

NICKY: You forget what I've seen to-night, mother.

FLORENCE: I don't care what you've seen.

NICKY: I've seen you make a vulgar, disgusting scene in your own house, and on top of that humiliate yourself before a boy half your age. The misery of losing Bunty faded away when that happened – everything is comparative after all.

FLORENCE: I didn't humiliate myself —

NICKY: You ran after him up the stairs because your vanity wouldn't let you lose him – it isn't that you love him – that would be easier – you never love anyone, you only love them loving you – all your so-called passion and temperament is false – your whole existence had degenerated into an endless empty craving for admiration and flattery – and then you say you've done no harm to anybody – Father used to be a clever man, with a strong will and a capacity for enjoying everything – I can remember him like that, and now he's nothing – a complete nonentity because his spirit's crushed. How could it be otherwise? You've let him down consistently for years – and God knows I'm nothing for him to look forward to – but I might have been if it hadn't been for you —

FLORENCE: Don't talk like that. Don't – don't – it can't be such a crime being loved – it can't be such a crime being happy —

NICKY: You're not happy – you're never happy – you're fighting – fighting all the time to keep your youth and your looks – because you can't bear the thought of living without them – as though they mattered in the end.

FLORENCE (*hysterically*): What does anything matter – ever?

NICKY: That's what I'm trying to find out.

FLORENCE: I'm still young inside – I'm still beautiful – why shouldn't I live my life as I choose?

NICKY: You're not young or beautiful; I'm seeing for the first time how old you are – it's horrible – your silly fair hair – and your face all plastered and painted —

FLORENCE: Nicky – Nicky – stop – stop – stop!

*She flings herself face downwards on the bed.* NICKY *goes over to her.*

NICKY: Mother!

134

FLORENCE: Go away – go away – I hate you – go away —
NICKY: Mother – sit up —
FLORENCE (*pulling herself together*): Go out of my room —
NICKY: Mother —
FLORENCE: I don't ever want to see you again – you're insane –
you've said wicked, wicked things to me – you've talked to me
as though I were a woman off the streets. I can't bear any
more – I can't bear any more!
NICKY: I have a slight confession to make —
FLORENCE: Confession?
NICKY: Yes.
FLORENCE: Go away – go away —
NICKY (*taking a small gold box from his pocket*): Look —
FLORENCE: What do you mean – what is it —?
NICKY: Don't you know?

> FLORENCE *takes the box with trembling fingers and opens it. She
> stares at it for a moment. When she speaks again her voice is quite
> dead.*

FLORENCE: Nicky, it isn't    you haven't   ?
NICKY: Why do you look so shocked?
FLORENCE (*dully*): Oh, my God!
NICKY: What does it matter?

> FLORENCE *suddenly rises and hurls the box out of the window.*

That doesn't make it any better.
FLORENCE (*flinging herself on her knees beside him*): Nicky, promise
me, oh, promise you'll never do it again – never in your life –
it's frightful – horrible —
NICKY: It's only just the beginning.
FLORENCE: What can I say to you – what can I say to you?
NICKY: Nothing – under the circumstances.
FLORENCE: What do you mean?
NICKY: It can't possibly matter – now.
FLORENCE: Matter – but it's the finish of everything – you're
young, you're just starting on your life – you must stop – you
must swear never to touch it again – swear to me on your
oath, Nicky – I'll help you – I'll help you —
NICKY: You!

*He turns away.*

FLORENCE (*burying her face in her hands and moaning*): Oh – oh – oh!

NICKY: How could you possibly help me?

FLORENCE (*clutching him*): Nicky!

NICKY (*almost losing control*): Shut up – shut up – don't touch me —

FLORENCE (*trying to take him in her arms*): Nicky – Nicky —

NICKY: I'm trying to control myself, but you won't let me – you're an awfully rotten woman, really.

FLORENCE: Nicky – stop – stop – stop —

*She beats him with her fists.*

NICKY: Leave go of me!

*He breaks away from her, and going up to the dressing-table he sweeps everything off on to the floor with his arm.*

FLORENCE (*screaming*): Oh – oh – Nicky —!

NICKY: Now then! Now then! You're not to have any more lovers; you're not going to be beautiful and successful ever again – you're going to be my mother for once – it's about time I had one to help me, before I go over the edge altogether —

FLORENCE: Nicky – Nicky —

NICKY: Promise me to be different – you've got to promise me!

FLORENCE (*sinking on to the end of couch, facing audience*): Yes – yes – I promise – (*The tears are running down her face.*)

NICKY: I love you, really – that's why it's so awful.

*He falls on his knees by her side and buries his face in her lap.*

FLORENCE: No. No, not awful – don't say that – I love you, too.

NICKY (*sobbing hopelessly*): Oh, mother —!

FLORENCE (*staring in front of her*): I wish I were dead!

NICKY: It doesn't matter about death, but it matters terribly about life.

FLORENCE: I know —

NICKY (*desperately*): Promise me you'll be different – promise me you'll be different —

FLORENCE: Yes, yes – I'll try —

NICKY: We'll both try.

FLORENCE: Yes, dear. – Oh, my dear —!

*She sits quite still, staring in front of her – the tears are rolling down her cheeks, and she is stroking* NICKY'S *hair mechanically in an effort to calm him.*

CURTAIN

# FALLEN ANGELS

## Characters

JULIA STERROLL

FREDERICK STERROLL

JANE BANBURY

WILLIAM BANBURY

MAURICE DUCLOS

SAUNDERS

———

*The action of the play takes place in the* STERROLLS' *flat*

# ACT I

*The scene is the dining-room of the* STERROLLS' *flat – the wall separating it from the drawing-room has been abolished, therefore the two rooms are used as one. There is a grand piano,* R. *The rest of the furniture can be left to the producer's discrimination.*

*When the curtain rises* FRED *is having his breakfast and* JULIA *is sitting in an arm-chair,* L., *reading the newspaper and dangling her legs over the arm. She is dressed plainly and appropriately for an ordinary London day in which nothing particular may be expected to happen. There must not be the faintest suggestion of the usual elegant silks and satins so beloved by the theatrical dressmaker.* FRED *is in golfing clothes.*

JULIA: You'll only get hiccups if you gobble like that.

FRED: I'm not gobbling.

JULIA: What time's Willy coming?

FRED: He ought to be here now.

> *There is a slight pause.*

JULIA (*rustling newspaper*): I say – Muriel Fenchurch is divorcing her husband.

FRED: That's uncommonly generous of him.

JULIA: Do you want any more coffee?

FRED: No thanks, dear.

> *There is another pause.* JULIA *goes on reading.*

JULIA: There was an old lady found dead on Clapham Common last night.

FRED: Another!

JULIA: Don't be silly, Fred, the last one was Wandsworth Common.

FRED: Oh!

JULIA: I think you'd better have some more coffee.

FRED: Why?

JULIA: Because I want you to see our new treasure.

141

FRED: Oh! all right, I didn't know we had one.

JULIA: She seems a nice girl, but rather grand. (*She rings.*)

FRED: Thank God what's-her-name's gone; I couldn't bear her.

*Enter* SAUNDERS.

FRED: Good morning.

SAUNDERS: Good morning, sir.

FRED: What's your name?

SAUNDERS: Jasmin, sir.

FRED: Oh!

JULIA: We have arranged that she shall be called Saunders.

FRED: Oh! good. I shan't want any more coffee, Saunders.

SAUNDERS: Yes, sir. (*She exits.*)

JULIA: She seems all right, doesn't she?

FRED: Quite. (*He rises from the table.*) I wish Willy'd learn to be punctual.

JULIA: Never mind, you've got the whole day; sit down quietly and smoke, and he'll be here in a minute.

*FRED sits in arm-chair, JULIA sits on the edge and lights his cigarette.*

FRED: What are you going to do?

JULIA: Nothing in particular. I'm lunching with Jane, and we shall probably go to a matinée.

FRED: There now, didn't I tell you your day would pan out perfectly normally?

JULIA: Yes, but I *did* have a presentiment when I first woke up.

FRED: But it was nothing definite, you said so.

JULIA: Of course it wasn't; you can't define a presentiment exactly, that's what's so horrid, the feeling of being unsettled.

FRED: I expect it's indigestion.

JULIA: No, I really felt quite odd, as though something damnable were going to happen.

FRED: If you go on thinking in that vein, something damnable *will* happen.

JULIA: You're being rather taciturn and important this morning.

FRED: I don't like to see you worrying yourself over nothing.

JULIA (*laughing*): I'm not really – I'm very happy.

FRED: Are you – honestly?

JULIA: Of course.

FRED: Sure?

JULIA: Positive.

FRED: Good! I think it's awfully silly of people to lead unhappy lives, don't you?

JULIA: Yes, I suppose so. We shall both know the first minute we go off one another.

FRED: We've been married five years.

JULIA: A divine five years.

FRED: Yes – wonderful.

JULIA: We're not in love a bit now, you know.

FRED: I don't know anything of the sort.

JULIA: It's true.

FRED: The first violent passion is naturally over —

JULIA: Thank God!

FRED: Why?

JULIA: It's so uncomfortable – passion.

FRED: Yes, but it's a thoroughly fundamental thing, one couldn't do without it.

JULIA: You mean we couldn't.

FRED: No, I don't, we can and are doing without it.

JULIA: One can't be really in love without passion, that's why I said we weren't any more.

FRED: Don't be annoying, Julia, you know perfectly well we've reached a remarkable sublime plane of affection and good comradeship, far above —

JULIA: Just ordinary 'being in love'. I quite agree.

FRED: We *are* in love.

JULIA: Hypocrite, we're not.

FRED: We are – in a different way.

JULIA: There is no different way. It's exactly the same with everybody, I've discussed it with Jane.

FRED: Damn Jane.

JULIA: By all means, but she knows – just as I do.

FRED: You're psycho-analytical neurotics both of you.

JULIA: That sounds lovely, Fred.

FRED: Do you always discuss everything with Jane?

JULIA: Yes, everything.

FRED: Even the most intimate relationships – us?

JULIA: Yes, you know I do, I always have.

FRED: I think that's dreadful – it shocks me.

JULIA: Nonsense, you discuss everything with Willy.

FRED: Yes, but differently.

JULIA: Less accurately, I expect, that's the only difference.

FRED: I'm sure married life was much easier in the Victorian days.

JULIA: If you think women didn't discuss everything minutely in the Victorian days just as much as they do now you're very much mistaken.

FRED: But it was all so much simpler.

JULIA: For the men.

FRED: For the women too; they didn't know so much.

JULIA: They didn't give themselves away so much, poor dears, they were too frightened.

FRED: Anyhow, on the whole I'd rather be as we are.

JULIA: That's right, dear.

FRED: But you're wrong when you say I don't love you any more.

JULIA: I didn't say that at all. I know you love me very much, and I love you, too – you're a darling. But we're not 'in love'. Can't you see the difference?

FRED: I suppose so, but I don't want to.

JULIA: Well, we won't go on about it any more – you shall go and play your golf and quarrel with Willy, and I'll stay at home and quarrel with Jane, and we'll all be awfully happy. Are you coming home to-morrow?

FRED: Perhaps to-night if the weather's bad.

JULIA: Well, you might telephone and let me know.

FRED: All right.

*There is the sound of the front door bell.*

JULIA: There is Willy.

FRED: I'll let him in and save Jasmin the trouble.

JULIA: Saunders.

FRED: Saunders, then. (*He goes out into the hall, and after a moment ushers in* WILLY, *also in plus fours and looking very nice in them.*)

WILLY: Good morning, Julia – how are you?

JULIA: I'm feeling grand. Fred and I have just had a little psychological romp – it was very stimulating.

FRED: It's depressed me for the day.

WILLY: Jane's been a trifle difficult this morning.

JULIA: In what way?

WILLY: She woke up with a presentiment.

FRED: Good Lord!

WILLY: She went on about it all through breakfast.

JULIA: How tactless of her – I at least waited until after breakfast.

WILLY: Have you had one, too?

JULIA: Yes, a beast! But don't ask me to explain it, it's quite intangible at present.

FRED: We'd better go, Willy, and leave them to their dreary forebodings, we'll be very hearty and jolly all day and drink a lot of beer at lunch.

WILLY: The car's downstairs.

FRED: Come on then.

WILLY: Have you got your clubs?

FRED: They're in the hall.

WILLY: Good-bye, Julia – don't encourage Jane too much for Heaven's sake!

JULIA: Whatever encouragement there is will be mutual – I feel in a particularly heart-to-heart mood to-day.

FRED: Good-bye, darling. (*He kisses her.*)

JULIA: Good-bye, love – don't forget to telephone.

> FRED *and* WILLY *go out amicably.* JULIA *rings the bell and goes over to the piano – she sits down and begins to play absently. Re-enter* SAUNDERS *with tray to clear away the breakfast things.*

JULIA: Does it feel awful to be in a new place, Saunders?

SAUNDERS: No, ma'am – not particularly.

JULIA: I'm so glad – I'm sure I should be terrified and break everything.

SAUNDERS: It's just getting used to things, ma'am.

JULIA: I hope you're not secretly hurt at our refusing to call you Jasmin?

SAUNDERS: Oh, no, ma'am – I don't mind.

JULIA: It's a sticky name, isn't it – for the house?

SAUNDERS: I've never thought about it much, ma'am.

JULIA: That's right, then you won't miss it, will you?

SAUNDERS: No, ma'am.

JULIA: If rather a strange-looking man calls during the morning will you take him straight to the bathroom?

SAUNDERS: Yes, ma'am.

JULIA: He'll probably be the plumber.

SAUNDERS: Very good, ma'am.

 SAUNDERS *goes out with the tray.* JULIA *begins to sing lightly.*

JULIA (*singing*):

 Même les Anges succombent à l'amour,
 C'est pourquoi donc je vous en prie –
 Dieu qui arrange les jours et les séjours
 Laisse moi encore une heure de paradis.
 Tous mes amours me semblent comme des fleurs,
 Leurs parfums restent douces quand même
 Donne moi tes lèvres, ton âme, et ton cœur,
 Parce que follement je t'aime – je t'aime – je t'aime.

*There is a ring at the front door bell. After a moment* JANE *enters in travelling clothes and carrying a suitcase. She looks extremely startled.*

JULIA (*still singing without noticing her*):

 Je t'aime – je t'aime – je t'aime —

JANE (*in a stifled voice*): Julia, stop singing that song.

JULIA: My dear, what a fright you gave me.

JANE (*tragically*): You don't know – that's all – you just don't know!

JULIA: Why, what on earth's the matter?

JANE: I should like a glass of water.

JULIA: What nonsense, you've only just finished breakfast.

JANE (*plumping her suit-case down*): We must both go away at once.

JANE (*amiably*): All right, where shall we go?

JANE: Don't be maddening, Julia, I'm serious.

JULIA: If you'd stop trying to get dramatic effects and just explain what it's all about —

JANE (*handing her a postcard*): Read that.

JULIA: It's the Blue Grotto at Capri.

JANE (*impatiently*): I know it is, read it.

JULIA (*turning it over*): Good God! (*She reads it carefully.*)

JANE: There now!

JULIA: This is frightful! (*She rings bell.*)

JANE: What are you ringing for?

JULIA: I want a glass of water.

JANE: What are we to do?

JULIA: Think – we must think!

> *Enter* SAUNDERS.

Two glasses of water please, Saunders.

SAUNDERS: Yes, ma'am. (*She goes out.*)

JULIA: When's he coming?

JANE: Now, I suppose – to-day – any moment!

JULIA: Oh, Jane, I wonder if he's changed.

JANE: I don't expect so – that type never does.

JULIA: Don't say 'that type' like that – it's most irreverent.

> *Re-enter* SAUNDERS *with two glasses of water on a salver.*

JANE (*taking one*): Thank you.

JULIA (*also taking one*): Thank you, Saunders.

> *Exit* SAUNDERS.

JANE: I packed just a few things very hurriedly – I thought perhaps Brighton for a day or two until our passports were properly viséd.

JULIA: Passports?

JANE: Yes, for America.

JULIA: Don't be ridiculous.

JANE: You must forgive me, darling, but I'm worked up – it was a most frightful shock, and the funny part of it was that I had a presentiment when I woke this morning.

JULIA: So did I.

JANE: There, you see!

JULIA: We must keep calm, and talk it over quietly, it's the only way. Have a cigarette. (*She hands* JANE *box.*)

JANE (*taking one*): Thanks, dear.

JULIA (*also taking one and lighting both*): We've got the whole day before us.

JANE (*fervently*): I only hope we have.

JULIA: You don't think he'll arrive before lunch?

JANE: He might, he never had the slightest restraint. Oh, after seven years, I do think it's cruel! (*She takes off her hat in front of the glass over the mantelpiece and fluffs out her hair.* JULIA *is sitting on the sofa.*)

JULIA: It might have happened before; that would have been much worse.

JANE: I wonder – perhaps we should have had more strength to – to – resist.

JULIA: Oh, no, we've never been exactly bursting with that kind of strength.

JANE (*intensely*): You know what we are, don't you? We're the slaves of coincidence – we always have been, it does make life so dreadfully difficult.

JULIA: Yes, but easier at moments; we can at least face it together.

JANE: It's going to be perfectly awful – facing *him* together!

JULIA: We must be firm; after all, we're not in love with him any more.

JANE: Not at the moment, but suppose when he arrives he's just as attractive and glamorous as ever? We shall go down like ninepins.

JULIA: I shan't, I've changed in seven years – I'm too fond of Fred.

JANE: I've been bolstering myself up like that all the morning, arguing that I'm too fond of Willy, and that everything is quite different now, but I don't know – I'm afraid, terribly afraid. You see, we might just as well face facts – we're not really *in love* with our husbands. I had a scene with Willy about it only last night. We're awfully happy, and there's a lovely firm basis of comradeship and affection and all that, but the real 'being in love' part is dead. You couldn't expect it to be anything else after all this time.

JULIA: Yes, I told Fred all that this morning.

JANE: Oh, Julia, I do wish we hadn't – when we did!

JULIA: It's a fat lot of good wishing that now.

JANE: Give me back the Blue Grotto.

JULIA (*handing it to her*): It's typical of him to send that, anyhow.

JANE (*looking at it*): Maurice! It gives me a fearful sort of illegitimate thrill even to look at his name.

JULIA (*warningly*): Now then, Jane.

JANE: I wonder if he realises that he's been the one Grand Passion in both our lives.

JULIA: Of course he does, it's almost his profession!

JANE: Our love for our husbands has been on an entirely different plane all along – much nicer and worthier and everything, but not half so soul-shattering.

JULIA: I wonder if he can speak English now.

JANE: I hope not, he was so lovely in French.

JULIA: What would Willy and Fred say if they knew?

JANE (*shuddering*): Don't!

JULIA: Fred would be sensible, I think, after the first shock had worn off.

JANE: Willy wouldn't.

JULIA: It isn't as if we'd been unfaithful *since* marriage, it all happened before.

JANE: Yes, but men never forgive that sort of thing, whenever it happened.

JULIA: It seems so unfair that men should have the monopoly of Wild Oats.

JANE: They haven't really, but it's our job to make them think they have.

JULIA: When I think of Italy, and the Cypresses and Moonlight and the wonderful romance of it all —

JANE: Don't dear, you'll only upset yourself.

JULIA: Do you remember me writing to you in Scotland and telling you all about it?

JANE: Yes.

JULIA (*far away*): How I adored him! And nobody knew – nobody knew a thing. I left Aunt Mary a week earlier than I said, and got out of the train at Pisa – he was waiting for me – we used to go and look at the Leaning Tower night after night – Carrara marble, dear – too marvellous!

JANE: I was so worried because I guessed —

JULIA: And that lovely song he used to sing all the time –

sometimes on the terribly cracked piano at the hotel, and sometimes just walking along the street. (*She goes to piano and begins to sing*):

> Même les Anges succombent à l'amour
> C'est pourquoi donc je vous en prie —

JANE: Don't, don't — he sang that to me afterwards —

JULIA (*still singing*):

> Donne moi tes lèvres, ton âme, et ton cœur —

JANE *joins in and they sing the last line together.*

BOTH: Parce que follement je t'aime — je t'aime — je t'aime —

SAUNDERS *enters with a postcard on a salver — she takes it to* JULIA.

JULIA (*jumps slightly — in stifled tones*): That will do, Saunders.

*Exit* SAUNDERS.

JANE (*with her eyes tight shut*): Don't tell me, dear, I know it's the Leaning Tower of Pisa.

JULIA: Of course it is.

JANE: What a devil!

JULIA (*reading*): J'arriverai à Londres cette semaine — J'espère avec tout mon cœur que me n'oubliez pas. — Maurice.

JANE: Cette semaine! And to-day's Saturday. Oh, God!

JULIA: Listen, Jane, we're in for a bitter time — we must summon up all our courage and face it properly.

JANE: Yes, give me another cigarette.

JULIA (*handing her box*): We must get the whole situation laid out quite clearly, like Patience, then we shall know where we are.

JANE (*lighting both cigarettes*): Yes — oh, yes!

JULIA (*sitting back on sofa*): Now then.

JANE: Now then what?

JULIA (*in business-like tones*): Two wretchedly happy married women —

JANE: Yes.

JULIA: Both during the first two years of their married lives having treated their exceedingly nice husbands to the requisite amount of passion and adoration —

JANE: Yes.

JULIA: As is usual in such cases – after a certain time the first ecstasies of passionate adoration subside, leaving in some instances an arid waste of discontent —

JANE: Lovely, darling!

JULIA: In some instances rank boredom and rampant adultery on both sides —

JANE: Don't be gross, dear.

JULIA: And in other rarer instances such as ours – complete happiness and tranquillity devoid of violent emotions of any kind with the possible exception of golf.

JANE: Quite.

JULIA: And there lies the trouble – the lack of violent emotion, fireworks, etc.

JANE: I don't want fireworks.

JULIA: Neither do I – not the nice part of me, but there's an unworthy, beastly thing in both of us waiting to spring – it sprang once before our marriage, and it will spring again – it hasn't been fed for a long, long time —

JANE (*shocked*): Julia!

JULIA: To put it mildly, dear, we're both ripe for a lapse.

JANE (*going into peals of laughter*): A Relapse, Julia. – Oh, dear!

JULIA (*also collapsing*): It's perfectly appalling, and we're laughing on the very edge of an abyss!

JANE: I can't help it, it's hysteria.

JULIA: By a semi-humorous malignity of fate we both happened to throw our respective bonnets over the same windmill —

JANE (*giggling weakly*): Oh, do stop —!

JULIA (*relentlessly*): And now, at a critical moment in our matrimonial careers, that windmill is coming to wreck us.

JANE (*wailing*): I don't want to be wrecked! I don't want to be wrecked!

JULIA: Shhh, dear! Saunders will hear you.

JANE (*panic-stricken*): Don't you see? What I suggested in the first place, it's the only way – we must go – at once – anywhere out of London.

JULIA: I shall do nothing of the sort, it would be so cowardly.

JANE: A blind goat could see through that, dear!

JULIA: All the same, I shall stay and face it.

JANE: If you do, I shall.

JULIA: There is not the least necessity for us both to suffer.

JANE: If you imagine I should enjoy being by myself in Brighton while you were gallivanting about London with Maurice —

JULIA: I should be too much upset to gallivant.

JANE: No, dear, it won't do.

JULIA: What do you mean, 'It won't do'?

JANE: We stand or fall together.

JULIA: I don't mind standing together, but I won't fall together, it would be most embarrassing.

JANE: Whatever happens, I am not going to be left out.

JULIA: Very well, then I'll go away and you stay.

JANE (*eagerly*): All right.

JULIA: What about standing or falling together?

JANE (*nobly*): I'm willing to sacrifice myself for you.

JULIA: Liar!

JANE: Julia, how can you —?

JULIA: I thought so.

JANE (*airily*): I don't know what you mean.

JULIA: Oh, yes, you do.

JANE: If you're going to be bad-tempered I shall go.

JULIA: I'm not in the least bad-tempered, I'm only seeing through you, that's all.

JANE: Seeing through me, indeed? What about you not going away because it would be cowardly? Huh!

JULIA (*sweetly*): Are you insinuating, dear, that I *want* to stay?

JANE: Not insinuating – I'm dead certain of it.

JULIA (*laughing forcedly*): Ha ha! Really, Jane —

JANE: You're simply longing for him.

JULIA: Jane!

JANE: You are, you know you are!

JULIA: So are you.

JANE: Certainly I am.

JULIA: Oh, Jane, we must be very careful.

JANE: I'm always careful.

JULIA: I don't mean about him, I mean about us.

JANE: Oh!

JULIA: Don't you see what's going to happen?

JANE: Yes – yes, I do.

JULIA: It's always the way, when sex comes up it wrecks everything. It's a beastly rotten thing—

JANE: It didn't wreck us before.

JULIA: We weren't together before – if we had been we should have been the blackest enemies in five minutes.

JANE: Yes, as it was you were a bit upset when I met him afterwards.

JULIA: I was awfully sweet about it.

JANE: It was too late for you to be anything else – I took jolly good care not to let you know until it was all over.

JULIA: Yes, that's true.

JANE: We've been friends, real friends, ever since we were eight and nine respectively—

JULIA: And in all probability this will break all that up.

JANE: Certainly – unless we circumvent it.

JULIA (*firmly*): I won't go away.

JANE: Neither will I – we're both firmly agreed on that point.

JULIA: It's only natural, after all, that we should want to see him again.

JANE: And it's also only natural that when we do see him again we shall fight like tigers.

JULIA: I wonder if we shall – really?

JANE: It's unavoidable – we almost started just now out of sheer anticipation.

JULIA: Oh, Jane darling, how miserable I am.

JANE: Nonsense, you're thoroughly thrilled and excited.

JULIA: Not altogether, I'm torn between my better self and my worse self. I never realised there were two of me until this moment so clearly defined. I want terribly badly to be a true, faithful wife and look after Fred and live in peace, and I want terribly to have violent and illicit love made to me and be frenziedly happy and supremely miserable.

JANE: We're both in exactly the same boat. But the most horrible contingency is that one of us may give in utterly and leave the other shrouded for ever in unrewarded virtue.

JULIA: Meaning the one he fancies most?

JANE: Exactly.

JULIA: Well, there won't be any virtue at all – just biting jealousy.

JANE: We must make a vow that however badly one or both of us behaves during the black and scarlet period before us – when it's all over and died down we can reinstate ourselves on the same concrete plane of friendship and intimacy without the slightest sacrificing of pride on either side.

JULIA: Oh, yes, yes, Jane – I vow it now.

JANE (*kissing her*): Darling! So do I – whatever we do, and whatever we may say when temporarily unhinged by sex —

JULIA: Whatever we do and whatever we say —

JANE: Afterwards – perfect friendship again.

JULIA: Perfect friendship again – and *no* apologies!

JANE: Not one!

JULIA (*suddenly*): Jane – I can't go through with it after all.

JANE: Now, Julia.

JULIA: It's no use – I can't – it will be frightful.

JANE: Agony.

JULIA: Let's do your plan, and fly.

JANE: Together?

JULIA (*impatiently*): Yes, oh, yes, together.

JANE: He'll think it so rude.

JULIA: Jane, don't be weak.

JANE: Frenchmen are so particular about that sort of thing.

JULIA: It can't be helped, one can carry good manners too far.

JANE: We ought to be hospitable.

JULIA: Well, as we can neither of us be hospitable without giving him the run of the house, we'd better leave him to freeze on the door-step!

JANE: *I* know! We can leave him a letter.

JULIA: Saying we've been called away.

JANE: Yes – that would ease my conscience.

JULIA: Quick then, you write it while I pack — Saunders – Saunders —

JANE: Your French is much better than mine.

JULIA: Never mind – I'll help —

    *Enter* SAUNDERS.

Saunders, I want you to pack a small suit-case – I've been called away —

SAUNDERS: Yes, ma'am.

*They both go off into bedroom, L., leaving door open.*

JANE (*at desk*): Shall I start, Mon cher Maurice?

JULIA (*off*): No, 'Notre cher', it's less compromising.

JANE (*after writing for a moment*): Listen – 'Notre cher Maurice – nous sommes désolée, mais il n'est pas possible pour nous vous voir cette fois —'

JULIA (*off*): Not 'cette fois', it sounds so sly.

JANE: What shall I put, then?

JULIA: While you are in London — No, Saunders, I shan't need those sort of things at all —

JANE: What's 'while'?

JULIA: Pendant.

JANE (*writing*): 'Pendant vous êtres à Londres.' Do let me put 'cette fois' now, it sort of rounds it off.

JULIA: All right. (*To* SAUNDERS.) Yes, it's on the dressing-table – no, the pink one —

JANE: Listen – 'Nous sommes mariée maintenant très heureusement —'

JULIA (*off*): Isn't that a little crude, dear?

JANE: I think he ought to know.

JULIA. Well, put 'Isn't it fun' after it.

JANE: I don't know how to.

JULIA (*off*): C'est amusant, n'est pas?

JANE: That sounds so facetious – and, anyhow, it isn't particularly.

JULIA: It probably will be to him, he'll rock with laughter.

JANE: Oh, very well. (*She writes.*)

JULIA: Put 'Have you got a beard yet?'

JANE (*laughing*): All right. (*She writes.*) Wouldn't it be awful if he had?

JULIA: Much safer. That's right, Saunders, in the top drawer among my stockings —

JANE: Is beard masculine or feminine?

JULIA: I'm not sure, make it feminine, he'll appreciate it more.

JANE (*writing hard*): That's all that's necessary now, don't you think?

JULIA: Tidy up, Saunders. (*She enters in travelling things and carrying a small suit-case.*) Yes, dear, finish it off gracefully.

JANE: 'Nous esperons pour vous voie quelquefois bientôt.' We must put that – it's mere politeness.

JULIA: Yes, now we'll both sign our names.

*They do so.*

I'll address the envelope while you put on your hat.

JANE (*putting on her hat hurriedly before glass*): We ought to explain to Willy and Fred.

JULIA: We haven't time to leave any more notes, we'll telephone —

JANE: Where from?

JULIA: Aberdeen – come on! Saunders, there's a note here for a foreign gentleman when he calls.

SAUNDERS (*off*): Very good, ma'am.

JULIA: Hurry up, Jane.

JANE: All right – I'm ready.

JULIA (*exultantly*): I'm glad! I'm tremendously glad – we're doing the right thing – don't you feel marvellous?

JANE: No – awful.

JULIA: Never mind – our better selves have won in spite of everything.

JANE: Yes, I suppose they have.

*They go towards the door with their bags. They almost reach it when there comes a loud ring and knock at the front door. They both stand still, as though they had been struck – looking at one another. Then with one accord they plonk their bags down.*

JULIA (*with determination*): Anyhow, it will be good for our French!

CURTAIN

# ACT II

*The scene is the same as Act I, and it is the evening of the same day.*

*When curtain rises,* JULIA *is looking out of the window.* JANE *is seated on the sofa. They are both elaborately dressed. The dinner-table is laid for two, and there are some lovely flowers in the room.*

JANE: I'm extremely hungry, Julia.

JULIA: So am I – ravenous.

JANE: It's getting on for nine.

JULIA: I know.

JANE: There's not the least likelihood of him arriving at this time.

JULIA: He might, especially if the Paris train were late.

JANE: We don't know whether he was coming from Paris.

JULIA: Where else would he be coming from?

JANE: Don't snap at me, Julia – he might be coming from the Channel Islands, or Brussels, or anywhere – he's frightfully cosmopolitan.

JULIA: I'm quite sure he's coming from Paris.

JANE: Well, anyhow, the idea was for him to arrive unexpectedly and discover us quietly dining together in charming domestic surroundings – not sitting twiddling our thumbs with eager strained expressions, and the room decorated like a Bridal Suite.

JULIA: That, dear, was not in the best of taste. Would you like a salted almond? (*She goes to table.*)

JANE: Yes, please – it may assuage the pangs a little.

JULIA (*throwing her one*): Here you are.

JANE (*missing it, and picking it up from the sofa*): Thanks.

JULIA: The table looks pretty, doesn't it?

JANE (*weakly*): Lovely, dear.

JULIA (*sitting down beside her*): It's been the most shattering day.

JANE: I shall never forget your face when, after all that suspense, the plumber arrived.

JULIA: I'm thankful he did all the same.

JANE: Why?

JULIA: Domestic reasons.

JANE: Why do you suppose Violet Coswick chose to-day of all days to come to tea?

JULIA: And talk exclusively of Paris and Frenchmen —

JANE: She has an awfully unpleasant mind, poor Violet, I suppose it must be the result of so much repression.

JULIA: Repression of what, dear?

JANE: Oh, everything.

JULIA: She lacks opportunities – it's her clothes, I think.

JANE: They don't lack opportunities, they grab them whole-heartedly.

JULIA: I've never seen so many things on any woman.

JANE: What was the meaning of that hat, anyhow?

JULIA: It appeared to be kept on by suction. Shall we have a cocktail?

JANE: It isn't very wise, is it? On empty stomachs.

JULIA (*ringing bell*): I shall get black depression if I don't.

JANE (*resignedly*): We shall just lapse into complete silliness, and when Maurice does come we shall giggle helplessly at him and our heads will wobble.

   *Enter* SAUNDERS.

JULIA: Cocktails, please, Saunders.

SAUNDERS: Yes, ma'am.

JULIA: Strong ones.

JANE: Julia!

SAUNDERS: Very good, ma'am.

   *Exit* SAUNDERS.

JULIA: I don't believe he ever will come.

JANE: Neither do I.

JULIA: It's probably all a sort of elfin joke – he was always being elfin.

JANE: And so terribly unreliable.

JULIA: I wouldn't trust him an inch.

JANE: I never did.

JULIA: But still, he was a darling.

JANE: Adorable, damn him!

JULIA: And he doesn't know many people in England.

JANE: I think he *will* come.

JULIA: So do I.

JANE: He'll kiss our hands and look up at us while he does it –
you remember?

JULIA: Oh, yes, I remember all right.

JANE: And he'll laugh and show all his teeth.

JULIA: Many more than are usual.

JANE: You know what we're doing, don't you?

JULIA: What?

JANE: We're working ourselves up.

JULIA: We have been all day.

JANE: I should like to scream now – scream and scream and
scream and roll about on the floor —

JULIA: So should I, but we must restrain ourselves.

JANE: It's want of food, you know.

JULIA: Yes, that's what it is.

SAUNDERS *comes in with cocktails.*

JANE: Oh, Julia – don't let's wait any longer.

JULIA: All right. (*She takes cocktail and hands it to* JANE.) Here you
are, dear. – Dinner, please, Saunders.

JANE: Quickly.

SAUNDERS: Yes, ma'am. Shall I open the champagne?

JANE (*beseechingly*): Julia!

JULIA (*firmly*): Yes, Saunders.

SAUNDERS *goes out.*

JANE: Listen! There's a taxi stopping outside.

JULIA: Quick!

*They both rush to the window and peer out.*

JANE: I can't see – it's so dark.

JULIA: He's got a black hat.

JANE: It must be – it must be!

JULIA: It's the beastly woman from upstairs – how dare she drive
about in taxis.

JANE: Look, there's another coming round the corner.

*They both crane round to see.*

*Re-enter* SAUNDERS *with oysters.*

SAUNDERS: Dinner is served, ma'am.

JULIA: It's no use – come and eat.

JANE: It was lovely of you to think of oysters, darling.

JULIA: They do give one a 'grand' feeling. It's awfully necessary for us to feel 'grand' to-night.

*They both sit down.*

JANE: Wouldn't it be dreadful if Fred and Willy came home?

JULIA (*with a warning look towards* SAUNDERS): Shhhh!

JANE: Drunk.

JULIA: What do you mean?

JANE: I say wouldn't it be dreadful if Fred and Willy came home drunk?

JULIA: Why should they?

JANE (*grimacing towards* SAUNDERS): Don't be silly, Julia.

JULIA: Oh, I see – yes, dreadful. I'd forgotten it was Saturday.

JANE: Saturday?

JULIA: Yes, naturally depressing in November because of the fog.

JANE: But only if you pay your subscription in advance.

SAUNDERS, *having served champagne and oysters, goes out.*

JULIA: Poor Saunders.

JANE: She looked extremely startled.

JULIA: You must be careful.

JANE: I'm sorry, darling, I quite forgot she was there.

JULIA: Wouldn't it be wonderful if he arrived suddenly now!

JANE: I should choke.

JULIA: You're sure you left a thoroughly clear message at your flat in case he went there?

JANE: Of course.

JULIA: We shall probably have a fearful shock when we do see him.

JANE: I don't see why, really.

JULIA: He's sure to have got fat, or bald, or something.

JANE: No, he'll be the same as ever; he wouldn't come at all if he weren't – he's much too conceited.

JULIA: Not conceited, a little vain perhaps, naturally.

JANE: With those eyes one can't blame him.

JULIA: And those hands —

JANE: And teeth —

JULIA: And legs! Oh, Jane!

JANE: Oh, Julia!

*Re-enter* SAUNDERS *with 'Œufs au plat Bercy' on separate dishes.*

JULIA: The cushions of the carriages are always so dusty.

JANE: She ought never to have been burnt at the stake because she was such a nice girl.

JULIA: I can hardly wait until strawberries come in again.

SAUNDERS (*putting dish before* JANE): Be careful, ma'am – it's very hot.

JANE: Thank you, I will.

JULIA: More champagne?

JANE: Yes, darling. (*She holds out her glass and* JULIA *fills it.*)

JULIA (*filling her own*): I'm feeling better now, aren't you?

JANE: Yes, I adore this little sausage with my egg.

JULIA: It is sweet, isn't it?

SAUNDERS *goes out.*

JANE (*leaning back*): It's all such a wonderful adventure.

JULIA: It hasn't started yet.

JANE: Oh, yes it has – I've enjoyed my day enormously.

JULIA: How can you? It's been damnable!

JANE: But frightfully exciting. I love something to break the monotony.

JULIA: Don't be 'young', Jane.

JANE: You're being awfully superior, but you're as thrilled as I am.

JULIA: I see such blackness ahead if we're not careful.

JANE: We mustn't lose our heads.

JULIA: Perhaps he won't want us to this time.

JANE: I have sudden beastly pangs about Fred and Willy.

JULIA: So do I.

JANE: We're being so disloyal.

JULIA: Only in thought so far.

*The telephone rings.*

BOTH: My God!

JANE (*rising*): I'll go.

JULIA (*also rising*): It's my house.

JANE: Quick – toss for it – rough or smooth, see! (*She picks up a fork.*)

JULIA: Rough.

JANE (*tossing it*): Rough it is.

JULIA (*at telephone*): Hallo! – Yes, Park 8720 – yes – (*To* JANE *in a hoarse whisper.*) It's a call office. – Hallo! – yes, speaking — (*She jumps.*) It is – it is —! Is that you, Maurice?

JANE (*rushing up and trying to hear*): It can't be – it can't be —

JULIA (*crossly*): Oh! Uncle Hugo, is that you – I thought it was someone else.

JANE: Damn!

JULIA (*impatiently*): No, he won't be home until to-morrow, he's playing golf with Willy.

JANE: Damn – damn – damn!

JULIA: Shut up, Jane. – Yes, all right, I'll tell him – Good-bye.

JANE: Stupid old fool.

JULIA: I hate all Fred's relations, anyhow.

*They go back to the table.*

JANE: He's probably gone straight to an hotel and had a lovely hot bath and changed his clothes and will come on here afterwards.

JULIA: I wonder.

JANE: Of course, he always has a hot bath after a journey.

JULIA: I hadn't forgotten, dear.

JANE: He'll probably wear a soft silk shirt with his dinner-jacket – so beautifully careless.

JULIA: Stop, Jane, I'm beginning to feel dreadful.

JANE (*dreamily*): I can see him now threading his way between the tables outside Florian's in the Piazza San Marco – we used to have coffee there always, then we used to stroll languidly along to the Piazzetta – I had a lovely green shawl – and then drift over the lagoon – and we'd hitch our gondola to a serenata and lie back and look up at the stars while darling little men in white shirts poured out their sentimental souls in the most shattering tenor voices. Sometimes we wouldn't stop

at all, but just glide on through the Picolo Canales until we
suddenly came out into that big lagoon behind Venice – away
from everywhere – just one or two buildings rising up like
ghosts out of the mist, then Maurice used to —

SAUNDERS *enters with Tournedos and sauce Bearnaise and Pommes
Dauphine.*

JULIA: The worst of a circus is, I'm always so *terrified* that they
ill-treat the animals.

JANE: Poor George and he *was* so charming before he married.

SAUNDERS *takes away plates.*

JULIA: I hope you haven't forgotten the sauce Bearnaise,
Saunders?

SAUNDERS: No, ma'am – it's here.

JANE: How delicious.

JULIA: Have some more champagne?

JANE: All right.

JULIA (*refilling both glasses*): We ought to have some of those little
wooden things in coloured paper to take the gassiness out.

JANE: They're such fun!

*There is suddenly a loud ring at the front door bell.* JULIA *gives a cry,
and* JANE, *who is drinking, chokes.*

JULIA: Jane, pull yourself together.

JANE (*choking badly*): I can't – it's agony —

JULIA: Leave the potatoes, Saunders, and answer the door.

SAUNDERS: Very good, ma'am.

JULIA (*to* JANE): Eat some bread quickly.

JANE (*recovering a little*): Oh, don't let him in – not yet —

JULIA: Eat some bread – here — (*She rushes round the table and
administers bread and water to* JANE.)

JANE (*weakly*): It's all right now. I'm better. (*She rises and grabs her
bag, then proceeds to powder her nose frantically.*)

*Re-enter* SAUNDERS.

SAUNDERS: It's a foreign gentleman, ma'am.

JANE: There, now!

JULIA: Why didn't you show him in?

SAUNDERS: He says he won't come in. He only wants to know if
there's a Madame Gambelitti living here.

JANE: What's he like?

SAUNDERS: Quite respectable, ma'am, but with a long moustache.

JULIA: Come on, Jane, we'll peep.

*They go to the door and peep round it into the hall – then return to the table crestfallen.*

JULIA: Why didn't you tell him there was no Madame What's-her-name here, and get rid of him?

SAUNDERS: You said you were expecting a foreign gentleman, ma'am, and I thought I'd better keep him in case.

JULIA: Well, get rid of him now.

SAUNDERS: Very good, ma'am.

*Exit* SAUNDERS.

JANE *(almost in tears)*: It's downright cruel, that's what it is.

JULIA: It's the first time that anybody not aggressively English has rung that bell since we've been here.

JANE: And he would come after his beastly Madame Gambelitti to-night of all nights. It's indecent!

JULIA: More champagne?

JANE *(loudly)*: Yes.

JULIA: Well, don't shout.

JANE: I shall if I want to, Julia; you mustn't be dictatorial.

JULIA *fills both glasses again.*

JULIA: Let's have a toast!

JANE *(rising and holding up her glass)*: Maurice Duclos.

JULIA *(also rising)*: Maurice Duclos! No heel taps.

*They both drain their glasses.*

JANE *(sitting down quickly)*: That was silly of us, Julia.

JULIA *(also sitting)*: Eat some steak quickly.

*There is silence for a moment while they devote themselves to their food.*

JANE: Wouldn't it be awful if a tree blew down and killed Fred and Willy on the golf links?

JULIA *(shocked)*: Jane, how can you!

JANE: It would serve us right.

JULIA: It would be too awful – I should never forgive myself.

JANE: Neither should I.

JULIA: There's a dreadful gale blowing.

JANE: Things like that do happen!

JULIA: No, they don't – not if you don't think about them. Mind over matter.

JANE: I do admire you, Jane, you're so strong – and sensible.

JULIA: Nonsense, dear, I'm just not *afraid* of life.

JANE: You're brave.

JULIA: No braver than you.

JANE (*verging on tears*): We must both be brave always, Julia.

JULIA (*slightly maudlin*): Whatever happens.

JANE: Even if Fred and Willy *were* killed we should have to bear it.

JULIA: Yes, Jane – we wouldn't break down – we'd face the world with a smile.

JANE: Not quite a smile, dear, it might be misunderstood.

JULIA: Poor darling Fred, I can see him now being carried in on a stretcher —

JANE: With Willy on another stretcher. Oh, dear — (*She breaks down.*)

JULIA: Jane dear – don't —

Re-enter SAUNDERS *with sweet – 'profiteroles au chocolat'.*

JANE: I've eaten much too much already.

JULIA: So have I, but we must go on, it will keep up our strength.

JANE: They look lovely. – Tinker, tailor, soldier, sailor —

JULIA (*giggling*): No, you do that with cherry stones.

JANE (*also giggling*): I like doing it with these.

JULIA: Have some more champagne?

JANE: No, thank you.

JULIA: Here you are. (*She pours it out.*)

JANE: Thanks, darling.

JULIA: What's so silly is that I'm beginning to feel sleepy.

JANE: I'm not – exactly – just cosy.

JULIA: Bring the coffee straightaway, Saunders.

SAUNDERS: Yes, ma'am.

*Exit* SAUNDERS.

JANE: What a pretty girl Saunders is!

JULIA: Yes, isn't she?

JANE: She ought to be a great success in life, she's so calm.

JULIA (*suddenly bursting out laughing*): Oh, dear —!

JANE: What are you laughing at?

JULIA: You look frightfully funny!

JANE: What's the matter with me? (*She gets up just a little unsteadily and looks at herself in the glass.*)

JULIA (*giggling hopelessly*): I don't know – you just do!

JANE: So do you.

JULIA (*also getting up and looking in glass*): It's our heads, I think – they're far too big.

JANE: We've had too much champagne.

JULIA (*agreeably*): Much too much.

JANE: Let's sit down again.

JULIA: All right.

>  *They return to the table.*

JANE: I feel awfully warm and comfortable.

JULIA: A child could play with me.

>  *The telephone rings.*

JANE: There now!

JULIA: It must be him this time.

JANE: It's my turn; come and stand close to me.

JULIA: All right – I'll sit on the edge of the sofa.

JANE (*at telephone – loudly*): Hallo!

JULIA: He isn't deaf.

JANE: Hallo! Yes, this is Park 8724.

JULIA: It isn't.

JANE: Keep quiet, I can't hear —

JULIA: Look on the thing; it's not 8724.

JANE (*gives a quick look at telephone number*): No, it isn't – it isn't – it's 8720 – hallo! Exchange — They've gone. Julia, it's a trunk call; what *am* I to do? – Exchange, hallo —!

JULIA: Hang the receiver up.

JANE: It will only go on ringing and ringing and ringing if I do. – Exchange, hallo! (*She bangs receiver up and down.*) Oh, this is agony!

JULIA: Here, give it to me. (*She snatches the telephone out of* JANE's *hand.*) Hallo! No, you've got the wrong number. – No, I'm not; I'm somebody quite different. (*She slams receiver down.*)

It's a shame! What on earth did you say we were Park 8724
for? You ought to know the number by now.

JANE: I couldn't help it; he jumped at me.

JULIA: You were in such a flutter because you thought it was
Maurice —

JANE (*with dignity*): I was as calm as a cucumber.

JULIA: You were shaking all over.

JANE: So were you – simply bobbing up and down on the sofa.

JULIA: Why you said it was Park 8724 I can't imagine.

JANE: I told you I couldn't help it.

JULIA: Don't argue, Jane, when you've been stupid over
anything it's much better not to argue.

JANE (*irately*): Stupid indeed! – I like that. Why, if you —

> *The telephone rings.*

JULIA: Leave it alone.

JANE: It may be him.

JULIA: No, it's only that trunk call again. It'll probably go on all
night because you told him it was Park 8720.

JANE: I didn't – I said Park 8724.

JULIA: Jane, how can you! You said 8720!

JANE: It *is* 8720.

JULIA: It isn't.

JANE: Look there. (*She shows her.*)

JULIA: I shall go mad, that's all, and it will serve you right.

> *The telephone continues to ring.*

JANE: Oh, stop it, for God's sake!

JULIA: There. (*She takes off receiver and puts it on table.*)

> *Enter* SAUNDERS *with coffee.* JULIA *and* JANE *both sit down at the
> table again.*

JANE: I don't mind what happens now – I'm just past everything.

JULIA: Have some coffee.

JANE (*taking it from* SAUNDERS): Thank you.

JULIA: A liqueur?

JANE (*giggling*): Don't be ridiculous.

JULIA: Cordial Médoc, Saunders.

JANE: Shall we have it in tumblers?

JULIA: I ordered it specially – it rounds off a dinner so nicely.

JANE: It certainly will.

SAUNDERS *goes to sideboard, pours out two liqueurs and puts them down on the table.*

JULIA: Thank you, Saunders – that will do now.

SAUNDERS: Very good, ma'am.

SAUNDERS *goes out with the remains of the sweet on a tray.*

JANE (*sipping her liqueur*): It's terribly strong!

JULIA (*airily*): It's supposed to make one feel rather – rather — (*She waves her hand vaguely.*)

JANE: How thoughtful of you, dear.

JULIA: Have some fruit?

JANE: I couldn't.

JULIA: Do, it rounds off the dinner so nicely.

JANE: For Heaven's sake stop rounding off the dinner, it's getting on my nerves.

JULIA: Don't be temperamental.

JANE: Do you think it would matter if I took off my shoes?

JULIA: Not at all – they always do in Japan, I believe.

JANE (*kicking off her shoes*): If Maurice had any instincts at all he'd arrive at this moment – looking marvellous.

JULIA: And make the most lovely sort of baffled scene!

JANE: What would baffle him?

JULIA: Us, of course, because we'd be so gloriously aloof and stately.

JANE: I shouldn't – I should give in without a murmur.

JULIA: Then he'd want me more.

JANE: If you feel that's the only way to make him, you'd better encourage me.

JULIA: You don't need any encouraging.

JANE: What do you mean by that?

JULIA: What I say.

JANE: Oh!

JULIA: Anyhow, I should never let you cheapen yourself.

JANE (*affronted*): How dare you, Julia.

JULIA: How dare I what?

JANE: Insult me.

JULIA: I didn't.

JANE: You did – you went too far – it was past a joke.

JULIA: It wasn't intended to be a joke – I hate jokes, bitterly.

JANE: Then you meant it?

JULIA: Meant what?

JANE: How can anyone carry on a conversation when you keep on saying what, what, what, what, what, what, what all the time! If you can't quite grasp what I say, you'd better go to bed.

JULIA: That was exceedingly rude, Jane.

JANE: I'm sorry, Julia, but you're annoying me.

JULIA: Unfortunately, this happens to be my flat.

JANE (looking round): Never mind, dear, you'll get used to it in time.

JULIA: Stop bickering, Jane.

JANE: How can you expect me not to bicker when you sit there abusing me.

JULIA: I never abused you.

JANE: Yes, you did – you insinuated that I was brazen.

JULIA: Well, so you are – sometimes – we all are, it's human nature.

JANE: Nothing of the sort.

JULIA: Don't contradict everything I say – it infuriates me.

JANE: Brazen! It was you who refused to run away this morning, anyhow.

JULIA: Why should I run away?

JANE (laughing loudly): That's funny.

JULIA (coldly): I'm glad you think so.

JANE: Why should you run away – ha-ha!

JULIA: I think you must be going to have a cold, Jane.

JANE: Why?

JULIA: Your voice is so strident.

JANE: I shall whisper for the rest of the evening.

JULIA: Do, it's more soothing.

JANE (in a hoarse whisper): Anyhow, there's this to be said – if you hadn't met Maurice first and gone on with him like that in Pisa —

JULIA: You're being insufferable.

JANE: Not at all – I'm merely pointing out that it's no use riding

169

a high horse now because the whole affair's been entirely your
fault from beginning to end.

JULIA (*rising*): I'm awfully disappointed in you, Jane, – I thought
you had a nicer mind than that.

JANE: Mind! What about yours? I suppose you imagine it's a
lovely gilt basket filled with mixed fruit and a bow on the top!

JULIA: Better than being an old sardine tin with a few fins left in
it!

JANE (*rising*): You'll regret that remark in your soberer
moments.

JULIA: Have a cigarette.

JANE (*taking one*): Thank you.

JULIA (*striking a match*): Here!

JANE (*with dignity*): Thank you.

JULIA (*grandly*): Perhaps you'd like a little music? Shall I put the
gramophone on?

JANE: Do, if you feel it would put you in a better temper.

JULIA (*ignoring her – conversationally*): I had such an amusing letter
from Aunt Harriet this morning.

JANE (*rudely*): Did you really? I thought she was dead.

JULIA (*with a superior frown*): I'm afraid you must be muddling her
up with someone else.

JANE: Go on, dear – tell me some more news. I love you when
you're offended.

JULIA (*sadly*): I'm not offended, Jane. A little hurt, perhaps, and
surprised —

JANE (*suddenly furious*): How dare you draw yourself up and
become the outraged hostess with *me!*

JULIA: I'm sorry – I must have lost my sense of humour –
perhaps because I'm tired – we've been together so much
lately, we've probably grated on one another's nerves.

JANE: Yes, you're right there. Where are my shoes?

JULIA (*disdainfully*): I really don't know – they can't have gone
far.

JANE: I should like to shake you, Julia, shake you and shake you
and shake you until your eyes dropped out!

JULIA: Indeed?

JANE: Yes, when you're superior and grand like that you rouse the very worst in me —

JULIA: Obviously.

JANE: You make me feel like a French Revolution virago. I'd like to rush up and down Bond Street with your head on a pole!

JULIA: You'd better pull yourself together and I'll ask Saunders to help you to your flat.

JANE: If she comes near me I'll throttle her.

JULIA: I've never seen you violent before – it's very interesting psychologically.

JANE (*with sudden determination*): I could bring you down to earth in one moment if I liked.

JULIA: Vulgarity always leaves me unmoved.

JANE: This is not vulgarity – it's something I was more ashamed of than vulgarity, but I'm not ashamed of it any more – I'm glad! I've kept something from you, Julia.

JULIA: I wish you'd go home, Jane.

JANE: I must have realised subconsciously all the time that you were going to turn out false and beastly —

JULIA: What are you talking about?

JANE: Where are my shoes?

JULIA: Never mind about your shoes – what do you mean?

JANE: Give me my shoes.

JULIA (*moving over to the mantelpiece*): They're probably under the table – you'd better get them and go.

JANE (*finding them and putting them on savagely*): And now I'm thankful to God I *did* keep it to myself.

JULIA: That's right.

JANE: You're still too grand to be curious, I suppose.

JULIA: Don't be cheap, Jane.

JANE: It concerns Maurice.

JULIA (*turning*): Oh! it concerns Maurice, does it?

JANE: Yes, I thought that would rouse you!

JULIA: I think you'd better tell me – if you don't want to wreck our friendship for ever.

JANE: It will wreck our friendship all right when I *do* tell you – and I don't care. It's this – *I know where he is!*

JULIA: It's a lie!

JANE: No, it isn't. He rang me up while I was dressing to-night.

JULIA: Jane!

JANE: Yes, I didn't want to tell you because I thought it would have hurt your feelings. But now I know that you haven't got any feelings to hurt – only a shallow sort of social vanity —

JULIA: Where is he, then? Tell me!

JANE: I shall do nothing of the sort. I don't want you to rush round there and make a fool of yourself.

JULIA (*losing all control*): How dare you! How dare you! I'll never speak to you again as long as I live. You're utterly completely contemptible! If it's true, you're nothing but a snivelling hypocrite! And if it's false, you're a bare-faced liar! There's not much to choose between you. Please go at once!

JANE: Go – I'm only too delighted. You must curb your social sense, Julia, if it leads you to drunken orgies and abuse!

JULIA (*in tears*): Go – go – go away —!

JANE: Certainly I shall – and it may interest you to know that I'm going *straight* to Maurice!

JULIA (*wailing*): Liar – Liar!

JANE: I'm not lying – it's true. And I shall go away with him at once, and you and Fred and Willy can go to hell, the whole lot of you!

> JANE *flounces out.* JULIA *hurls herself on to the sofa in screaming hysterics.*


**CURTAIN**

# ACT III

*The same scene. It is the next morning.* JULIA *is finishing her breakfast gloomily. She rings the bell at her side. Enter* SAUNDERS.

JULIA: When I say a 'Soft-boiled egg', Saunders, I don't mean an *un*-boiled egg.

SAUNDERS: I'm sorry, ma'am.

JULIA: There was also a long dark hair in the marmalade.

SAUNDERS (*anxiously*): Was there, ma'am?

JULIA: I haven't the remotest idea how it got there, we are both distinct blondes; perhaps it was Mr Robertson's.

SAUNDERS: Yes, ma'am.

JULIA: Anyhow, please search the marmalade in future.

SAUNDERS: Very good, ma'am.

> JULIA *goes over to the telephone.*

JULIA (*at telephone*): Park 5703 – yes, please – 03 — Damn! (*She slams the telephone down and goes over to the window and drums her fingers on the pane – it is pouring with rain. She picks up the paper, looks at it in disgust for a moment, then throws it away. She goes once more to the telephone.*)

JULIA: Hallo! – Park 5703 – yes, please. – Oh! (*She holds the receiver away from her ear as the engaged signal is deafening. After a pause:*) It can't possibly *still* be engaged! – Very well – hallo – My good girl, you suffer from being both incompetent *and* stupid! (*She slams down receiver. There is a ring at the front door bell. She jumps. After a moment* WILLY *enters.*)

WILLY: Good morning, Julia.

JULIA: Willy! What on earth are you doing here? Where's Fred?

WILLY (*gloomily*): I left him at the Grand Hotel, Littlestone. Where's Jane?

JULIA (*coldly*): I don't know.

WILLY: You don't know?

JULIA: I haven't the faintest idea – she might be anywhere by now.

WILLY: What d'you mean 'By now'?

JULIA: Just 'By now'.

WILLY: What's the matter?

JULIA: Nothing.

WILLY: What's happened?

JULIA: Everything probably – by now!

WILLY: What are you talking about?

JULIA: Oh, don't be tiresome!

WILLY: I made sure Jane would be with you. Where's she gone?

JULIA: Do stop cross-questioning me – anyone would think I'd murdered her and put her in a box.

WILLY: Well, from the furtive way you're behaving I shouldn't be in the least surprised.

JULIA: Anyhow, what do you mean by leaving Fred all alone in the Grand Hotel, Littlestone?

WILLY: We had a row last night.

JULIA: Oh, did you!

WILLY: Yes, Fred infuriated me.

JULIA (*with sarcasm*): I'm sure I'm very sorry – I'll speak to him severely.

WILLY: And I felt I couldn't bear to meet him at breakfast and go all over it again – so I crept out and left by the early train.

JULIA: What did you row about?

WILLY: Nothing.

JULIA: That's the worst kind.

WILLY: Have you quarrelled with Jane?

JULIA: Yes, bitterly.

WILLY: What about?

JULIA: Nothing!

WILLY: Oh!

JULIA: We got drunk.

WILLY: What!

JULIA: Extremely drunk.

WILLY: Julia!

JULIA: Jane was much worse than I was, and – well, we quarrelled.

WILLY (*incensed*): If I can't go away for a quiet game of golf without you making Jane drunk —

JULIA: I didn't make her drunk – it was voluntary.

WILLY: Disgusting, I call it.

JULIA: And she banged out of the flat.

WILLY: Where is she now?

JULIA: I don't know, and I don't care.

WILLY: Don't be callous, Julia.

JULIA: She's probably at home in bed sleeping it off.

WILLY: She isn't – I've just been there.

JULIA: I thought you came straight here.

WILLY: No, I had a large bag and golf clubs.

JULIA: Are you sure she isn't at home?

WILLY: Perfectly, but I didn't worry because I thought she'd be with you.

JULIA (*turning away*): Then it *was* true, then —

WILLY: What was true?

JULIA (*biting her lip angrily*): Oh! – Oh!

WILLY: What in God's name's the matter?

JULIA: I was going to ring her up and make friends again. I didn't believe for a moment – I didn't think that – Oh!

WILLY: Didn't believe *what!*

JULIA: She must have been deceiving me steadily all through dinner. How dare she! Oh, oh, oh!

> JULIA *begins striding up and down the room.*

WILLY: Julia, will you stop still and explain what's happened?

JULIA (*stopping*): Explain! Oh, yes, I'll explain all right – the sly, underhand little —!

WILLY (*with dignity*): Will you please remember that you are referring to my wife.

JULIA: Your wife! – Huh! Optimist!

WILLY: Julia!

JULIA (*irately*): Yes, my poor Willy – my poor, poor Willy.

WILLY: You're maddening me, Julia.

JULIA (*beginning to stride again*): To have behaved like that – after all these years. Oh, it's contemptible!

WILLY (*catching her by the shoulders*): What's happened to Jane? Where's she gone?

JULIA: I should like to break it to you gently, Willy – she's gone off with a man!

WILLY: What!

JULIA (*defiantly*): A Frenchman.

WILLY: Nonsense, she can't have.

JULIA: I tell you she has.

WILLY: I don't believe it – you're unhinged, that's what it is.

JULIA: I'm perfectly hinged. It's true.

WILLY: I'm sorry, Julia, but I don't believe it. I know Jane too well; she'd never rush off like that at a moment's notice.

JULIA (*bitterly*): She knew where he was all the time, and she went to him.

WILLY: She was pulling your leg.

JULIA: Don't be so pig-headed, Willy, this is one of the few big moments in your life, and you're behaving like a ninny!

WILLY: If you think stamping up and down the room and blackguarding Jane is a big moment in my life you're very much mistaken.

JULIA (*exasperated*): It's true! She's known him for years. She was in love with him before she married you – before she ever met you.

WILLY: Don't be ridiculous!

JULIA: Your smug complacency is beyond belief. I suppose you feel quiet sure that no woman could bear to leave you?

WILLY: Jane couldn't – she'd hate it.

JULIA: There's going to be a shattering awakening for you.

WILLY: I say, Julia, don't go on ramping any more – just calm down and explain things quietly. I'll pour myself out some coffee, if I may.

*He does so.* JULIA *watches him in silence.*

JULIA: Willy – I – Oh! (*She bursts into tears.*)

WILLY: What's up now?

JULIA: I'm a beast – a traitress — (*She sobs.*)

WILLY: No, you're not – you're just thoroughly hysterical – you'll be better in a moment. (*He drinks some coffee.*)

JULIA (*controlling herself*): Listen, Willy! – I'm sorry – but I'm afraid what I said just now was the truth.

WILLY (*amiably*): I'm trying hard to understand. I can't help feeling that there's something awfully silly behind all this – it doesn't seem to ring true.

JULIA (*with sarcasm*): Perhaps you think I'm playing an amusing practical joke on you?

WILLY: No, it isn't that, but you've either deceived yourself into believing it or else you're making a mistake.

JULIA: But, Willy —

WILLY: If Jane really had left me, I know I should have some sort of feeling about it – but I haven't.

JULIA: That'll come later all right.

WILLY: Who is this man she's supposed to be with?

JULIA: He's a Frenchman – Maurice Duclos. Jane and I both knew him before we married.

WILLY: Did you know him well?

JULIA: Extremely well.

WILLY: And Jane? Was Jane in love with him then?

JULIA: Yes, violently! We both were.

WILLY: Did you – er – did you —?

JULIA: Yes, Willy.

WILLY: Where?

JULIA: Pisa.

WILLY: And did Jane ever —?

JULIA: Yes, Willy.

WILLY: Good God, where?

JULIA: Venice.

WILLY: This is horrible – incredible —

JULIA: Willy, I'm sorry I —

WILLY (*abruptly*): You'd better save your apologies for Fred. I'm going to find Jane.

JULIA: I'll come too.

WILLY: Has she seen this man since we've been married?

JULIA: No – at least – I don't know – she's such a liar.

WILLY: When did *you* last see him?

JULIA: Seven years ago on the railway station at Pisa. We were both going to Paris, and at the last moment he said he wanted a Salami sandwich, and as I hated garlic, we had a row. He was far too temperamental, anyhow, so I pushed him out on to the platform just as the train was starting. I repented it bitterly at the time – but now I'm glad.

WILLY: I think you ought to be ashamed of yourself.

JULIA: I didn't push him very hard.

WILLY: I don't mean about that – I mean the whole affair.

JULIA: Are you daring to disapprove of me, Willy?

WILLY: Yes. You're devoid of the slightest moral sense.

JULIA: What about Jane?

WILLY: Jane's different – she's just weak. You probably set her a bad example.

JULIA: Willy!

WILLY (*hotly*): I wouldn't mind betting you met the beastly man first and then told Jane all about it and generally egged her on.

JULIA: She didn't need any egging – she met him and never said a word to me for ages afterwards.

WILLY: She was probably too ashamed and repentant.

JULIA: Repentant my foot.

WILLY: Anyhow, it's more than you are – you're positively glorying in your – your – shame!

JULIA: If I'd known what a smug little man you were I'd never have let Jane marry you at all.

WILLY: And if I'd known how utterly lacking you were in all the finer feelings I'd never have let Fred come near you.

JULIA: I should think it would be as well to stop hurling abuse at me and go in search of your weak but strictly virtuous wife, who, if she hasn't succeeded in finding Maurice Duclos, is probably roaming about the streets in deep evening dress and hiccuping.

WILLY: You must come with me.

JULIA: I shall do nothing of the sort.

WILLY: You said you would.

JULIA: That was before your insults.

WILLY: Julia, do come?

JULIA: Where could we go first – Vine Street?

WILLY: She can't have gone far.

JULIA: Judging by her condition when she left this flat she's probably gone farther than our wildest dreams.

WILLY: Please come, Julia.

JULIA: I'll come back to your flat – she may have left a note or something.

WILLY: I never thought of that.

JULIA: Wait a moment. (*She goes into the bedroom and issues forth in a small hat and a coat over her arm.*)

WILLY: Look here, Julia, I'm sorry for what I said just now.

JULIA: So you ought to be.

WILLY: But I still don't believe it all – quite.

JULIA: I want you to understand one thing clearly. I'm not coming with you just to help you. I'm coming because I wish to find Jane and tell her exactly what I think of her.

WILLY: I say, Julia, don't be beastly to her. She's probably feeling pretty awful.

JULIA: I don't care if she's feeling heavenly, she won't be when I've finished with her!

> *They go out.* SAUNDERS *just catches sight of them as they vanish.* SAUNDERS, *humming to herself, begins to pile the breakfast things on a tray. The telephone rings.*

SAUNDERS (*at telephone*): 'Hallo! – yes – yes, sir. – No, sir, she isn't in at present. – I don't know, sir, she didn't say. – Yes, sir, what name, sir? – One moment, sir, I'll write it down –' (*She writes on block.*) 'Maurice Duclos – Park 9264. – Yes, sir, I'll tell her.' (*She hangs up the receiver and continues to clear away. She is on her way to the door when* FRED *comes in.*)

FRED: Good morning, Saunders.

SAUNDERS: Good morning, sir.

FRED: Where's the mistress?

SAUNDERS: She's gone out, sir.

FRED: Gone out? But it's pouring.

SAUNDERS: Yes, sir.

FRED: Where's she gone?

SAUNDERS: I don't know, sir.

FRED: She's with Mrs Banbury, I expect. Run up, will you, and tell her I've come back?

SAUNDERS: What number is it, sir?

FRED: Number five – two floors up.

SAUNDERS: Very good, sir. (*She goes out.*)

> FRED *lights a cigarette and wanders about the room aimlessly. He*

*goes over to the piano and plays absently the tune of 'Même les Anges' with one finger. He also hums it a little.*

JANE *enters rather draggled, in evening dress and a cloak.*

JANE: Fred! What are you doing?

FRED (*turning*): Playing the piano. Good heavens!

JANE: What?

FRED: Have you been out all night?

JANE: Yes.

FRED: Lucky for you I left Willy at Littlestone.

JANE: Oh, you did, did you?

FRED: Yes, sleeping like a hog. I left early in the car.

JANE: Why?

FRED: We had rather a row last night. If you'll forgive me saying so, your husband is a fool sometimes.

JANE: I've always found him extremely intelligent.

FRED: Where have you been?

JANE: Mind your own business, Fred!

FRED: Don't jump down my throat – it was quite a harmless question.

JANE: I object to your dictatorial tone.

FRED: Well, to come in like that at eleven o'clock in the morning is a little —

JANE: If I choose to come in naked on a tricycle it's no affair of yours. Where's Julia?

FRED: I don't know, she went out before I arrived.

JANE: Out – where?

FRED: I haven't the faintest idea. I thought she'd probably be with you.

*Re-enter SAUNDERS.*

SAUNDERS: The mistress isn't at Mrs Banbury's, sir. (*She sees* JANE.) Oh!

JANE: Don't look so surprised, Saunders. You left the door open so I walked in.

SAUNDERS: Yes, ma'am.

FRED: What time did the mistress go out, Saunders?

SAUNDERS: Just before you came in, sir.

FRED: Was she alone?

SAUNDERS: No, sir, there was a gentleman with her.

JANE (*tensely*): A what?

SAUNDERS: A gentleman, ma'am.

FRED: Who was it?

SAUNDERS: I don't know, sir, he didn't give any name when I opened the door; he just walked straight in.

JANE: What was he like?

SAUNDERS: About medium height, ma'am, and dark.

JANE (*ominously*): Dark was he!

FRED: Why, what's the matter?

JANE: I'm sorry for you, Fred, extremely sorry for you.

FRED (*startled*): That will do, Saunders.

SAUNDERS: Very good, sir. (*She goes out.*)

FRED: What do you mean, Jane?

JANE: Don't speak to me for a moment, just don't speak to me – I'm trying to control myself, and I should like a cigarette.

FRED (*giving her one – very puzzled*): What's all this mystery about?

JANE (*austerely*): There is no mystery, I'm afraid, any more – it's all far too clear.

FRED: Jane – tell me at once – what's happened?

JANE: You'll know all too soon, Fred dear. Julia *was* my friend – I have no intention of being disloyal.

FRED: Jane – tell me what's happened!

JANE (*sadly*): I'm sorry, Fred, but I can tell you nothing. Julia may be double-faced, treacherous, and thoroughly immoral. But I repeat, she was my friend.

FRED (*relieved*): Oh, I see – you had a row last night, too.

JANE: Yes, we did.

FRED: What about?

JANE: I don't know – Julia spoke rather indistinctly.

FRED: Do you know where she's gone now?

JANE: I have a shrewd suspicion, but my lips are sealed.

FRED: Tell me at once!

JANE: I can't possibly. I — (*She catches sight of* MAURICE's *name on the telephone block. She gives a gasp of fury.*) Oh! – Oh!

FRED: What's the matter now?

JANE: So she knew – all the time – Oh!

FRED (*frantically*): Knew *what*?

JANE: How dare she – how dare she – it's contemptible – it's –

Oh! — (*She takes up the telephone block and hurls it to the ground.*)
The sneaking hypocrite! Oh! the despicable squalor of it all –
to be deceived like that by one's best friend, and for such a
sordid purpose. – Oh! – Oh! – Oh! (*She positively stamps with
rage.*)

FRED *picks up the block and reads the name on it.*

FRED: Who's this?

JANE: Don't speak to me – don't speak to me!

FRED: What does it mean?

JANE: It means that Julia has deserted you, Fred.

FRED: Deserted me?

JANE: Yes, she's gone off with that man Maurice Duclos – she's
known him for years – long before you were married – in
Italy.

FRED: Are you mad, Jane?

JANE: No – I'm terribly sane.

FRED: You don't seriously expect me to believe that Julia would
leave me suddenly without rhyme or reason?

JANE: She'd do anything! She hasn't a single scruple or a pang of
conscience anywhere – she'd lie, slander, forge, thieve,
murder, anything! She's a thorough out-and-out bad lot – she's
a – a —

JANE *bursts into violent tears.*

FRED: Pull yourself together, Jane, you're overwrought just
because you've had a little row with Julia —

JANE: Go away – go away – leave me alone.

FRED: You know perfectly well you like her better than anyone
else in the world, and always will.

JANE: Don't, Fred – stop!

FRED: I expect she's feeling just the same as you at this very
moment.

JANE: Not she, she's far too busy.

FRED: Jane, do control yourself.

JANE (*making an effort*): I came here first – even before going
home – because I wanted to make up the row. I've had a
wretched night all by myself in an hotel in Bayswater.

FRED: Why on earth Bayswater?

JANE: Because the taxi man took me there. I'll tell you

everything – it's awful. Julia and I were both drunk, and before we were married we both had an affair with the same man, and he's come to England, and we were terrified we'd fall in love with him again, and we worked ourselves up and waited for him, and Julia got grand after dinner, and ordered me out of the house, and I pretended I knew where he was and was going straight to him, and I went to the Granville Hotel, Bayswater.

FRED: Was he there?

JANE: Don't be such a fool; of course he wasn't.

FRED: Where is he then?

JANE: With Julia.

FRED: Impossible.

JANE: Nothing of the sort – here's his name in capitals on the telephone block and Saunders saw them go out together.

FRED: You say you both knew him in Italy before you married?

JANE: Yes, Fred.

FRED: And you both —

JANE: Yes, Fred.

FRED: How dare you stand there and say 'Yes, Fred'!

JANE: Well, it's true.

FRED: You appal me absolutely! Your dreadful matter-of-fact callousness. – 'Yes, Fred.' Oh, my God!

JANE: Don't be melodramatic.

FRED: Melodramatic! It's horrible – awful —

JANE: You were playing the love song he used to sing to us both when I came in – 'Même les Anges succombent à l'amour —'

FRED: I suppose you feel proud of yourself, having led Julia into that blackguard's clutches!

JANE: Led her! Ha-ha – that's funny.

FRED: Yes, led her – deliberately. You've got a depraved mind.

JANE: You're insufferable and pompous, you like wallowing in a quagmire yourself and you think everybody else likes wallowing in a quagmire.

FRED: Don't be ridiculous. You ought to be humble and ashamed instead of truculent.

JANE: Humble and ashamed. Why? Do you expect me to believe you led a model life before marriage?

FRED: That's beside the point.

JANE: No it isn't. If you had, Julia would never have married you at all; you'd have been too dull!

FRED (*shocked*): Jane!

JANE: Yes, it's no use going on like that – it's just silly – the great thing is what are you going to do now?

FRED: Do! I'm going to find Julia.

JANE: That'll be nice.

FRED: And you're coming with me.

JANE: Oh, no, I'm not. I've seen quite enough of Julia to last me for a long time.

FRED (*firmly*): You're coming with me. (*He takes her arm.*)

JANE: Let go.

FRED: Come on.

JANE: I can't go like this.

FRED: You'll have to.

JANE (*losing all control and bursting into hysterical tears*): Let me go – how dare you pull me about. Fred, Fred, let go at once —

FRED: I'm quite determined.

JANE: Oh! help! help! help! —

> They struggle for a moment or two.
> Re-enter JULIA and WILLY.

JULIA: Fred!

WILLY: Jane! Where have you been?

JANE (*slowly – aghast*): It was *you* who went out with Julia and not – not —

JULIA (*coldly*): Good morning, Jane.

JANE: Julia – Julia – I've done the most awful thing!

JULIA (*turning away*): I'm not at all surprised.

FRED (*to* WILLY): How did you get up here?

WILLY: I left by the early train.

JANE: Julia, you must listen – I haven't been where you think – I've been all by myself at an hotel in Bayswater.

JULIA: What?

JANE: I came back here to make it up with you and found Fred – and Saunders said you'd just gone out with a dark man, and then I saw that! (*She shows her telephone block.*)

JULIA (*under her breath*): What are we to do now? (*Loudly.*) Jane, I

think it only fair for you to know that I have told Willy
everything.

JANE: Julia!

JULIA: Yes, everything.

JANE: I've told Fred a good deal, too.

JULIA: Jane!

FRED: I want to get this cleared up, please. Willy, what has Julia
told you?

WILLY: About Jane and a snivelling Frenchman in Venice.

JANE (to JULIA): Hypocrite!

WILLY: What's Jane told you?

FRED: About Julia and a Frenchman in Pisa.

JULIA (to JANE): I'll never look at you again as long as I live.

JANE (hysterically): It's not true, any of it – it's all a joke – we
made it up between us – just to – just to —

FRED: She's lying. Julia, tell me the truth.

JULIA (firmly): Certainly I will – it's all a ridiculous fuss about
nothing. Jane and I have been perfectly faithful to you both –
always.

WILLY: Before marriage?

JANE: We couldn't be faithful to you before we met you, could
we?

FRED (loudly): Is this Frenchman story true?

JULIA: Jane – Jane – I'm sorry, d'you hear? I'm sorry for
everything. We've got to stand together now; they're going to
be perfectly beastly.

JANE: All right. Willy, listen to me, I —

JULIA: Fred, you must listen —

    SAUNDERS enters.

SAUNDERS (announcing): Mr Maurice Duclos.

    There is a dead silence. Enter MAURICE, beautifully dressed, most
    attractive, and exceedingly amiable.
    SAUNDERS goes out.

MAURICE (kissing JULIA's hand): Julia! Après sept ans – c'est
émotionant!

JULIA (snatching her hand away): Oh!

MAURICE (kissing JANE's hand): Jane! Je suis enchanté – ravi – Ma
chère, Jane!

JANE (*helplessly*): Julia!

JULIA (*beginning to laugh*): This is agony! Sheer agony —!

JANE (*with an effort*): Willy, let me present Monsieur Duclos – my husband.

WILLY (*coldly*): Good morning.

MAURICE (*puzzled*): How do you do.

JULIA (*hysterically*): My husband – Maurice, this is *my* husband.

MAURICE (*shaking* FRED'*s hand warmly*): How do you do. I had no idea – I haven't seen Julia for so long —

WILLY (*sharply*): When did you last see Jane?

MAURICE: I beg your pardon?

JANE: Shut up, Willy!

JULIA: You speak English very well now.

MAURICE: Yes. – Seven years. – It seems like yesterday.

> *There is an awful silence.*

JANE (*conversationally*): Do you think we've changed?

MAURICE: Not at all. (*To* WILLY.) I met your wife abroad, years ago. It is so strange renewing old friendships.

WILLY: Damned strange.

JANE: Willy!

> MAURICE *raises his eyebrows slightly and looks at* JULIA, *who makes a meaning grimace at him.*

MAURICE (*to* FRED): My first day in London – and look at it – it's too bad.

FRED: I should like to have a little chat with you sometime, Monsieur Duclos – there are several things I want explained.

MAURICE: I shall be charmed.

> *There is another awful silence.*

WILLY: I can't stand this any longer! (*To* MAURICE.) Look here, you've arrived at a very opportune moment. We've just discovered —

MAURICE: What have you discovered? (*He gives a quick glance at* JULIA *and* JANE, *who look appealingly at him.* JANE *grimaces wildly.*)

JULIA: I'll explain. Maurice, our husbands have found out that you and Jane and I were very intimate friends in Italy seven years ago. They've just found out this moment. I must apologise for their surly behaviour, but they're naturally upset.

MAURICE (*laughing*): *Mon Dieu!* It's succeeded beyond your wildest dreams, hasn't it?

WILLY: What do you mean?

JANE *and* JULIA *look at him blankly.*

MAURICE (*to* JULIA, *still laughing*): It was cruel of you to ask me here this morning – without warning me – cruel of you. It would serve you right if I gave you away.

FRED: You needn't trouble, they've done that for themselves.

MAURICE (*to* JANE): Please, please, let me tell them the truth now – it places me in such an embarrassing position.

JULIA (*eagerly*): Yes, yes – you'd better – tell them the truth —

JANE (*mystified*): I'm going mad!

JULIA: Be quiet, Jane.

WILLY: I'm afraid we know the truth; there's nothing much more to be said.

MAURICE: Do you love your wife, monsieur?

WILLY: Mind your own business.

FRED: What do you mean? What are you getting at?

MAURICE (*to* JULIA): I have your permission to speak?

JULIA: Yes – yes —

MAURICE: Well, I'm afraid it has all been rather what you would call a 'Put-up job'!

WILLY: Put-up job?

MAURICE: Yes, you see I haven't known Jane and Julia for a very long while – we are great friends – they confide in me.

FRED: The hell they do!

MAURICE: You would make it much easier, monsieur, if you were not so angry. I give you my word there is nothing to be angry about.

WILLY: I'm glad you think so – we have rather a different sense of values in England.

MAURICE: An obvious remark, monsieur, and not very much to the point.

FRED: What is the point?

MAURICE: Has not the suspicion ever crossed your minds that here in England husbands take their wives a little too much for granted sometimes?

WILLY: So they ought to.

MAURICE: It is a little dull for the wives. In France, of course, it is all arranged so differently – there are so many diversions.

FRED: What are you trying to say?

MAURICE: Perhaps Jane and Julia require a bit more attention than you are prepared to give?

WILLY: Rubbish!

JANE: It isn't rubbish, is it, Julia?

JULIA: Certainly not.

MAURICE: You've been married now for how long?

    JULIA *holds up five fingers behind* FRED'*s back – unperceived.*

Five years, is it not?

FRED: What I want to know is, whether this revolting story's true. Is it or isn't it?

MAURICE: Of course it isn't. We made a plan, Julia, Jane and I —

WILLY: Damned impertinence.

MAURICE (*ignoring him*): Five years brings one to rather a critical matrimonial period as a rule. The first Romance is over – everything seems slightly 'gauche'. Our plan was to rouse you up to a sense of your responsibilities – don't you see?

FRED: That was extremely kind of you.

JULIA: Fred darling, don't be cross any more – it's all such absurd nonsense.

WILLY: I don't understand at all.

JULIA: We've muddled it so dreadfully – or at least you did by coming home unexpectedly – it's taken all the wind out of our sails. Jane was going to break it to Fred that I'*d* run off with Maurice, and I was going to break it to Willy that *she'd* run off with Maurice – as it was you appeared much too early, before we were properly rehearsed. It's all so supremely ridiculous – please forgive us.

FRED (*to* MAURICE): How long have you been in London?

MAURICE: Three weeks.

FRED: Was this what you were hinting at when you said yesterday morning that you had a presentiment, and that I didn't love you any more?

JANE (*laughing loudly*): Yes, don't you see? She was paving the way; that's what she was doing!

JULIA: Shhhh, Jane!

JANE (*hysterically*): I won't shhh – it's so stupid, but we were right, it's cleared the air – they were much too sure of us – much, much, much, much, much too — Oh dear —

JULIA: Would you like something to drink, Maurice? Fred is still too flurried to be hospitable.

FRED: I'm sorry – it never struck me! Whisky and soda?

MAURICE: No, thank you – I really only came down for a minute. I have the flat exactly above this one for a year.

JANE: Oh dear! Ha-ha-ha-ha-ha-ha-ha — (*She sinks hysterically into a chair.*)

MAURICE: And Julia and Jane promised to help me choose an attractive cretonne for my curtains.

JULIA: Yes, we did, didn't we? Pull yourself together, Jane.

MAURICE (*to* WILLY): Perhaps you'd all come up – it's rather untidy at present – but you won't mind?

WILLY: No, thanks, I've got to change.

MAURICE: They're sending for the patterns back at twelve o'clock.

JULIA: We'll come up now.

FRED: Look here, Julia, I —

JULIA: Would you rather I didn't, Fred?

FRED: No, no – it's all right. (*To* MAURICE.) I must apologise to you for being so boorish. It was all very puzzling.

JULIA: Come on, Jane.

JANE (*still giggling weakly*): Oh dear! oh dear! —

MAURICE: Will you all lunch with me to-day? It is so dull being alone.

WILLY: Thanks, but I think I —

FRED: Yes – it's very nice of you – we'd be delighted.

WILLY: Look here, I —

FRED: Shut up, Willy.

JULIA (*kissing* FRED): You are a darling. Come along, Maurice – we shan't be more than ten minutes, Fred.

JANE: Don't be cross, Willy.

WILLY: I don't quite see why —

JANE: Don't try to see any more —

WILLY: But —

JANE: No more buts —

WILLY: But *why* are you in evening dress?

JANE (*wildly*): That was part of the plan, dear – you were to discover me dead drunk in the downstairs hall – we were going to rehearse this morning —

    *Exit with* MAURICE *and* JULIA.

FRED (*beginning to laugh*): It's damned funny – it really is —

WILLY: What?

FRED: The way we arrived and wrecked their little game.

WILLY: But look here, Fred —

FRED: Have a drink?

WILLY: All right.

FRED (*giving him drink*): You never know what Jane and Julia will do next when they start discussing things analytically.

WILLY: It isn't what they'll do next – it's what they did last! Thanks.

FRED: I don't think he's a bad chap, that Frenchman —

WILLY: I wouldn't trust him an inch.

FRED (*laughing*): The lies they told!

WILLY: You seem to have completely wiped it from your mind seriously – the whole thing —

FRED: I never believed Jane from the first when she told me that lurid story about Italy.

WILLY: It seems very queer to me still.

FRED: Oh, dry up!

WILLY: But it does – even if they'd got away with their scheme – what good would it have done them?

FRED: Made us jealous.

WILLY: Don't be an abject fool, Fred. He was bluffing us – the whole damned thing's true from beginning to end – I'm sure of it.

FRED: Why?

WILLY: I've never seen Jane hysterical like that before – she must have been upset over something —

FRED: Are you serious?

WILLY: Yes, I am. Do you realise that we've let them both go up to his flat – alone?

FRED (*startled*): Willy – I —

    *His speech is cut short by the sound of music above. They both listen.*

MAURICE's voice can be plainly heard singing the last phrase of 'Même les Anges'. He is singing it with great feeling – 'Je t'aime – je t'aime – je t'aime.' FRED and WILLY gaze at one another with stricken faces.

CURTAIN

# EASY VIRTUE

## Characters

COLONEL WHITTAKER

MRS WHITTAKER

JOHN                    *Their son.*

MARION                  *Their eldest daughter.*

HILDA                   *Their youngest daughter.*

SARAH HURST

CHARLES BURLEIGH

PHILIP BORDON

FURBER

MR HARRIS

NINA VANSITTART

THE HON. HUGH PETWORTH

BOBBY COLEMAN

LUCY COLEMAN

HENRY FURLEY

MARY BANFIELD

MRS HURST

MRS PHILLIPS

LARITA WHITTAKER

———

*The action of the play takes place in the hall of* COLONEL
WHITTAKER'*s house in the country.*

# ACT I

*The* WHITTAKERS' *house is typical of wealthy upper-middle-class England. The furniture is good and the chintz obvious, but somehow right for the atmosphere. There are three French windows down the right-hand wall. A flight of stairs up L., with the lobby leading to the front door. Down L. double doors open into the dining-room. A big bureau where* MRS WHITTAKER *does her accounts, etc., occupies a space between two of the windows. There is a comfortable sofa set in the centre, with a table behind it, on which are books and papers and flowers of some sort. A statuette of Venus de Milo on small pedestal L.*

*When curtain rises, it is a morning in early April. The hall looks quite gay with spring flowers, but rain can be seen beating against the windows.*

MRS WHITTAKER, *attired in a tweed skirt, shirt-blouse, and a purple knitted sports-coat, is seated at her bureau. She is the type of woman who has the reputation of having been 'quite lovely' as a girl. The stern repression of any sex emotions all her life has brought her to middle age with a faulty digestion which doesn't so much sour her temper as spread it. She views the world with the jaundiced eyes of a woman who subconsciously realises she has missed something, which means in point of fact that she has missed everything.*

MARION *is seated on the sofa, reading her letters. She is largely made and pasty, with big lymphatic eyes. In fifteen years' time she will have the reputation of having been 'quite lovely as a girl'. Her clothes are slightly mannish.*

COLONEL WHITTAKER *is reading* The Times. *He is a grey-haired man of about fifty – his expression is generally resigned.*

MRS WHITTAKER: I've written a strong letter to Mrs Phillips.
MARION: What have you said?
MRS WHITTAKER: Listen. (*She reads.*) 'Dear Mrs Phillips – I feel it

my duty to write to you with regard to the advisability of sending the unfortunate Rose Jenkins to London. As you know, she was in my service for a year, and I was quite convinced when I discharged her that a girl of her character could ultimately come to no good. I was therefore extremely surprised when I heard that you had engaged her. As you have appealed to me for advice in the matter, I suggest that you should get rid of her at once, as her presence in the village might quite conceivably corrupt the morals of the other girls. I will endeavour to use my influence with Mrs Faddle, who, as you know, is a prominent member of the Y.W.C.A., and perhaps later on a respectable berth of some sort may be obtained for her. I sadly fear, however, that our efforts on her behalf will be useless, as recent unpleasant events prove that the wretched girl is entirely devoid of any moral responsibility.

'Sincerely yours,

'Mabel Whittaker.'

MARION: I must go and see Rose Jenkins and have a talk to her.

MRS WHITTAKER: I'm afraid you wouldn't do any good.

MARION: You never know. A straight-from-the-shoulder chat might make her see things in a better light.

COLONEL: Why not leave the poor girl alone?

MARION: Because, father, if there's any chance of helping someone to see the truth, I consider it shirking to disregard the opportunity.

MRS WHITTAKER: It's no use arguing with your father, Marion – he doesn't understand.

COLONEL: No, I don't. What is the truth?

MRS WHITTAKER: The truth is, Jim – that Rose Jenkins, by her immoral behaviour, has caused unpleasantness in the village, and therefore must suffer accordingly.

COLONEL: It's her own village – she was born here.

MRS WHITTAKER: That's not the point.

COLONEL: Yes, it is – it's for her parents to decide what's to be done with her.

MARION: Mother's right, you know, father. It's better for her to be sent to London.

COLONEL: I'm glad you think so.

MRS WHITTAKER: I wish you wouldn't be so tiresome, Jim dear. I'm sure I've enough worries and responsibilities without —

COLONEL: I fail to see that the Rose Jenkins business is any affair of yours – she isn't in your service any more.

MRS WHITTAKER: I think we won't discuss it any further.

COLONEL: Very well, dear.

MRS WHITTAKER: Do you think that letter's all right, Marion?

MARION: Perfectly. You've put it very clearly.

MRS WHITTAKER: Mrs Phillips is so hopelessly lacking in stamina. (*She puts letter in envelope and sticks it down.*)

COLONEL: I'm going down to see Jackson for a minute.

MRS WHITTAKER: You'd better tell him what we decided about that bed in front of the sundial.

COLONEL: All right. I suppose Hilda took the dogs with her to the post office, didn't she?

MRS WHITTAKER: I expect so – you'll probably meet her.

    COLONEL WHITTAKER *goes out.*

MARION: Poor old father.

MRS WHITTAKER: He's so fearfully annoying about things.

MARION: Edgar's exactly the same. Men never will see.

MRS WHITTAKER: When is Edgar coming back?

MARION: I don't know – I had a long letter from him this morning. It will mean another four or five months out there, I'm afraid.

MRS WHITTAKER: Do you think he's really behaving himself?

MARION: I had a straight talk with him the day before he sailed – I think I made him realise things a bit better.

MRS WHITTAKER: Who would have imagined he'd turn out like that?

MARION: Oh, Edgar's all right – it's his upbringing. We'll always be pals – he's not really a marrying man, you know. I think I realised that all along, and now I've found other things in life to occupy my mind, thank God!

MRS WHITTAKER: It couldn't have been John's upbringing altogether – could it?

MARION: John's different – he's exactly like father.

MRS WHITTAKER: Yes, I'm afraid he is.

MARION: He was always weak, you know.

MRS WHITTAKER: I've tried to shut my eyes to it.

MARION: It's no use doing that, mother – everything must be faced.

MRS WHITTAKER: I lie awake at nights, wondering what's going to happen eventually.

MARION: You mustn't worry.

MRS WHITTAKER: Worry! It's on my mind always – naturally I've got over the first shock, to a large extent.

MARION: She may not be so bad, after all.

MRS WHITTAKER (*bitterly*): It's the greatest catastrophe that ever happened – your father's affairs were nothing to this – nothing.

MARION: Have you heard from John lately?

MRS WHITTAKER: Not since that postcard two weeks ago.

MARION: He's bound to bring her home soon.

MRS WHITTAKER: He's taken good care to explain nothing about her in his letters. If he hadn't been apprehensive of what we should think of her, he would have brought her home at once, instead of waiting three months.

MARION: He did say she was ill.

MRS WHITTAKER: Ill! Yes, I expect she was.

MARION: I'm glad I shall be here, anyhow.

MRS WHITTAKER: So am I. I wouldn't have faced it alone – and Jim's no help; he never has been, especially over anything of this sort.

MARION: Is Sarah coming to-day?

MRS WHITTAKER: Yes; she's bringing a man over to lunch – they've got a houseful of people.

MARION: I suppose she was broken-hearted when she heard?

MRS WHITTAKER: She was splendid; she wrote me the sweetest letter – saying that John's happiness was the thing to be considered before anything else, and that she was sure it would all turn out wonderfully.

MARION: That was to comfort you.

MRS WHITTAKER: Yes.

> *Enter* HILDA. *She possesses all the vivacity of a deficient sense of humour. She is nineteen, and completely commonplace.*

HILDA: Here's a wire, mother – they gave it to me at the post office.

MRS WHITTAKER (*startled*): A wire?

HILDA (*giving it to her*): They were going to send the boy with it, but I said, 'Oh no, don't do that, because I'm just going straight through the village and round.'

*MRS WHITTAKER reads it and closes her eyes.*

MARION: What is it? What's the matter? ... John?

MRS WHITTAKER (*nodding*): Yes.

*She gives it to her.*

HILDA: Let me see – let me see. (*She cranes over MARION's shoulder.*) To-day – this morning – they're arriving this morning!

MARION (*handing the wire back*): How typical of him.

MRS WHITTAKER (*bowing her head*): This is terrible.

MARION: When was it handed in?

HILDA (*snatching the wire from MRS WHITTAKER*): Ten-five. They must have sent it just as they were starting.

MRS WHITTAKER: Ring the bell, Hilda.

HILDA (*jumping up and doing so*): It's terrifically exciting.

MARION: Why on earth didn't he let you know before? He must be mad! Nothing's ready, or anything.

MRS WHITTAKER: I've long ago given up expecting any consideration at Johnnie's hands.

MARION: Are you going to stick to your original plan about the schoolroom?

MRS WHITTAKER: Yes. – Don't drum your heels, Hilda.

HILDA: I'm thrilled!

*Enter FURBER.*

MRS WHITTAKER: Furber, Mr John is arriving with his wife almost immediately. Will you see that fires are lit in the schoolroom and dressing-room?

FURBER: Yes, ma'am.

MRS WHITTAKER: If by any chance they're late, we'll wait lunch.

FURBER: Very good ma'am.

*He goes out.*

MARION: Sarah! What about Sarah?

MRS WHITTAKER: What shall we do? Put her off?

MARION: She's bound to meet her sooner or later —

MRS WHITTAKER: Yes, but we don't know yet – what she's like.

MARION: Sarah doesn't matter – it might be a good thing for her to be here – in one way.

MRS WHITTAKER: Go and find your father, Hilda.

HILDA: Where is he?

MRS WHITTAKER: With Jackson, I think. Also tell Jackson to send in some flowers at once.

HILDA: All right – lovely! I'll arrange them.

*She rushes off girlishly.*

MRS WHITTAKER (*putting out her hand*): Marion – I shall need your help – badly.

MARION (*patting her*): Cheer up, mother.

MRS WHITTAKER: I feel so unequal to it all to-day – I didn't sleep a wink last night, and I woke with a racking headache.

MARION: Shall I get you some aspirin?

MRS WHITTAKER: No; it wouldn't do me any good – the blow's fallen, you see – the blow's fallen.

MARION: Don't mother!

MRS WHITTAKER: I feel as though I were going mad. John – my John – married to this – this – woman! It's unthinkable.

MARION: She may be a good sort.

MRS WHITTAKER: It's no good bolstering ourselves up – I know in my heart —

*She cries a little.*

MARION (*embracing her dutifully*): It will all come right in the end, mother, if only you have enough faith.

MRS WHITTAKER: Faith! All my life I've had to battle and struggle against this sort of thing. First your father – and now John – my only son. It's breaking my heart.

MARION: We must just put our trust in Divine Providence, dear. I'll have a straight talk to John. If she really is – well, quite hopeless – something must be done.

MRS WHITTAKER: Nothing can be done – I tell you I know – she's got him, and she'll stick to him.

MARION: If she's the sort of woman we imagine, she's probably realised her mistake already.

MRS WHITTAKER: Why should she have married him? Except for
what she can get out of him – money and position. He's been
made a fool of, just as your father was made a fool of –
hundreds of times. We know she's older than John – I don't
suppose there was any love, as far as she was concerned; she's
just twisted him around her little finger.

MARION: It's no use upsetting yourself *now* – you must pull
yourself together and face it bravely.

MRS WHITTAKER: I thought he would at least have had the
decency to give me fair warning.

MARION: I expect they came over from France yesterday.

*Enter* HILDA *and* COLONEL WHITTAKER.

HILDA: I've told father the news.

COLONEL: I suppose they're motoring down.

MARION: Yes.

HILDA: It was luck me going to the post office like that, wasn't it?
I nearly as anything didn't go out at all this morning – what
with the rain and everything.

COLONEL: Are their rooms ready?

MRS WHITTAKER: I've told Furber to have fires lighted.

HILDA: It's too exciting for words – wondering what she'll be
like.

MRS WHITTAKER (*bitterly*): I wish I could share your feelings.

HILDA: And it's so romantic – the old schoolroom being turned
into a boudoir for John's wife.

MRS WHITTAKER: Sitting-room, not boudoir.

HILDA: Sitting-room, then. Do you think she'll be dark or fair?

MRS WHITTAKER: I don't know.

MARION: Do be quiet, Hilda.

HILDA: I think fair and larky!

MRS WHITTAKER: I see no reason to suppose anything of the
sort.

HILDA: But guessing at people is such fun – Jackie Coryton and I
do it lots – she's awfully good at it. What do *you* think she'll be
like, Marion?

MARION: Stop asking absurd questions.

HILDA: I'm dying to see. I wonder if she drinks.

MRS WHITTAKER (*sharply*): Hilda!

HILDA: Well, you never know – living abroad like that.

MARION: Can't you see mother's upset and doesn't want to be worried?

COLONEL: I fail to see the object of working yourself up into a state before you've set eyes on her.

MRS WHITTAKER: You wouldn't see, Jim, because you don't care – you never have cared. As long as you're comfortable you don't mind if your son goes to the dogs.

COLONEL: He had to marry somebody – she's probably a very interesting woman.

MRS WHITTAKER: I've no doubt you'll find her so.

HILDA: She may be frightfully sweet.

MRS WHITTAKER: When you've reached my age, Hilda, you'll probably realise that the sort of women who infest French watering-places are generally far from being 'frightfully sweet'.

HILDA: Cannes isn't exactly a French watering-place – I mean it's better than that – I mean everyone goes there.

COLONEL: Everything's changing nowadays, anyhow.

MRS WHITTAKER: I fail to see that that makes the slightest difference.

MARION: Father means that social barriers are not quite so strongly marked now, and perhaps, after all —

MRS WHITTAKER: I know quite well what your father means.

HILDA: But everybody's accepted so much more – I mean nobody minds so much about people – I mean —

MRS WHITTAKER: You don't know what you mean – you don't know anything about it.

HILDA: But, mother —

MRS WHITTAKER: Your attitude towards the whole affair is ridiculous, Hilda, and I'm surprised at you. (*She sniffs.*)

HILDA: Oh, mother, don't cry – it will only make your eyes all red —

FURBER *enters, with a tray on which there are some vases, a jug of water and some flowers.*

FURBER: Jackson sent these in just after breakfast, ma'am.

HILDA: These will be enough, mother. I'll arrange them.

MRS WHITTAKER: Tell Jackson not to pick any more.

FURBER: Very good, ma'am. (*He goes out.*)

> HILDA *pounces on the flowers with girlish enthusiasm.*

HILDA: Aren't they lovely? – I expect she's used to orchids and things. These are so fresh – they'll be a gorgeous surprise.

MARION: We ought to warn Sarah – it might be a shock for her.

MRS WHITTAKER: Yes – you'd better telephone.

MARION: I'll just say that we should like her to come, but if she feels that she'd rather not, we quite understand.

MRS WHITTAKER: Don't splash that water all over the table, Hilda.

MARION: What's the number?

MRS WHITTAKER: 60.

MARION (*at telephone*): Hulo – 60 please.

HILDA (*conversationally*): I saw Mrs Phillips coming out of Smith's.

MRS WHITTAKER (*tiding up the papers on bureau*): Did you?

HILDA: She went over to talk to Mrs Jenkins. Rose was peeling potatoes in the porch.

MARION: Hullo! – is that you, Sarah? It's Marion. Listen, old girl; prepare yourself for a shock. John's coming home with Larita, or whatever her name is, this morning. – Oh, I thought it would be rather.... I'm glad you feel like that, anyhow. We wanted to know if you'd come over to lunch just the same.... Yes, of course, bring him.... All right. Good-bye, old thing. (*She hangs up receiver.*) That's that.

MRS WHITTAKER: Have you seen my glasses anywhere.

MARION: Aren't they on the desk?

MRS WHITTAKER: They must have slipped down behind —

HILDA: Did Sarah seem upset?

MARION: She laughed.

MRS WHITTAKER (*shocked*): Laughed!

MARION: I think she's pretending – even to herself – that she doesn't mind.

MRS WHITTAKER: If only everything had been different – it might have been Sarah he was bringing home.

HILDA: It wouldn't have been half so exciting.

MARION: I wish to Heaven it were. She's a damned good sort, that girl.

HILDA: What's the man's name who's coming over with her?

MARION: Charles Burleigh.

HILDA: I'm dying for lunch – it's going to be too thrilling for words.

MARION (*finding glasses*): Here are your blinkers, mother.

MRS WHITTAKER (*forcing a wan smile at* MARION'S *ebullient phraseology*): Thank you, Marion.

COLONEL: I wonder how John's looking.

MRS WHITTAKER (*jumping*): What a fright you gave me, Jim. I'd forgotten you were here.

COLONEL: The return of the Prodigal is always such a momentous occasion, isn't it?

MRS WHITTAKER: I wish you wouldn't talk like that – it's not amusing.

COLONEL: I'm sorry. I thought perhaps a little light irony might alleviate the prevailing gloom.

MRS WHITTAKER: If you think constant reminders of your callousness over the whole affair —

COLONEL: I'm not callous, Mabel; I'm just waiting with a more or less open mind.

MRS WHITTAKER (*bitingly*): Open mind!

HILDA: There – those look sweet, don't they? I'll take them up.

MRS WHITTAKER: Take the tray into the kitchen first.

HILDA: All right.

> *She rushes off with the tray.*

MARION: What's the time?

COLONEL: A quarter past twelve – if I may be so bold.

MARION: They might be here at any minute now.

MRS WHITTAKER: I'm going upstairs to look at the schoolroom. Tell Hilda to bring that other vase – I'll take these.

> *She goes upstairs.*

COLONEL (*lighting his pipe*): I'm glad your mother's getting cross. I prefer irritability to hysteria.

MARION: I don't think you're being very decent to mother, father.

COLONEL: You know, Marion, you're the only thoroughly Christian woman I've ever known who has retained her school-girl phraseology.

*Re-enter* HILDA, *breathlessly.*

HILDA: Where's mother?

MARION: She's gone up to the schoolroom with the flowers. Will you take that other vase up?

HILDA: All right. Don't you feel *terrifically* excited, father?

COLONEL: Terrifically.

HILDA *runs joyously upstairs with the vase.*

MARION: Hilda's irrepressible.

COLONEL: How is Edgar?

MARION: He's all right. Why do you ask – suddenly like that?

COLONEL: I have such a friendly feeling for him since you broke off your engagement.

MARION: Do you imagine I don't see when you're sarcastic and bitter, father? It's been growing lately. You're always saying unkind things.

COLONEL: Am I?

MARION: You must be very unhappy.

COLONEL: Perhaps that accounts for it.

MARION: Then are you?

COLONEL: Do you want to have a straight talk to me, Marion?

MARION: I suppose you despise me for trying to help other people?

COLONEL: You and your mother are always trying to help lame dogs over stiles – even if they're not lame and don't want to go.

MARION: You don't appreciate mother.

COLONEL: I appreciate you both enormously.

MARION: Mother's played fair all her life, anyhow.

COLONEL: And I haven't. I quite see that.

MARION: I'm glad you admit it.

COLONEL: I'm surprised that you're glad – it generally annoys people to be agreed with.

MARION: Don't you ever think of other things, father?

COLONEL: What sort of other things?

MARION: You know quite well what I mean.

COLONEL: Don't try to save my soul, Marion. I can defend myself.

MARION: I don't mind your taunts a bit.

COLONEL: Good!

MARION: But mother does.

COLONEL: My dear girl, your mother stood by me through my various lapses from grace with splendid fortitude.

MARION: You realise that?

COLONEL: I realise the fact but distrust the motive.

MARION: What motives could she possibly have had other than loyalty and affection?

COLONEL: I don't believe you know.

MARION: I certainly don't.

COLONEL: Well, I won't disillusion you.

MARION: Father —

COLONEL (*politely*): Yes?

MARION: She needs your help and support now – badly.

COLONEL: Why?

MARION: You can seriously stand there and ask why?

COLONEL: She has built up in her mind a black-hearted monster of a woman who has enslaved her babe, and she expects me to combine in a superhuman effort to oust her.

MARION: Nothing of the sort, father.

COLONEL: As I said before, I'm waiting with an open mind – and whatever John's wife is or has been, I shall do my utmost to make her happy and comfortable here.

> *Re-enter* MRS WHITTAKER *and* HILDA.

HILDA: The car's coming up the drive – I saw it from the landing window.

MARION: Now for it!

MRS WHITTAKER (*appealingly*): Jim.

COLONEL (*amiably*): Yes, dear?

MRS WHITTAKER: Nothing – it doesn't mater.

HILDA: Oh, I wonder what she'll be like – I wonder —

COLONEL: We shall soon see.

> *They wait in silence. Then* JOHN *bursts in. He is young, good-looking, with great charm; his eagerness is perhaps a shade overdone.*

JOHN: Mother!

> *He kisses her.*

MRS WHITTAKER: But, John, where —

JOHN: She's still in the car – powdering her nose. She said she wanted me to get the first joys of reunion over. Father!

*He shakes hands with the* COLONEL.

COLONEL: I'm glad you're back, John.

JOHN: I do so hope you'll like her.

*He kisses* MARION *and* HILDA.

HILDA: I know I shall.

JOHN: I feel terrified. It will be so wonderful if you do like her, and so awful if you don't.

MRS WHITTAKER: It's a little late to think of that now.

JOHN (*his face falling*): Mother!

LARITA *comes in. She is tall, exquisitely made-up and very beautiful – above everything, she is perfectly calm. Her clothes, because of their simplicity, are obviously violently expensive; she wears a perfect rope of pearls and a small close travelling-hat.*

MRS WHITTAKER: How-do-you-do.

LARITA (*taking both her hands*): How-do-you-do seems so hopelessly inadequate, doesn't it, at a moment like this? But perhaps it's good to use it as a refuge for our real feelings.

MRS WHITTAKER (*coldly*): Did you have a nice crossing yesterday?

LARITA (*sensing her attitude and smiling emptily*): Perfectly horrible.

MRS WHITTAKER: I'm so sorry. This is my eldest daughter, Marion, and Hilda. No doubt you've heard John speak of them.

LARITA (*shaking hands with* MARION): But of course I have – hundreds of times. (*She kisses* HILDA.) You're like Johnnie, you know.

*The family wince at the diminutive.*

MRS WHITTAKER: And this is my husband.

LARITA (*shaking hands with the* COLONEL): You looked dazed – I suppose I'm very unlike what you expected – or perhaps not?

COLONEL: I'm delighted to welcome you home.

LARITA (*gratefully*): Oh, thank you.

HILDA (*excitedly*): You're not a bit like what I expected.

LARITA: I'm very much older, probably. (*She looks at* MRS WHITTAKER.) I'm awfully sorry about that.

JOHN: Don't be silly, Lari.

LARITA: There *have* been a good many happy marriages even though —

JOHN: It doesn't matter how many there have or haven't been, as long as ours is.

LARITA: That's right, Johnnie darling.

MRS WHITTAKER: You must be tired after your journey. Perhaps you'd like to go upstairs.

HILDA (*eagerly*): We've turned the old schoolroom into a boudoir for you.

LARITA: How divine! It will be full of memories of Johnnie as a grubby little boy.

COLONEL: I'm sure you'd rather smoke one cigarette and get to know us all a little better first.

*He offers her his case.*

LARITA (*smiling*): You're right – I should. Do you mind if I smoke one of my own? I have a special kind. Try one. (*She produces a beautiful case.*)

COLONEL (*taking one*): Thanks.

LARITA (*looking round*): Would anyone else like one?

MRS WHITTAKER: No, thank you.

LARITA (*sitting down*): You know, it's such a relief being here at last. I've been wondering so frightfully what it was going to be like —

*The* COLONEL *lights her cigarette.*

MRS WHITTAKER: I'm so sorry it's such bad weather.

LARITA: The house looked fascinating from outside – I'm longing to go all over it.

JOHN: I'll take you after lunch.

LARITA: I want Mrs Whittaker to show it to me.

JOHN: Oh, Lari darling, not Mrs Whittaker. It's mother now.

LARITA: Not quite yet, Johnnie – I don't think.

MARION: Did you get down without any mishaps?

LARITA: Yes, it was a perfect run.

HILDA: Have you ever been in England before?

LARITA: Oh yes, several times. I used to come here a lot with my first husband.

MRS WHITTAKER: Your first husband?

LARITA: Yes.

MRS WHITTAKER (*stiffening*): I never realised you had been married before. John told us so little.

LARITA: That was awfully tiresome of you, Johnnie.

JOHN: He was a perfect brute to her, mother.

MRS WHITTAKER: How dreadful! It must have been almost a relief when he died.

LARITA: He didn't die – he divorced me.

MARION (*horror-struck*): Divorced you!

LARITA: Yes, I ran away. I was very young and silly – I should have waited, shouldn't I? and borne it stoically. It would have been braver.

JOHN: I don't see that at all. He was an absolute devil.

HILDA: I think it's the most thrilling thing I've ever heard!

LARITA: It does sound picturesque now.

MRS WHITTAKER: I suppose you went back to your parents?

LARITA: No – I couldn't go as far as that. They were both dead.

COLONEL (*kindly*): It's awfully nice of you to tell us this.

LARITA: Johnnie ought to have explained it all, really – it would have cleared the way.

JOHN: You can't write things like that in letters.

MRS WHITTAKER: No, I suppose not.

LARITA (*to* MRS WHITTAKER): You must have been very anxious and surprised and worried. We should have come home at once, only I stupidly got ill – pleurisy, you know. I've had it before – perfectly infuriating.

MARION: Beastly thing, pleurisy.

LARITA: But Johnnie was absolutely wonderful to me, and here we are at last. Can your butler speak French?

MRS WHITTAKER: I beg your pardon?

LARITA: I say, can your butler speak French? You see, my maid— Do go and rescue Louise, Johnnie; she's probably having a bad time.

JOHN: All right. Take Lari up, mother. (*He goes off.*)

HILDA: No, let me – do let me.

LARITA: I should love you to.

MRS WHITTAKER: I hope you'll find everything quite comfortable.

LARITA: I'm sure I shall. Come along, Hilda.

*She takes her hand.*

HILDA: I've put some flowers up there, but the rooms aren't very warm yet, I'm afraid. You see, the fires have only just been lighted.

MRS WHITTAKER: I think perhaps I'd better come.

LARITA: No, please don't trouble. Hilda will look after me perfectly all right – won't you Hilda?

HILDA (*eagerly*): Rather. Do let me, mother.

MRS WHITTAKER: Very well. Lunch will be ready quite soon.

LARITA (*as she goes upstairs with* HILDA): Lovely. I'm ravenous. I was too excited to eat any breakfast.

*They go off. There is silence for a moment.*

MARION: She seems a good sort – I like her.

MRS WHITTAKER: Do you, Marion?

MARION: Don't you?

MRS WHITTAKER: She's exactly what I expected – in every detail. (*She turns away.*)

COLONEL: Surely not in *every* detail? She wasn't drunk —

MRS WHITTAKER: Jim, please!

MARION: Father – how can you say things like that?

COLONEL: Larita's an extraordinarily pretty name.

MRS WHITTAKER: Excellent for musical comedy.

*She turns her back and goes over to the window.* JOHN *enters, and sees that* LARITA *has gone.*

JOHN (*eagerly*): Well?

COLONEL: I congratulate you, John.

JOHN (*shaking his hand violently*): Oh, father, thank you – I – *am* glad!

MARION: I hope you managed the French maid all right?

JOHN: Oh yes. I'm used to her. Mother — (*He goes to her.*)

MRS WHITTAKER (*turning and kissing him without warmth*): Well, John, I hope you'll be very happy.

JOHN: I am, mother – frightfully.

MRS WHITTAKER: She's very beautiful.

JOHN: Do you think so, honestly?

MRS WHITTAKER: Yes, of course.

JOHN: And you've no idea what a darling she is. All the time she was ill she was splendid – so brave and everything.

MARION: Is she a Catholic?

JOHN (*nonplussed*): I say – I'm afraid I don't know. You see, we weren't married in church.

MARION: Oh!

JOHN (*pulling himself together*): What a fool I am! She's a Catholic, of course; I remember now.

MRS WHITTAKER: Sarah's coming over to lunch.

JOHN: Is she? How ripping. I've been longing to see her again. I want her to meet Lari, too.

MRS WHITTAKER: The Hursts have been entertaining a lot this winter. Sarah's been very much in demand. They gave a most successful dance in London.

JOHN: Good old Sarah!

MRS WHITTAKER: If you've got any aspirin in your room, Marion dear, I should like some. My headache's rather bad.

MARION: All right. Will you come up, or shall I fetch it?

MRS WHITTAKER: I'll come up.

JOHN: I'm so sorry, mother. I suppose I ought to have let you know before that we were coming.

MRS WHITTAKER: It doesn't matter.

JOHN: I did so want it to be a surprise.

MRS WHITTAKER: I hope you'll see that your – Larita has everything she wants, John.

JOHN: Rather! Thanks, mother, – of course I will.

MRS WHITTAKER: That's right.

*She goes upstairs with* MARION.

JOHN: I suppose mother's upset, isn't she?

COLONEL: A little, I think.

JOHN: You think she'll get over it, though, don't you?

COLONEL: I expect so. Don't worry.

JOHN: It must have been an awful shock for her – for you both.

COLONEL: My dear boy, this sort of thing's always a shock – it's unavoidable.

JOHN: You like Lari, though, don't you, father?

COLONEL: She seems charming.

JOHN: Oh, she is – she's more than that – she's wonderful.

COLONEL: She's older than I thought.

JOHN: Yes, but that doesn't matter really, does it? – I mean if people really care for one another.

COLONEL: I don't know. It might – later on.

JOHN (*haltingly*): You mean – children?

COLONEL: Not altogether.

JOHN: I don't suppose we shall have any children.

COLONEL: No – I don't suppose you will.

JOHN: But Marion's married, and Hilda will be soon.

COLONEL (*gently*): That's not quite the same thing, is it?

JOHN: Are you cut up about it?

COLONEL: What's the use of being cut up, John? When a thing's done, you've got to stand by it.

JOHN: Father – I do love her terribly; she's my life's happiness.

COLONEL: That's all right, then. Run up and look after her – she's probably feeling a little shattered.

JOHN: All right. Thanks, father.

> *He goes upstairs, two at a time.*
>
> *The* COLONEL *sighs, takes* The Times *and goes off into the library.*
>
> FURBER *enters, followed by* SARAH HURST *and* CHARLES BURLEIGH. SARAH *is boyish and modern and attractive.* CHARLES BURLEIGH *is a pleasant-looking man somewhere between thirty and forty.*

SARAH: Where's everybody, Furber?

FURBER: I don't know, miss. Mr and Mrs John have just arrived. They're probably all upstairs. I'll tell them you're here.

SARAH: No, don't do that – we'll wait.

FURBER: Very good, miss.

SARAH: How's your neuritis, Furber?

FURBER: It's been rather bad, miss.

SARAH: I meant to bring you over that stuff, but I forgot. I'll send it to-night.

FURBER: Thank you very much, miss.

> *He goes out.*

CHARLES: I suppose this is a slightly momentous day in the lives of the Whittakers.

SARAH: Very momentous.

CHARLES: Is your heart wrung with emotion?

SARAH (*lightly*): Don't be a beast, Charles.

CHARLES: I think it's spirited of you to come.

SARAH: I want to see her.

CHARLES: I feel secretly embarrassed – as though I oughtn't to be here at all.

SARAH: Nonsense – you're moral backing for me.

CHARLES: Thank you, Sarah, – it's an attractive rôle.

SARAH: I wasn't really officially engaged to John – it was just a sort of understood thing.

CHARLES: I see.

SARAH: And I've had a nice three months to get over being upset about it.

CHARLES: And you have?

SARAH: Entirely.

CHARLES: Well, that's a comfort, isn't it?

SARAH: A great comfort.

CHARLES: Shall we be discovered intimately looking over the *Tatler* together?

SARAH: No – that would be overdoing it.

CHARLES: Perhaps it would.

SARAH: I'm extremely hungry.

CHARLES: That's a healthy sign.

SARAH: Whatever she's like, you must be awfully nice, and pay a lot of attention to her.

CHARLES: Certainly.

SARAH: I think I'm going to get the giggles.

CHARLES: For Heaven's sake, don't.

SARAH: It is funny, you know.

CHARLES (*gloomily*): Excruciatingly.

SARAH: You'll realise just *how* funny it is when you see Mrs Whittaker.

CHARLES: I shall try to control myself.

SARAH: And Marion. – Oh, dear Marion!

CHARLES: Shut up, Sarah – you're unnerving me.

SARAH: I can't help it.

*She giggles hopelessly.*

CHARLES: Pull yourself together. Someone's coming.

HILDA *rushes downstairs.*

HILDA: Sarah!

SARAH: Hullo!

HILDA (*breathlessly*): Oh, Sarah, she's too beautiful for words!

SARAH: No, really.

HILDA: And the most heavenly clothes.

SARAH: This is Mr Burleigh – Hilda Whittaker.

HILDA (*shaking hands*): How-do-you-do. We're all fearfully excited, you know – John's new wife just arrived.

CHARLES: Yes; Sarah told me.

HILDA: She's got a scream of a French maid – I nearly died!

SARAH: How's Mrs Whittaker?

HILDA: She's got a headache. John's talking to her in her room. I've got to dash down to the garage to give a message to the chauffeur – he's a new man. Come with me.

*She proceeds to drag her hand.*

SARAH: I can't leave poor Charles all alone.

HILDA (*persistently*): You must – it's only for a minute. I've got such lots to tell you.

SARAH: All right. Do you mind, Charles?

CHARLES: Very much.

HILDA: She shan't be long – honestly. I haven't seen Sarah for ages, and I shan't get another opportunity of talking to her.

SARAH (*laughing*): Charles is such a timid man, it'll do him good. Come on.

CHARLES: Here, I say – Sarah —

SARAH: We shan't be *very* long!

*She goes off with* HILDA.

CHARLES (*alone*): Oh, God!

*He wanders about the hall, then finally sits down on the sofa with the Tatler.*

LARITA *comes downstairs, having taken off her hat and generally reinstated herself.*

CHARLES *rises to his feet.*

LARITA: Oh, how-do-you-do.

CHARLES (*shaking hands*): How-do-you-do.

LARITA: Are you lunching here?

CHARLES: Yes; I came over with Sarah Hurst. I'm staying with them – a few miles away.

LARITA: I've heard Johnnie speak of them.

CHARLES: You've only just arrived, haven't you?

LARITA: Yes, this morning. We came over from Paris yesterday. (*There is a slight pause.*)

CHARLES: It's always rather an anti-climax, isn't it? – arriving anywhere.

LARITA: Why? Do I look bored?

CHARLES: Not at all.

LARITA: I know what you mean, though; one feels sort of dead.

CHARLES: It's only temporary.

LARITA: Oh yes – I hope so.

CHARLES: Do you know if anyone else is lunching?

LARITA: Only you and Miss Hurst, I believe – outside of the family.

CHARLES: Good!

LARITA: Why do you say 'Good' so emphatically?

CHARLES: It must be bad enough for you to have to meet a bunch of brand-new relations – let alone total strangers. I feel quite an interloper.

LARITA: Please don't. I don't mind meeting new people a bit – on the contrary, it's rather a comfort, in a way – it eases things a little.

CHARLES (*offering case*): Will you smoke?

LARITA: I'll smoke one of my own, if you don't mind. I get a bad throat if I change. I smoke far too much.

*She takes a cigarette out of her case.*

CHARLES (*lighting hers and his own*): That's an enchanting case.

LARITA: It *is* a darling.

CHARLES: Cartier?

LARITA: No; Lacloche. I've had it for years.

CHARLES: Were you in Paris long?

LARITA: Only a week. I had to get some new clothes and fortify myself.

CHARLES: Naturally.

LARITA: Where is everybody?

CHARLES: I don't know.

LARITA: They're discussing their first impressions of me, I expect. It must be horrid for them.

CHARLES: I don't see why.

LARITA (*smiling*): You do – perfectly well.

CHARLES: I suppose it's always rather a shock for people when their sons marry.

LARITA: Do you know Johnnie?

CHARLES: No.

LARITA: He's an angel.

CHARLES: I don't know any of them – I'm more of a stranger than you.

LARITA: I'm so glad. It gives us a sort of bond in common, doesn't it?

CHARLES: Yes.

LARITA: Tell me about Sarah Hurst.

CHARLES: How shall I begin?

LARITA: Don't look apprehensive. I know about her and Johnnie – when they were young, and everything.

CHARLES: She's a charming girl – unaffected.

LARITA: Thank God for that.

CHARLES: Not very emotional – and quite a sense of humour.

LARITA: I'm looking forward to seeing her.

CHARLES: Are you?

LARITA: No.

CHARLES (*laughing outright*): I quite understand.

LARITA: I know you do. Is she pretty?

CHARLES: Not exactly. More attractive than pretty.

LARITA: Dark or fair?

CHARLES: Fairish. She's rather like a young edition of a very old friend of mine. She lives in Paris. I wonder if you've met her.

LARITA: Who?

CHARLES: Cécile de Vriaac.

LARITA (*delighted*): Cécile! Do you know Cécile?

CHARLES: I've known her for years.

LARITA: How extraordinary! What's your name?

CHARLES: Charles Burleigh.

LARITA: Of course! She has shown me snapshots of you. I knew I recognised your face, somehow. She *is* such fun, isn't she?

CHARLES: I'm devoted to her.

LARITA: And Freddy!

CHARLES: Oh Freddy!

*They both laugh.*

LARITA: That's all over now.

CHARLES: No? – Is it?

LARITA: Yes – last August, in Venice – or rather the Lido, to be accurate.

CHARLES: I don't wonder. That beach would kill any passion.

LARITA: You know Zushie Wincott, of course?

CHARLES: Rather! What's become of her?

LARITA: I tremble to think – judging by the way she was behaving in Cannes at Christmas.

CHARLES: With George, I suppose?

LARITA: No, not *with* George – *at* George.

CHARLES: Poor old Zushie! She's rather a dear, really.

LARITA: She's so utterly uncontrolled – always making scenes. I loathe scenes.

CHARLES: You first met John at Cannes, didn't you?

LARITA: Yes. He'd been Banco-ing recklessly and losing everything. I was well up on the day, so I lent him some plaques, and it changed his luck.

CHARLES: In more ways than one.

LARITA: I wonder.

CHARLES: I'm sure of it.

LARITA: It's sweet of you to say so. I'm dreadfully fond of him you know.

CHARLES: I can see that.

LARITA: Can you? How?

CHARLES: By the way you talk of him.

LARITA: He's awfully young and – well, almost ingenuous sometimes. I think that must have been what attracted me to him at first – it was refreshing.

CHARLES (*nodding*): Yes.

LARITA: And then we kept on meeting, you know. Cannes is a small place – and I was so tired of everybody.

CHARLES: People run dreadfully in grooves.

LARITA: Always the same faces – and the same expressions and the same motives.

CHARLES: Motives?

LARITA: You know what I mean.

CHARLES: Yes.

LARITA: It's amusing and fun for a little while, and then one begins to realise that perhaps – after all – it's a trifle cheap.

CHARLES: It's certainly astonishing how quickly one becomes disillusioned over everything.

LARITA: Everything?

CHARLES: Well, practically everything.

LARITA (*with a sigh*): Yes, that's true.

CHARLES: Are you going to live here indefinitely?

LARITA (*slowly*): I don't know. Through the summer, anyhow.

CHARLES: I hope you'll be very happy.

LARITA: Thank you. (*She looks out of the window.*) I wish it wasn't raining.

CHARLES: There's a ridiculous picture of Harry Leftwich in the *Tatler*, walking along the terrace at Monte Carlo with that dark woman who went to share a studio with Maud Callish in the Rue Bonaparte.

LARITA: Oh, Suzanne – do let me see – Suzanne Fellini —

*She comes over to the sofa, and they both bend over the* Tatler.

CHARLES (*finding it*): There.

LARITA: Yes, that's Suzanne – doesn't she look fierce? It's so absurd when people are photographed with their legs sticking straight out in front of them like that.

CHARLES: (*laughing*): Poor dears!

LARITA: Oh, do look at her hat.

*They both laugh a good deal.*

MRS WHITTAKER *comes downstairs, followed by* JOHN *and* MARION. MRS WHITTAKER'*s face freezes slightly.* CHARLES *gets up.*

MRS WHITTAKER: How-do-you-do. You are Mr Burleigh?

CHARLES (*calmly*): Yes; your youngest daughter came and spirited Sarah away. I don't know where they've gone.

JOHN (*going to* LARITA): I couldn't think where you were, Larita.

LARITA: I thought everyone was down here.

MRS WHITTAKER (*to* LARITA): I suppose you and Mr Burleigh have introduced yourselves?

LARITA: Oh yes; we've discovered lots of mutual friends.

MRS WHITTAKER: How nice. (*To* CHARLES.) This is my eldest daughter.

CHARLES (*shaking hands*): How-do-you-do.

MRS WHITTAKER: And my son.

JOHN: How are you? (*He also shakes hands.*)

> HILDA *and* SARAH *re-enter.*

SARAH (*kissing* MRS WHITTAKER): Hilda dragged me off to see a perfectly strange chauffeur. Have you all met Charles?

CHARLES: Yes, you're too late – it's all over.

SARAH: Hallo, John – I'm terribly pleased to see you.

JOHN (*taking her hand*): Sarah, I want you to meet my wife, Larita. I do hope you'll be friends.

LARITA (*shaking hands*): I hope so, too.

SARAH: Of course we shall. You're utterly different from what I imagined.

LARITA (*smiling*): Am I really?

SARAH (*laughing*): Yes – I pictured you fair and fluffy.

LARITA: How absurd!

> FURBER *enters.*

FURBER: Lunch is served.

MRS WHITTAKER: Let's all go in, then. Tell the Colonel, Furber.

FURBER: Yes, ma'am.

> *The* COLONEL *enters.*

HILDA: Come on, father; lunch is ready.

> SARAH *takes* LARITA'S *arm and walks into the dining-room with her.* LARITA *throws a look over her shoulder at* CHARLES, *who smiles. Everyone goes in talking.* FURBER *waits, and then follows them, closing the folding doors after him.*

## CURTAIN

# ACT II

SCENE: *Three months have passed since Act I. It is a warm summer day – warm for England, anyhow – which means that unless you hurl yourself about on tennis-courts or indulge in some sort of strenuous exercise all the time, you get extremely cold. The sun-awning has been let down over the veranda.*

LARITA *is lying on the sofa, reading* Sodom and Gomorrah, *by Marcel Proust. Outside in the garden tennis noises can be heard, occasional shouts and laughter.* LARITA *throws her cigarette-end out to the veranda, but it goes on the carpet, so she has to get up and throw it again, which she does with a slight display of temper. She lights herself another and lies down again; then discovers that Marcel Proust has eluded her and is reclining carelessly on the bureau. With an expression of resigned fury she gets up again and fetches it. When she is once more ensconced on the sofa,* MRS WHITTAKER *enters.*

MRS WHITTAKER Why don't you go and watch the tennis, Larita?

LARITA: The excitement's so intense, my nerves won't stand it.

MRS WHITTAKER (*at window*): I wish you wouldn't throw cigarette-ends on to the veranda; it looks so untidy. (*She picks it up and throws it into the garden.*)

LARITA: I'm sorry.

MRS WHITTAKER: Fancy lying indoors on a lovely day like this.

LARITA: It's very chilly outside.

MRS WHITTAKER: Not in the sun.

LARITA: I get a headache if I sit in the sun.

MRS WHITTAKER: I wonder you don't play tennis with the others.

LARITA: I'm so awfully bad that it annoys everybody.

MRS WHITTAKER: You'd soon improve if you practised.

LARITA: I don't know that the end would altogether justify the means.

MRS WHITTAKER: Have you seen Marion?

LARITA: Not since lunch.

MRS WHITTAKER: I wonder where she is.

LARITA: Upstairs, I think.

MRS WHITTAKER: She had a letter from Edgar this morning.

LARITA: Did she?

MRS WHITTAKER: He's coming home.

LARITA: How lovely.

MRS WHITTAKER (*shooting a suspicious glance at her*): You've never met him?

LARITA: Never. I meant it was lovely for Marion that he was coming home – not for me.

MRS WHITTAKER: Where's Jim?

LARITA: He went out, I think.

MRS WHITTAKER: How irritating! I wanted to talk to him particularly.

LARITA: Perhaps he didn't know.

MRS WHITTAKER: I think we shall have to get rid of Jackson.

LARITA: What a pity! He seems such a nice man

MRS WHITTAKER: He's been neglecting the garden disgracefully.

LARITA: It must be awfully difficult to be a gardener.

MRS WHITTAKER: I'm worried to death about to-night.

LARITA: I'm so sorry. Why?

MRS WHITTAKER: If it's wet we can't have the buffet on the veranda

LARITA: Perhaps it will be fine.

MRS WHITTAKER: Only half the things I ordered have arrived from Fortnum's.

LARITA: Can I do anything?

MRS WHITTAKER: No, thank you, Larita. I'm quite used to all responsibilities of this sort falling on to my shoulders. The children are always utterly inconsiderate. Thank Heaven, I have a talent for organisation.

> *She goes out with a martyred expression.* LARITA, *with a sigh, once more plunges into her book. Enter* MARION, *downstairs.*

MARION: Hallo! old thing. Why aren't you watching the tennis?

LARITA: I'm afraid of discouraging them.

MARION: Have you seen mother?

LARITA: Yes, she's just gone into the garden.

MARION: I think she's getting a bit fussed about to-night.

LARITA: She has a talent for organisation.

MARION: Things are certain to turn out all right, if you don't worry about 'em.

LARITA: That must be a very comforting philosophy.

MARION: You seem a bit snappy, old girl. Has anything upset you?

LARITA (*putting down her book*): I'm sorry – I didn't mean to be snappy. What shall we talk about?

MARION: I'm afraid I haven't time to talk now – too many things to see to. You know, only half the stuff's arrived from Fortnum's.

LARITA: Why not telephone them?

MARION: I have.

LARITA: Are they sending the rest down?

MARION: Yes.

LARITA: Well, that's all right, then, isn't it?

MARION: Have you seen father?

LARITA: He went out, I think.

MARION: Typical of him to shelve everything on to mother and me.

LARITA: Perhaps he'll come back soon bristling with ideas.

MARION: I think mother's wrong about having the buffet on the veranda – it's sure to rain. (*She goes out.*)

> LARITA *lies back and closes her eyes. She is about to read again when* JOHN *rushes in from the garden, very hot.*

JOHN: Hullo! Why don't you come and watch the tennis.

LARITA: There seems to be a conspiracy among everybody to lead me on to that very exposed tennis-court.

JOHN: Well, you needn't come if you don't want to.

> He begins to go upstairs.

LARITA: Where are you going?

JOHN: To get Sarah's sweater – she left it in the schoolroom before lunch.

LARITA: You might bring down my fur coat.

JOHN: Fur coat? What on earth for?

LARITA: I'm cold.

JOHN: I don't wonder – lying about indoors all day.

LARITA: Don't be intolerant, darling.

> JOHN *goes off.*
>
> LARITA *bites her lip and looks extremely unhappy. After a moment* JOHN *returns, with* SARAH's *sweater over one arm and* LARITA's *coat over the other.*

JOHN: Here you are. (*He gives it to her.*)

LARITA: Thank you, Johnnie. (*She puts it on.*)

JOHN: You wouldn't be cold if you took some exercise.

LARITA: Come for a walk with me.

JOHN (*irritably*): How can I? We're in the middle of a set.

> JOHN *goes out.*

LARITA (*calling*): Johnnie!

JOHN (*reappearing*): What is it?

LARITA (*hopelessly*): Nothing. It doesn't matter.

> JOHN *goes out.*
>
> LARITA *sits on the sofa, her fur coat round her and her chin cupped in her hands; her eyes fill with tears, so she takes a handkerchief from her bag and blows her nose.*
>
> COLONEL WHITTAKER *enters. He regards her thoughtfully for a moment.*

COLONEL: Hullo! What's the matter?

LARITA (*jumping*): Oh – I never heard you.

COLONEL: You seem plunged in gloom.

LARITA (*lightly*): It's only a mood.

COLONEL: Cheer up.

LARITA: You won't ask me why I'm not watching the tennis, will you?

COLONEL: No, my dear. Nor will I inquire why you are wearing your fur coat – the reasons are obvious: you are bored and cold.

LARITA: Exactly.

COLONEL: Shall we play bézique?

LARITA (*shuddering*): No, thank you.

COLONEL: Do. It's such a thrilling game.

LARITA: I don't remember how —

COLONEL: Neither do I – that will give it an added piquancy.

> *He goes to the bottom drawer of the bureau and produces a bézique set.*

LARITA (*laughing*): You really are absurd.

COLONEL: Stay where you are, and I'll bring up this dear little table. (*He does so.*)

LARITA: It is sweet, isn't it?

COLONEL (*sitting down opposite her*): I forget how to deal. It's either nine or thirteen.

LARITA: I believe it's eleven.

COLONEL (*dealing her two cards and himself two*): Turn them up.

LARITA (*turning them up*): Card.

COLONEL (*turning his up*): Nine.

LARITA: I'm more used to this sort of bézique.

> He deals out four more cards.
>> Turning up eight.

Eight.

COLONEL (*passing her the pack*): There now.

LARITA (*dealing*): I feel my nostrils quivering like a war-horse.

COLONEL: Card, please.

LARITA (*turning up her cards*): Useless.

COLONEL: Are you preparing to have a run?

LARITA: Certainly.

> She deals again.

COLONEL (*turning up*): Eight.

LARITA (*also turning up*): I'm so sorry – nine!

COLONEL: Devil.

LARITA (*dealing again*): Faites vos jeux.

COLONEL (*turning up*): Carte.

LARITA: Nine!

COLONEL: Lucky at cards, unlucky —

LARITA: Don't say that to me – it's a malicious treason.

> She deals again.

COLONEL: Carte.

LARITA (*giving him one and herself one*): Now then.

COLONEL: Damn!

LARITA: Nine!

COLONEL: There's something underhand about this.

LARITA: I shall have you turned out of the Casino if you accuse me of cheating.

COLONEL: One more go, please.

LARITA (*dealing*): There!

COLONEL: Eight.

LARITA (*laughing*): My poor friend! Nine.

COLONEL (*hurling the pack on to the floor*): Disgusting.

COLONEL: Don't be a cad!

*They both go down on to the floor and proceed to pick up the cards.*

COLONEL: I should like to get a shoe and a couple of seedy croupiers, and start a gambling-hell in this village.

LARITA: It would be grand.

MRS WHITTAKER *enters.*

MRS WHITTAKER: What on earth are you doing?

COLONEL: Gambling.

LARITA: I'm afraid the Colonel forgot he was an English gentleman, and lost his temper.

MRS WHITTAKER: Have you been down to the village, Jim?

COLONEL: Yes.

MRS WHITTAKER: Well, all I can say is, you might have told me you were going – you could have seen Harry about fixing the Japanese lanterns.

COLONEL: I did see Harry.

MRS WHITTAKER: What did he say?

COLONEL: He's coming up at half-past five.

MRS WHITTAKER: Well, I think you might have let me know.

*Going. She goes upstairs.*

COLONEL: It is *such* fun giving a dance.

LARITA: You must control your excitement.

COLONEL: There, that's all, I think. (*He rises.*)

LARITA: There's an angry Queen of Hearts secreting herself under the sofa. (*She retrieves it and rises.*) I feel better now, thank you.

COLONEL: Splendid.

LARITA: Who's coming to-night?

COLONEL: The county. You'll see dresses that will make your mouth water.

LARITA: I must be careful – it will be my social début.

COLONEL: What will you wear?

LARITA: Something non-committal and austere.

COLONEL: Not black?

LARITA: No – that would clash with the Dowager's.

COLONEL: White?

LARITA: Too *ingénue*.

COLONEL: There's always lavender.

LARITA: Yes – much more appropriate.

COLONEL: Your friend Charles Burleigh's coming.

LARITA: Yes, I know – I'm awfully glad. He's a nice man.

COLONEL: I tremble for you sometimes.

LARITA: Why?

COLONEL: This life must be so deadly for you.

LARITA: Don't say that.

COLONEL: It is though – isn't it?

LARITA: Now and then – perhaps.

COLONEL: Do you regret everything?

LARITA: What's the good? I must get used to it.

COLONEL: I try my best, with bézique and small-talk, to make things brighter for you.

LARITA: I know you do. You've been a darling all along.

COLONEL: Do you think you'd be happier if you and John settled down in London?

LARITA: I don't know. I feel frightened of making any definite plans. Everything depends on John.

COLONEL: I'll talk to him.

LARITA: No, please don't; let him decide on his own whatever he wants to do.

COLONEL: He must see you're being bored stiff.

LARITA: I'm not – all the time. I just get moods —

COLONEL (*patting her hand*): I understand.

LARITA: I wouldn't mind how bored and out of place I was – if only —

COLONEL (*gently*): If only what?

LARITA: If only John were with me a little more.

COLONEL: He's inconsiderate – but he doesn't mean to be.

LARITA: He's been a bit sick of me, I'm afraid.

COLONEL: What nonsense!

LARITA: I ought to be so much more adaptable – but it's difficult.

I've tried terribly hard during the three months I've been here, but I've only succeeded in making everyone more or less used to me. I've established a sort of truce, that's all.

COLONEL: That in itself is an achievement. We're an insular, hidebound set.

LARITA: Nobody really likes me – except you.

COLONEL: Sarah does.

LARITA: Yes, I'd forgotten Sarah. It's queer of her, isn't it?

COLONEL: She places a high value on intelligence where no one else recognises it.

LARITA: Marion is persistently pleasant because she feels she owes it to her religious views.

COLONEL: Marion – though I says it as shouldn't – is a fool.

LARITA: I've got an unworthy passion for popularity – it hurts my vanity not to be an unqualified success.

COLONEL: Rubbish! – it's nothing to do with your vanity.

LARITA: Please – I want it to be my vanity that's hurt, and nothing else.

COLONEL: You mustn't expect results too soon, you know. Three months is a very short time.

LARITA (*suddenly, with vehemence*): Oh, what's the use of going on about it? – throwing dust and trying to obscure the truth. You know and I know – it's all a rotten failure! (*She goes upstairs.*)

> The COLONEL *shrugs his shoulders and lights a cigarette.*
> MARION *comes in from the garden.*

MARION: I think if we had the lanterns just along the veranda and across to the cedar it would be all right, don't you?

COLONEL: Quite. There aren't enough to go further, anyhow.

MARION: Mother thought there ought to be a few round the summer-house.

COLONEL: Fairy lamps would be much better there, and there are more of them.

MARION: I wish you'd tell her what you think. (*She sees* LARITA's *book and picks it up.*) Hullo! what's this? *Sodom and Gomorrah.* Why does Lari read such silly muck?

> She *flings it down again.*

COLONEL (*gently*): Don't be sweeping, Marion. Marcel Proust happens to be one of the few really brilliant novelists in the world.

MARION: Pity he chooses such piffling subjects, then.

COLONEL: Have you ever read him?

MARION: No – but all French writers are the same – sex – sex – sex. People think too much of all that sort of tosh nowadays, anyhow. After all, there are other things in life.

COLONEL: You mean higher things, don't you, Marion? – much higher?

MARION: I certainly do – and I'm not afraid to admit it.

COLONEL: You mustn't be truculent just because you've affiliated yourself with the Almighty. (*He goes into the library.*)

MARION *snorts crossly, and* MRS WHITTAKER *comes downstairs.*

MRS WHITTAKER (*obviously*): Oh, there you are, Marion.

MARION: Father's intolerable.

MRS WHITTAKER: What's the matter?

MARION: He never loses an opportunity of jeering at me.

MRS WHITTAKER: He's an exceedingly selfish man – he knows perfectly well how rushed and worried I am, and he never attempts to help. I found him in here, on the floor, with Larita.

MARION: On the floor?

MRS WHITTAKER: Yes; they'd been playing cards, and dropped them, or something.

MARION: I wish Larita wouldn't slack about indoors all day. It isn't healthy.

MRS WHITTAKER (*seeing* Sodom and Gomorrah): Whose is that book?

MARION: Hers, of course.

MRS WHITTAKER: Well, please take it up to her room. I don't like that kind of literature left in the hall – especially when there are young people about.

MARION: You'd think she'd make some effort to adapt herself to our ways, wouldn't you? instead of —

MRS WHITTAKER: Please don't let's discuss her, Marion; you know it upsets me – and Heaven knows I've got enough on my mind to-day.

MARION: I should like to give her a little advice about things.

MRS WHITTAKER: Do, dear; but wait until after to-night – we don't want a scene.

MARION: I don't think she'd cut up rough if I was tactful. You see, she doesn't quite understand —

MRS WHITTAKER: How can you expect her to?

MARION: And father's always encouraging her, and saying ridiculous things, and making her laugh.

MRS WHITTAKER: Your father has a certain horrible streak in him that nothing will eradicate – no one's more aware of that than I. It's caused me years of suffering.

MARION: I know, mother.

MRS WHITTAKER: Birds of a feather —

MARION (*alarmed*): But I think Larita's all right – really, mother, don't you? I mean —

MRS WHITTAKER: My dear Marion, I flatter myself I'm a woman of the world. We have no proof of the sort of life Larita has led, and we don't want any proof – she is John's wife, and as long as he cares for her nothing can be done —

MARION: What do you mean by 'nothing can be done'?

MRS WHITTAKER: This was never anything but a mad infatuation – and mad infatuations don't last.

MARION: But, mother, he's married to her.

MRS WHITTAKER: There is such a thing as divorce.

MARION: I don't approve of divorce, and I never have.

MRS WHITTAKER: Neither do I – but in a case like this it's rather different.

MARION: I think she's fond of him, you know.

MRS WHITTAKER: Time will show.

   HILDA *comes in from the garden; she is flushed and hot.*

HILDA: Philip and I won the set. Is there any lemonade, or anything?

MRS WHITTAKER: You'd better go into the pantry and get some. Furber's very busy.

HILDA: Where's Larita?

MRS WHITTAKER: I don't know.

HILDA: She was making sheep's eyes at Philip all through lunch.

MRS WHITTAKER: You mustn't say things like that, Hilda.

HILDA: Well, she was. I nearly *died* of shame.

MARION: You'd better go and fetch the lemonade.

HILDA: You'd think she'd know how to behave at her age.

MRS WHITTAKER: Hilda, that will do.

HILDA: I'm fed up with her. Look how she went on with Harry
Emsworth. She'd better be careful, I can tell you —

*Enter* JOHN, SARAH *and* PHILIP BORDON — *he is a callow, lanky
youth.*

JOHN: Where's the drink?

HILDA: I'm just going to fetch it.

SARAH (*sinking down*): I'm dead.

PHILIP: It's jolly hot.

JOHN: Why didn't you play, Marion?

MARION: Too busy. Anyhow, you were four.

SARAH: Give me a cigarette, John.

JOHN: I've only got stinkers.

SARAH: I'll take one of Lari's; she won't mind.

*Takes one from* LARI'*s case on the sofa.* JOHN *lights it.*

MRS WHITTAKER: I wonder if two extra girls will be enough,
with Furber and Ellen.

MARION: I should think so.

MRS WHITTAKER: We can get Mrs Pollock's married daughter,
you know. They're only just down the road.

MARION: It won't be necessary.

*Re-enter* HILDA, *with tray of drinks.*

HILDA: Furber had it all ready.

JOHN: Put it on the veranda, Hilda.

PHILIP: Let me help.

*He and* HILDA *retire on to the veranda with the drinks.*

MRS WHITTAKER: Come into the library, Marion, and help me
with the dinner list.

MARION: Father's in there.

MRS WHITTAKER: We'll go up to my room, then. If Harris
comes, don't let him go before I've seen him, John.

JOHN: All right, mother.

MRS WHITTAKER (*as she and* MARION *go upstairs*): We shall have to
put Lady Gibbons next to your father.

MARION: He hates her.

MRS WHITTAKER: It can't be helped.

> *They go off.*

SARAH: Bring me some lemonade in here, John – it's so nice and cool.

JOHN (*going out on to the veranda*): I wish you were dining too.

SARAH: I've got to be at home and help mother with our party. I ought to be there now, really.

JOHN (*off*): Wouldn't you rather have ginger-beer?

SARAH: No – lemonade, please.

JOHN: Right.

> *After a moment he returns with lemonade for* SARAH *and ginger-beer for himself.*

SARAH (*taking it*): Thanks.

JOHN: Pretty hot player, Philip.

SARAH: He nearly killed me.

JOHN: Keep a lot of dances for me to-night, won't you?

SARAH: Of course.

JOHN: It ought to be fun, if it keeps fine.

SARAH: Where's Lari, I wonder?

JOHN: Reading somewhere, I expect.

SARAH: She looked divine at lunch.

JOHN: It's funny you liking her. I was afraid you wouldn't.

SARAH: Why?

JOHN: Oh, I don't know – she's so utterly different.

SARAH: I expect that's the reason.

JOHN: I wish she wouldn't slack indoors so much.

SARAH: I don't see that it matters, if she wants to.

JOHN: It's all very well in the winter, but in this sort of weather —

SARAH: You mustn't be grumpy just because people don't like doing exactly the same things as you.

JOHN: I'm not grumpy.

SARAH: Yes, you are – a little.

JOHN: It's annoying, though.

SARAH: Don't let it be.

JOHN: You're such a sport, always ready for anything.

SARAH: But I haven't got Lari's beauty or charm or intelligence.

JOHN: Here, I say!

SARAH: I mean that.

JOHN: She is clever, isn't she?

SARAH: Yes, and being clever she's a little bored.

JOHN: She wouldn't be if only she entered into things.

SARAH: Perhaps she can't enter into things. You must remember this sort of life is entirely new to her.

JOHN: Yes, I know, but —

SARAH: You're all right, because you're on your own ground. I think you ought to give a bit more.

JOHN: How do you mean?

SARAH: Do what she wants now and then, instead of only what you want.

JOHN: But I do. I took her for miles in the car yesterday – she said she needed air.

SARAH: That's right.

JOHN: So you see —

SARAH: Don't make excuses; you know what I mean.

JOHN: I don't.

SARAH: Well, I can't explain; it's something you must find out for yourself.

JOHN: I do think it's most frightfully decent of you to stand up for her.

SARAH: That wasn't my object.

JOHN: I say, you have changed lately; you never used to go on like this.

SARAH: Like what?

JOHN: Well, all serious and preachy.

SARAH (laughing): I'm sorry you think I'm preachy: you see, I'm growing up, and you're not.

JOHN: Oh yes, I am.

SARAH: Well, not in the way you should, then.

JOHN: You've got ever so much nicer-looking.

SARAH: Thank you.

JOHN: Are you going to marry, too?

SARAH: Certainly.

JOHN (anxiously): Who? Charlie?

SARAH: Good Heavens, no! He's much too old.

JOHN: Oh!

SARAH (*repentantly*): I'm awfully sorry. I didn't mean that exactly.

JOHN: It's all right.

SARAH: He's not my type at all; if I loved him, I wouldn't care how old he was.

JOHN: I can't imagine you married.

SARAH: What a pity! I have a vivid mental picture of it.

JOHN: Is there anybody you *are* in love with?

SARAH: Not at the moment, but I'm keeping my eyes open.

JOHN: I've often meant to ask you something, but I hadn't the courage.

SARAH: Well, don't then.

JOHN: I must.

SARAH: Give me a cigarette first.

JOHN: Stinker?

SARAH: Yes; anything.

JOHN (*giving her one*): Here.

SARAH: Thanks. Go ahead.

JOHN: Did you think I behaved like a cad, marrying Lari like that, without letting you know?

SARAH: Of course not.

JOHN: Are you sure?

SARAH: Quite. I understood perfectly.

JOHN: It's been on my mind rather.

SARAH: You took your opportunity and married for love, John, and I respect you for it. If we'd married, it would have been for friendship and convenience.

JOHN: Would it?

SARAH (*firmly*): Yes – we knew one another far too well.

JOHN: Do you think that's a disadvantage?

SARAH: In married life, certainly.

JOHN: I don't.

SARAH: It would have been so dull and ordinary – no excitement at all.

JOHN: I don't want excitement.

SARAH: I do. I want thrills and glamour and passionate love-letters – all the trappings.

JOHN: I could have written you love-letters.

SARAH: Well, why didn't you?

JOHN: I don't know. I —

SARAH (*triumphantly*): The fact that you didn't proves that you couldn't – you didn't feel that way about me, ever.

JOHN: It was a different sort of feeling.

SARAH: Don't be a hypocrite, John, and try and deceive yourself.

JOHN: I did love you, all the same.

SARAH (*rising*): How touching.

JOHN: I do still.

SARAH: Shut up, John!

JOHN: You see, I'm beginning to realise I've made rather a mess of things.

*He puts his face in his hands.*

SARAH (*furiously*): Shut up, I tell you, or I'll never speak to you again. That's behaving like a cad, if you like – an utter cad!

JOHN (*miserably*): Sarah —

SARAH: You ought to be ashamed of yourself! Haven't you got any sense of decency? Let me tell you one thing – you're not fit to wipe Lari's boots.

LARITA *appears at the top of the stairs in time to catch the last sentence.*

LARITA (*lightly; coming down*): Hallo! – what are you two squabbling about?

SARAH: John's infuriating – he always gets bad-tempered when he loses a set.

LARITA: I ought to have watched, after all, to keep him in order.

SARAH: I stole a cigarette out of your rich and rare case, Lari.

LARITA: That was revolting of you. I don't think I can forgive it.

HILDA *and* PHILIP *come in from veranda.*

HILDA: Aren't you going to play any more, John?

JOHN (*eagerly*): Yes, rather.

SARAH: I should stay and talk to Lari if I were you, John – you've neglected her shamefully.

PHILIP: I'll stay with Mrs John.

LARITA: You're all very kind and considerate – I really only want someone to hold my knitting.

*She makes a gesture of winding wool.*

HILDA: I want Philip to play.

LARITA: I'll come and glare at you all with eyes starting out of my head like prawns.

SARAH: No, don't. There's nothing so hideously dull as watching people play games you're not particularly interested in. Come on, Hilda – you and I will play Philip. He can beat us easily.

HILDA (*satisfied*): All right.

SARAH: Come along.

LARITA (*lightly*): Thanks, Sarah darling. (*She blows a kiss to her.*)

SARAH, HILDA, *and* PHILIP *go off.*

JOHN (*noticing* LARITA *is still wearing her coat*): Are you still cold?

LARITA: No, not really. I'll take this off if it annoys you. (*She does so.*)

JOHN: I don't mind.

LARITA: What shall we do? Go for a nice drive in the motor?

JOHN: Would you like to?

LARITA: No, dear – don't look so scared; I should hate it.

JOHN: I'm sorry if you think I've been neglecting you lately, Lari.

LARITA: Sarah put that into your head; I didn't.

JOHN: But have I?

LARITA: No. I think I've been neglecting you.

JOHN: I'm afraid I've been thoughtless and beastly.

LARITA (*smiling*): Dear Johnnie. (*She pats his hand.*)

JOHN: I say, you have got some strong scent on.

LARITA: It's very good, though, isn't it?

She leans forward so that he can smell it better.

JOHN (*with forced enthusiasm*): Lovely.

LARITA: Why are you looking so depressed?

JOHN: I'm not depressed.

LARITA: I hope you haven't been overtiring yourself – at tennis?

JOHN: Of course I haven't.

LARITA (*seriously*): Kiss me, Johnnie.

JOHN: All right.

He does so.

LARITA: I think I'd better put on my fur coat again.

JOHN: What's the matter with you to-day, Lari?

LARITA: Don't you know?

JOHN: No.

LARITA: We're married.

JOHN: What do you mean?

LARITA: That's what's the matter with both of us.

JOHN: There's nothing the matter with me.

LARITA: Isn't there?

JOHN: I feel a bit tired, that's all.

LARITA: Yes, I believe you do.

JOHN: I think you were right – I *have* been rather strenuous to-day.

LARITA: Poor darling!

JOHN: And we've got this awful dance to-night.

LARITA: Aren't you looking forward to it?

JOHN: Not particularly.

LARITA: Let's run away secretly to Deauville.

JOHN: How can we?

LARITA (*smiling*): It's all right. I didn't mean it; that was a joke.

JOHN: Oh, I see.

LARITA: You mustn't be dull. (*She laughs.*)

JOHN: Oh, do stop twitting me!

LARITA: Twitting! What a ridiculous expression.

JOHN: You're always in some mood or another.

LARITA: Surely that's quite natural?

JOHN: I suppose it's my fault, really, for leaving you alone so much. But still, I *do* think —

LARITA: If you're going to be magnanimous, do it gracefully.

JOHN: There you are, you see. Whenever I try —

LARITA (*sharply*): You weren't trying hard enough.

JOHN: Anyone would think I'd been deliberately planning to annoy you.

LARITA: Deliberately or not – you've succeeded.

JOHN: I don't see what I've done.

LARITA: You play tennis eternally – tennis – tennis – tennis! Such a pretty game.

JOHN: It's healthier than sitting indoors, anyway.

LARITA: I believe it develops the muscles to an alarming extent.

JOHN: You don't want me to be flabby, do you?

LARITA: Mentally or physically?

JOHN: Lari, look here, I —

LARITA: I'm getting flabby mentally – and I can't bear it.

JOHN: Well, it's not my fault.

LARITA: Yes, it is.

JOHN: How?

LARITA: Come away – come abroad again.

JOHN: We can't – you know we can't – possibly.

LARITA: Why?

JOHN: It's unfair of you to ask me.

LARITA: Yes, it is – I suppose.

JOHN: After all, this is my life, and it always will be.

LARITA: Will it?

JOHN: Of course.

LARITA: And mine?

JOHN: Naturally.

LARITA: How secure that sounds.

JOHN: Secure?

LARITA: Yes. Words are such silly things. When you said 'Naturally' like that it sounded like everything I want in the world; but I know in my heart it meant nothing.

JOHN: I don't understand.

LARITA: That's why it mcant nothing.

JOHN: Are you really dissatisfied?

LARITA: Yes.

JOHN: You're not happy here at all?

LARITA: No.

JOHN: Why?

LARITA: Because you've stopped loving me.

JOHN (startled): Lari!

LARITA: It's true.

JOHN: But you're wrong – I haven't stopped loving you.

LARITA (lightly): Liar!

JOHN: Look here, you're hysterical and upset because I've been neglecting you.

LARITA: No, dear, it isn't that.

JOHN: I've never heard anything so ridiculous in my life.

LARITA: Neither have I.

JOHN: Why, we've only been married six months.

LARITA: It might be six years.

JOHN: It looks more as though you'd stopped loving me.

LARITA: Oh, John, don't be *silly*.

JOHN (*hotly*): I'm not silly! You're always irritable and snappy these days – you never used to be.

LARITA: I'm sorry.

JOHN: If you were a bit more interested in everything here and didn't retire into your shell so much, you'd be far happier.

LARITA: Does your mother want me to be interested?

JOHN: Of course she does.

LARITA: Then why does she snub me and discourage me whenever I make the slightest effort?

JOHN: She doesn't mean to. You're too sensitive.

LARITA: Sensitive! (*She laughs.*)

JOHN: Yes, you think everybody's against you.

LARITA: So they are – except your father and Sarah.

JOHN: Marion's been sweet to you, and Hilda —

LARITA: Hilda evinced a high-school passion for me when I first arrived – which has since reacted into black hatred.

JOHN: Rot!

LARITA: It isn't rot. Marion is gratuitously patronising.

JOHN: She's nothing of the sort.

LARITA: Her religious views forbid her to hate me openly.

JOHN: It's beastly of you to say things like that.

LARITA: I'm losing my temper at last – it's a good sign.

JOHN: I'm glad you think so.

LARITA: I've repressed it for so long, and repression's bad. Look at Marion.

JOHN: I don't know what you mean.

LARITA: No – you wouldn't.

JOHN: But I suppose it's something unpleasant.

LARITA: Quite right – it is.

JOHN: Well, will you please remember that Marion is my sister.

LARITA: I shouldn't think of her at all if she weren't.

JOHN: You're behaving like a child.

LARITA: I can't tell you what a wonderful relief it is.

JOHN: It's damned inconsiderate.

LARITA: Yes – my turn now!

JOHN: Look here, Lari —

LARITA: Don't try and stop me. Let me go on and on – or I shall burst.

JOHN: Don't talk so loudly.

LARITA: Why not? No one would be in the least surprised to find me rolling about on the floor, soaked in drugs and hiccoughing. They almost expect it of me. Surely a little shouting won't matter – it will gratify their conception of my character.

JOHN: I've never seen you like this before.

LARITA: No, it doesn't happen often.

JOHN: Thank God for that!

LARITA: Splendid! Repartee helps. I like you to play up. This is our first row, you know.

JOHN (sullenly): I hope it will be our last.

LARITA: It may be – quite possibly.

JOHN: As far as I can see, you're just thoroughly bad-tempered because I haven't been dancing attendance on you all the time.

LARITA: If you can only see as far as that, you're extraordinarily short-sighted.

JOHN: All the same, I'm right.

LARITA: How I wish you were!

JOHN: If things have been upsetting you for so long, why on earth didn't you tell me before?

LARITA: I was hoping against hope that you'd see for yourself.

JOHN (turning away irritably): Oh, what's the use of arguing and bickering like this? It doesn't lead anywhere.

LARITA: You never know – it might lead to the end of everything.

JOHN: Do you want it to?

LARITA: Do you?

JOHN: No, I don't. All I want is peace and quiet.

LARITA: You're far too young to make a remark like that seriously.

JOHN: I can't help my age.

LARITA: You said just now that you loved me still.

JOHN: I certainly don't when you go on like this.

LARITA: I wanted to see how much it would stand.

JOHN: Wasn't that rather silly?

LARITA: No, it *wasn't* silly. Three months ago you'd never have spoken to me as you have to-day. Whatever I'd done. I've been watching your passion for me die. I didn't mind that so much; it was inevitable. Then I waited very anxiously to see if there were any real love and affection behind it – and I've seen the little there was slowly crushed out of you by the uplifting atmosphere of your home and family. Whatever I do now doesn't matter any more – it's too late.

JOHN: Look here, Lari —

LARITA: I've shown myself to you quarrelsome and cheap and ugly for the first time – and it hasn't hurt you; it's only irritated you. You're miles away from me already.

JOHN: You're utterly unreasonable – you imagine things.

LARITA: Do I?

JOHN: I realise that I'm to blame for leaving you alone so much – and, honestly, I'm sorry.

LARITA: Do you really believe that that accounts for it all?

JOHN: Yes.

LARITA: Well, let's pretend it's true – for a little longer.

JOHN: There's no need to pretend.

LARITA: Give me my handkerchief, will you? – it's in my bag.

JOHN (*finding it*): Here you are.

LARITA: Thanks. (*She dabs her eyes and blows her nose.*) I hope I'm not going to have a cold.

JOHN: I'll see that you don't get miserable and upset any more.

LARITA (*half smiling*): Will you, Johnnie?

JOHN: Yes – and I'll talk to mother.

LARITA: No, don't do that.

JOHN: I will. I don't think she's been quite fair.

LARITA: Please don't say a word – promise me you won't. It wouldn't do the slightest good. She's your mother, and I do see her point, you know.

JOHN: As a matter of fact, I should rather like to go abroad again in September – Venice or somewhere.

LARITA: It would be lovely. (*She laughs.*)

JOHN (*suspiciously*): Why are you laughing?

LARITA: Because I feel happier.

JOHN: Or Algiers – I've never been to Algiers.

LARITA: If we went to Algiers, we could stay with the Lessings.

JOHN: I don't know them.

LARITA: They're darlings. She's an American. She used to design people's houses. We had great fun in New York.

JOHN: I never knew you'd been to New York.

LARITA: I must have told you – I was there for ages.

JOHN: You didn't. Was it before you married?

LARITA: No; after.

JOHN: I thought you lived in Paris all the time.

LARITA: Not all the time.

JOHN: Why did you go?

LARITA: Oh, I don't know – the tall buildings and the champagne air – so fascinating.

JOHN: Did you go alone?

LARITA: Yes – but the boat was crowded.

JOHN: Why didn't you tell me?

LARITA: I thought I had. It doesn't matter though, does it?

JOHN: What did you do there?

LARITA: Really, Johnnie – nothing particular.

JOHN: You never told me much, you know – about anything.

LARITA: I'll write my memoirs one day; then all will be disclosed.

JOHN: Is Francis alive now?

LARITA: Oh yes; he's kicking about somewhere.

JOHN: You never hear from him?

LARITA: Of course not. I don't consider it chic to receive chatty letters from ex-husbands.

JOHN: I only wondered.

LARITA: Well, you needn't have.

JOHN: Mother's always trying to pump me about your early life.

LARITA: And what do you say?

JOHN: Nothing. I feel rather a fool.

LARITA: Never mind, dear.

JOHN: It's natural that she should be curious, I suppose.

LARITA: Oh, quite.

JOHN: And that I should be, too.

LARITA: I never realised you were.

JOHN: You are my wife, after all.

LARITA: Yes, isn't it lovely?

JOHN: Do you regret anything?

LARITA: Hundreds of things.

JOHN: But seriously —

LARITA: The home atmosphere is certainly having its effect on you.

JOHN: How do you mean?

LARITA: You never cross-questioned me before.

JOHN: I'm not cross-questioning you.

LARITA: Yes, you are – a little.

JOHN: I'm sorry. I won't any more.

LARITA: It betrays a certain lack of trust.

JOHN: Lari, how can you!

LARITA: You see, when we married, we married because we loved one another – no explanations were necessary on either side.

JOHN: They're not necessary now, only —

LARITA: Only you're feeling a little uncomfortable – is that it?

JOHN: No, not exactly.

LARITA: It's all a question of values.

JOHN: Values?

LARITA: Yes, the scales are awfully erratic. When we met and fell in love, nothing else mattered as long as we were together. But when the first fine careless rapture wears off, other things begin to obtrude themselves – one has to readjust oneself to see clearly. What had happened to either of us in the past didn't count a bit at first – why should it? – everything was new and exciting. Now it's not new and exciting any more; we've grown used to one another, so to alleviate the monotony we start prying about behind the scenes – trying to find out things about each other that haven't any real bearing on the case at all. It's inevitable with such a hideously intimate relationship as marriage.

JOHN: I don't want to find out anything.

LARITA: You may not want to, but you'll persevere until you do. It's human nature.

JOHN: I'd hoped there was nothing to find.

LARITA: There's always something – somewhere.

JOHN: Don't let's say any more about it.

LARITA: Very well.

*She takes out her powder-puff and powders her nose.*

JOHN: I trust you absolutely.

LARITA: Whatever happens in the future, dear, I want you to remember one thing – I've never deceived you and I've never lied to you. There are many things that I've purposely left unexplained, because they don't concern you in the least and don't apply in any sense to our life together.

JOHN: Darling!

*He kisses her very sweetly, and she smoothes his hair.*

LARITA: You've rubbed all the powder off my nose.

JOHN: I don't care a bit.

LARITA: Go and play some more tennis – you've been in the house far too long; it isn't healthy.

JOHN: Don't be a beast.

LARITA: Away with you – I'm going to rest before tea.

JOHN: I'll come and rest too.

LARITA: No, you won't. We should go on talking and talking and talking until our heads fell off.

JOHN: Oh, all right.

*He kisses her hand lightly and goes into the garden.*

LARITA *is about to go upstairs when* MARION *comes down.*

MARION: Hallo! old girl.

LARITA: Hallo!

MARION: Are you going upstairs?

LARITA: I *was*. I thought of lying down a little.

MARION: You're always lying down.

LARITA: Yes, isn't it strange? I expect there's something organically wrong with me.

MARION *(anxiously)*: I hope there isn't.

LARITA *(beginning to go)*: Well, I'll see you later on —

MARION *(touching her arm)*: Don't go. I've been wanting to talk to you.

LARITA: To me? Why – what about? – anything important?

MARION: No; just everything.

LARITA: That ought to take several years.

MARION *(laughing forcedly)*: I didn't mean it literally.

LARITA: Oh, I see.

MARION: Have you got a cigarette on you?

LARITA: Yes, certainly. Here. (*She hands her case.*)

MARION (*taking one*): Thanks.

LARITA (*amiably*): Why aren't you watching the tennis?

MARION (*insensible of irony*): I've been too busy all the afternoon.

LARITA: How are all the preparations for to-night going?

MARION: All right. You're sitting next to Mr Furley.

LARITA: Splendid. Is he nice?

MARION: He's a damned good sort – rather High Church, you know; almost ritualistic.

LARITA: He won't be ritualistic at dinner, will he?

MARION: And you've got Sir George on the other side of you.

LARITA: Sir George who?

MARION: Sir George Bentley. He's awfully well up in dead languages and things.

LARITA: I do hope I shall be a comfort to him.

MARION: Very interesting man, George Bentley.

LARITA: How many are dining altogether?

MARION: Only twelve – we haven't really room for more comfortably.

LARITA: I hope it will all be an enormous success.

MARION: You won't be offended if I ask you something – just between ourselves?

LARITA: That depends, Marion. What is it?

MARION: Speaking as a pal, you know.

LARITA (*vaguely*): Oh yes – well?

MARION: Don't encourage father too much.

LARITA: In what way – encourage him? I don't understand.

MARION: Well, you know – you and he are always getting up arguments together.

LARITA: Why shouldn't we?

MARION: It annoys mother so when he tries to be funny.

LARITA: I've never noticed him trying to be funny – he's a very intelligent man.

MARION: Sometimes when you're discussing certain subjects, he says things which are not quite —

LARITA: You say 'certain subjects' in rather a sinister way, Marion. What subjects do you mean particularly?

MARION: Well, sex and things like that. You were talking about the Ericson divorce case the other day at lunch, when Harry Emsworth was here —

LARITA: It's an extraordinarily interesting case.

MARION: Yes, but one doesn't discuss things like that openly in front of strangers – I mean to say, it doesn't matter a bit when we're by ourselves; no one could be more broad-minded than I am – after all, what's the use of being in the world at all if you shut your eyes to things?

LARITA (*crisply*): Exactly.

MARION: You're not angry, are you?

LARITA: Angry? – no.

MARION: You see, I like you, Lari; we get on well together. I grant you we see things from different points of view, but that's only natural.

LARITA: Yes – oh yes.

MARION: I knew you'd be a sport about it and not mind. You see, my philosophy in life is frankness. Say what you've got to say, and have done.

LARITA: In other words – moral courage.

MARION: Yes, that's it.

LARITA: Why didn't you attack the Colonel on these little breaches of etiquette? He seems to be more to blame than I.

MARION: A woman always understand better than a man.

LARITA: Surely that's a little sweeping.

MARION: It's true, all the same. I knew you'd see.

LARITA: You weren't by any chance afraid that he'd laugh at you?

MARION: Good Heavens, no! I don't mind being laughed at.

LARITA: How extraordinary! I hate it.

MARION: What does it matter? If you've got something to say, say it.

LARITA: According to your code, the fact of having spoken like that about your father doesn't strike you as being disloyal in any way, does it?

MARION: Not between pals like us.

LARITA: Of course, yes – pals. I keep forgetting.

MARION: I believe you *are* angry.

LARITA: I'm not – but I'm very, very interested.

MARION: Look here, Lari, it's like this. Father's been a bit of a dog in his day. Mother's had a pretty bad time with him, and she's stood by him through thick and thin.

LARITA: How splendid!

MARION: Some men are like that – no moral responsibility. Edgar, you know, was just the same.

LARITA: You say 'was'. Has he reformed?

MARION: I think I've made him see – but it's been a tough struggle.

LARITA: What have you made him see?

MARION: I've made him see that nothing matters if you keep your life straight and decent.

LARITA: There are so many varying opinions as to what is straight and decent.

MARION: God admits of no varying opinions.

LARITA: Your religion must be wonderfully comforting. It makes you so sure of yourself.

MARION: If you're going to take up that tone, we won't discuss it.

LARITA: No – we'd better not.

MARION (*gently*): You mustn't jeer at religion, old girl. (*She puts her hand on her arm.*)

LARITA (*shaking her off*): I don't jeer at religion – but I jeer at hypocrisy.

MARION: *I'm* not a hypocrite – if that's what you mean.

LARITA (*quietly*): I'm afraid you are, Marion – and a disloyal one, too, which makes it all the more nauseating.

MARION: How dare you speak to me like that!

> *Enter* PHILIP BORDON *from the garden.*

PHILIP (*to* LARITA): Hallo! – I wondered if you were still here.

LARITA: You must be exhausted. You've been at it steadily all the afternoon.

PHILIP: John and Sarah are playing a single now, and Hilda's sitting on the steps, scoring.

> MARION, *livid with rage, takes a writing-block off the bureau and marches into the library.* PHILIP *looks after her in some surprise.*

What's up?

LARITA: We've been arguing about the dinner guests – it's all very difficult.

PHILIP: I wish I was dining.

LARITA: But you're coming directly afterwards, aren't you?

PHILIP: Rather! About ten of us.

LARITA: Good Heavens!

PHILIP: Will you keep a dance for me?

LARITA: Certainly.

PHILIP: What number?

LARITA: I don't know.

PHILIP: Three?

LARITA: Perhaps you won't be here in time.

PHILIP: Say five, then, and six.

LARITA (*laughing*): Not two running! We should be bored stiff with each other.

PHILIP: Five and seven, then?

LARITA: All right.

PHILIP: You won't forget?

LARITA: Of course not.

PHILIP: I'm sure you dance wonderfully.

LARITA: Why?

PHILIP: Because of the way you move.

LARITA: Oh, thank you very much.

PHILIP: I mean it.

LARITA: Well, it's very sweet of you. (*She sits on sofa.*)

PHILIP: May I sit next to you?

LARITA: Certainly, if you like. (*She makes room for him.*)

PHILIP (*sitting down*): I'm afraid I'm awfully hot and sticky.

LARITA (*laughing out loud*): I don't mind as long as you keep your end.

PHILIP: Don't laugh at me.

LARITA: I'm sorry – but you are rather funny.

PHILIP (*gloomy*): Everyone says that.

LARITA: Never mind. Be frank – speak straight from the shoulder – say what you have to say, and have done.

PHILIP (*surprised*): I beg your pardon?

LARITA: It's all right – I was only quoting.

PHILIP: Oh, I see.

LARITA: You must forgive me if I'm a little distrait – I've had a rather trying afternoon.

PHILIP: Everybody fussing round, I suppose, over the dance?

LARITA: Yes – more or less.

PHILIP: People take things so damned seriously.

LARITA: You don't think it's a good plan to take things seriously?

PHILIP: Oh, sometimes, of course, but —

LARITA: I'm inclined to agree with you.

PHILIP: Life's too short to worry over things.

LARITA: It *is* miserably short, isn't it?

PHILIP: Rather!

LARITA: I sometimes wonder why we're here at all – it seems such a waste of time.

PHILIP: You're laughing again.

LARITA: Not altogether.

PHILIP: No one ever thought old John would marry anyone like you.

LARITA: Do you know that remark positively made me jump.

PHILIP: You're so different and so alive. He's a lucky devil.

LARITA: You must be careful with your compliments. If you go peppering them about like that they'll lose value.

PHILIP: They're not compliments – they're true.

LARITA: Do you always go on like this?

PHILIP: Of course not. I wouldn't dare.

LARITA: Forgive me for asking – but do you lead a straight and decent life?

PHILIP (*alarmed*): What!

LARITA: It's *so* important. Whenever you feel yourself slipping, think of me.

PHILIP: I don't quite understand.

LARITA: On second thoughts, it would be better if you thought of Marion.

PHILIP: I'd rather think of you.

LARITA: Good! I must leave you now – I've been trying to get to my room for the last hour. (*She rises.*)

PHILIP (*catching her hand*): Please don't go yet.

> HILDA *bounces in in time to see* LARITA *withdrawing her hand from* PHILIP's *grasp.*

LARITA: I must, really.

HILDA (*furiously*): Oh!

PHILIP (*rising*): Hallo! Have they finished?

HILDA: I wondered where you were – I might have known.

> *She shoots a malignant glance at* LARITA.

LARITA (*frowning*): Hilda!

HILDA: I hope I'm not intruding.

LARITA (*irritably*): This is too much!

HILDA: Yes, it is!

LARITA: If you adopt that rather rude tone to me, Hilda, I'm afraid I shall have to poach on Marion's preserves and have a straight talk to you.

PHILIP: Look here, Hilda —

HILDA: Don't speak to me!

> FURBER *enters with various tea-things.* MRS WHITTAKER *comes downstairs.*

MRS WHITTAKER: Has anyone seen my little blue notebook? I can't think where I left it.

> FURBER *finds it on the bureau.*

FURBER: Is this the one, ma'am?

MRS WHITTAKER: Yes – thank you, Furber. It's really too annoying, Harris has never come – you'd better send down after tea.

FURBER: Very good, ma'am.

> SARAH *and* JOHN *come in.*

JOHN (*to* LARITA): Did you get your rest, darling?

LARITA: No – but it doesn't matter.

SARAH: Mrs Whittaker, Philip and I must really go now. I've left mother all alone with herds of strange people.

MRS WHITTAKER: Won't you have some tea first? It's all ready.

SARAH: No, honestly! – I daren't. She'll be cross as it is.

MRS WHITTAKER: Very well. Be in good time to-night.

SARAH: I don't intend to miss one dance. Come along, Philip.

PHILIP (*shaking hands with* MRS WHITTAKER): Good-bye, and thanks awfully.

MRS WHITTAKER: Until to-night.

PHILIP: Rather! (*He goes to* LARITA.) I say —

*He looks at* HILDA, *who glowers at him.*

LARITA: Good-bye for the moment – you must make me laugh some more to-night.

PHILIP: Remember – five and seven.

LARITA: I won't forget.

SARAH: Come *on*, Philip! See you later Lari.

LARITA: Yes. Good-bye.

SARAH *and* PHILIP *go off.* FURBER *brings in the teapot.*

JOHN: I'm going up to have a bath – I don't want any tea.

MRS WHITTAKER: Oh, John – just one cup.

JOHN: No, mother. I've had tons of ginger-beer during the afternoon. Come up after, Lari.

LARITA: All right, dear.

JOHN *bounds off upstairs.*

MARION *and the* COLONEL *come in from the library.* MARION *is fuming.*

COLONEL: If you don't like my opinions, you shouldn't ask for them.

MARION: I'm not used to having that sort of thing said to me.

MRS WHITTAKER (*with a look towards* FURBER): Marion, please!

MARION (*flopping down*): Father's impossible!

FURBER *goes out.*

MRS WHITTAKER: I do wish you'd control your temper in front of the servants, Marion.

HILDA: Other people besides Marion ought to control themselves.

MRS WHITTAKER: What do you mean, Hilda?

HILDA: Ask Lari – she knows what I mean.

MRS WHITTAKER: Come and sit down and have your tea.

HILDA: Disgusting, I call it!

MARION: What's disgusting?

HILDA: Ask Lari.

LARITA (*quietly*): Hadn't you better explain yourself, Hilda, instead of referring everyone to me?

HILDA: I pity John – that's all.

COLONEL (*angrily*): Have you gone mad, Hilda?

MRS WHITTAKER: What on earth's the matter?

HILDA: I came in suddenly, and found Lari canoodling on the sofa with Philip.

MRS WHITTAKER: Don't use such expressions, Hilda – I'm surprised at you. Come and sit down, Larita.

LARITA: I think I'll go to my room, if you don't mind.

HILDA: She's frightened because she knows I've found her out.

    LARITA *stifles an exclamation of rage.*

COLONEL: Stop, Hilda! I forbid you to say another word.

HILDA (*hysterically*): I won't stop – I know something none of you know, only I wasn't going to say anything about it – until after the dance. (*She goes, in dead silence, to the bookcase, takes down a book, and takes a newspaper cutting out of it; she gives it to* MRS WHITTAKER.) Look at that, mother. I got it from Sir George when I went there on Tuesday – he keeps all the back numbers of *The Times*, in files. I cut it out when he was in the garden.

MRS WHITTAKER (*reading cutting*): Marion – Jim —

    *She puts out her hand.*

        MARION *approaches and reads the cutting too. The* COLONEL *turns away.*

LARITA: I should like some bread-and-butter, please.

COLONEL: Here you are, my dear. (*He hands it to her.*)

HILDA: And I'm glad I did – glad.

COLONEL (*ignoring her*): Do you want any jam with it?

LARITA: No, thanks; I always drop it all over myself.

HILDA (*shrilly*): It's no use pretending to be so calm. You know the game's up now, don't you?

LARITA (*serenely*): 'Specially strawberry – the runny kind.

MRS WHITTAKER: Hilda, be quiet.

    *She sits back and closes her eyes.*

MARION: We'd better have this out and face it, hadn't we?

LARITA: By all means. What happened?

MARION (*handing her cutting*): I suppose you don't deny that that's you?

LARITA (*glancing at it and handing it back*): I've always hated that photograph.

MARION: You'd better read it, father.

COLONEL: Certainly not. I haven't the faintest desire to see it.

LARITA (*taking it and handing it to him*): Please do – all my friends know about this. I ought to have told you before, really, but it didn't seem necessary.

COLONEL: Really, I'd rather not.

LARITA: Please – it's necessary now.

> *There is silence while the* COLONEL *reads the cutting.* LARITA *drinks a little tea.*

COLONEL: Well, what of it? (*He tears up the cutting.*)

HILDA: Father!

LARITA: That was unkind. Hilda went to such a lot of trouble to get it.

MRS WHITTAKER: This is appalling!

COLONEL: Why? Larita's past is no affair of ours.

MRS WHITTAKER: You seem to forget – she's married to our son – our son — (*She breaks down.*)

MARION (*putting her arm round her*): Mother, don't give way.

COLONEL: I must apologise for this unpleasant scene, Lari.

LARITA: It had to occur, sooner or later.

MRS WHITTAKER (*raising her head; to* LARITA, *bitterly*): I hope you're satisfied.

LARITA: I'm not at all satisfied. I think – with the exception of the Colonel – that you're all behaving ridiculously.

MARION: It's easy to adopt a light tone – when you've brought degradation on to us.

COLONEL: Don't be a fool, Marion.

MARION: I'm not surprised at your attitude, father. Larita's your sort, isn't she?

LARITA: That's one of the nicest things that have ever been said to me.

MRS WHITTAKER: Don't talk like that, Marion – it's useless.

MARION (*firmly*): The question is – what's to be done? (*To* LARITA.) Does John know about this?

LARITA: Mind your own business.

> FURBER *enters.*

FURBER (*announcing*): Mr Harris.

> MRS WHITTAKER *gives a gasp of horror, and* HARRIS *enters. He is a thick-set, affable little man.*

HARRIS (*brightly*): Sorry I couldn't come up before Mrs Whittaker, but we've 'ad a busy day down at the White 'Art, what with one thing and another.

> There is silence for a moment, then MARION speaks.

MARION (*with an effort*): My mother's not feeling very well, Harris; perhaps you'd call a little later.

HARRIS (*sympathetically*): Oh, I *am* sorry to 'ear that – but time's getting on, you know – I've got to get back inside of 'arf an hour. If you'd just tell me where you want the fairy lights put, I could run 'em up right away.

MARION (*helplessly*): I don't really think —

LARITA (*rising*): I can show you from here —

HARRIS: Oh, thanks very much – if it isn't troubling you —

LARITA: Not at all. Look – (*she moves to the window*) we want chains – between those four big trees – and some on the arch leading to the rose garden.

HARRIS (*jotting it down*): Mixed colours, or shall I make it a scheme?

LARITA: Mixed colours would be better, I think.

HARRIS: Right you are.

LARITA: And if you could arrange some round the summer-house — (*To* COLONEL.) Just a few, don't you think?

COLONEL: Oh yes, certainly; it will brighten it up.

HARRIS (*still jotting*): Rose h'arch – summer-'ouse. – What about the Chinese lanterns?

LARITA: Furber can manage those, I think. We've got them all here.

HARRIS: Righto, then, that's that. I'll get 'em up in no time. It ought to look very pretty and gay.

LARITA: I'm sure it will.

HARRIS: Can I go out this way?

LARITA: Oh yes, by all means.

HARRIS: Thanks very much. Sorry to have troubled you. Hope you'll be feeling better by to-night, Mrs Whittaker. Good afternoon. (*To* HILDA.) Good afternoon, miss.

HILDA (*jumping*): Oh – good afternoon.

> HARRIS *goes importantly out on to the veranda and out into the garden.*
>
> LARITA *sits down again and goes on with her tea.*

MRS WHITTAKER *has been busy regaining her self-control; her face is slightly suffused with rage.*

MRS WHITTAKER (*with forced calm*): Larita, will you oblige me by going to your room, please? We will discuss this later.

LARITA: Certainly not. I haven't finished my tea.

MRS WHITTAKER: Doubtless you imagine that you are carrying off this – this abominable situation with a high hand, but your callousness only goes to prove that your senses must be blunted to all decent feelings.

LARITA (*quietly*): Nothing I have ever done warrants your speaking like that.

MRS WHITTAKER: You have married my son!

LARITA: I married John because I loved him.

MARION: Under false pretenses.

LARITA: There were no false pretenses.

MRS WHITTAKER: Do you think he'd have married you if he'd known?

LARITA: I expect so.

MARION: Then why didn't you tell him?

LARITA: Because I didn't consider it necessary. We took one another on trust. What happened before I met him concerns no one but myself. I've never let John down in any way – I love him.

MRS WHITTAKER: You married John because you wished to break away from your disgraceful life and gain a position to which you were not entitled.

LARITA: It's natural that you should think that, but it's not true.

COLONEL: Larita, please go upstairs, and let me deal with this.

LARITA: No – honestly, I'd rather stay. I understand Mrs Whittaker's attitude perfectly, and I sympathise with it. It's horrible for her – but I don't want her to labour under any misapprehension.

MARION: In the face of everything, I'm afraid there's very little room for misapprehension.

LARITA: Your life is built up on misapprehensions, Marion. You don't understand or know anything – you blunder about like a lost sheep.

MARION: Abuse won't help you.

LARITA: That's not abuse – it's frankness.

MRS WHITTAKER: This is beside the point.

LARITA: Not altogether – it's an attitude of mind which you all share.

COLONEL: Instead of jumping to the worst conclusions at once, wouldn't it be better to give Larita a little time to explain? We may be doing her an injustice.

LARITA: That's kind of you. I haven't the faintest intention of making excuses or trying to conceal anything – that newspaper cutting was perfectly accurate – as far as it went. I *was* concerned in that peculiarly unpleasant case. I changed my name afterward for obvious reasons. The papers rather over-reached themselves in publishing the number of my lovers – only two of the list really loved me.

MRS WHITTAKER: You were responsible for a man killing himself.

LARITA: Certainly not. It was his weakness and cowardice that were responsible for that – not I.

MRS WHITTAKER: It's incredible – dreadful – I can hardly believe it.

LARITA: I felt like that at the time, but it's a long while ago.

MARION: Fifteen years! John was a child.

LARITA: Thank you. I quite realise that.

MRS WHITTAKER: And how have you lived since this – this – scandal?

LARITA: Extremely well.

MRS WHITTAKER: Your flippancy is unpardonable.

LARITA: So was your question. I've only explained so far because, as you're John's mother, I felt I owed it to you; but if you persist in this censorious attitude I shall say no more.

MRS WHITTAKER: Do you realise what you've done?

LARITA: Perfectly, and I regret nothing. The only thing that counts in this instance is my relationship with John. Nothing that has occurred in the past affects that in the least.

MRS WHITTAKER: Your marrying him was an outrage.

LARITA: Why? I've told you before, I love him.

MRS WHITTAKER: You prove your love by soiling his name irreparably.

LARITA: Nonsense.

COLONEL: Do you think it's quite fair, Mabel, to set ourselves up in judgment on Larita? We know none of the circumstances which led to these bygone incidents.

MRS WHITTAKER: You've failed me too often before, Jim, so I'm not surprised that you fail me now.

LARITA: The Colonel's not failing you – it's just as bad for him as for you. You don't suppose he *likes* the idea of his only son being tied up to me, after these – revelations? But somehow or other, in the face of overwhelming opposition, he's managed to arrive at a truer sense of values than you could any of you ever understand. He's not allowed himself to be cluttered up with hypocritical moral codes and false sentiments – he sees things as they are, and tried to make the best of them. He's tried to make the best of me ever since I've been here.

MARION: That hasn't astonished us in the least.

LARITA: No doubt, with your pure and unsullied conception of human nature, you can only find one meaning for the Colonel's kindness to me.

MARION: I didn't say that.

LARITA: You think it, though, don't you? Only this afternoon you asked me not to encourage him.

MRS WHITTAKER: Marion!

LARITA: You disguised your unpleasant lascivious curiosity under a cloak of hearty friendship – you were pumping me to discover some confirmation of your petty suspicions. One thing my life has taught me, and that is a knowledge of feminine psychology. I've met your type before.

MARION: How dare you! How dare you!

MRS WHITTAKER (*rising*): This is insupportable.

LARITA (*sharply*): Yes, it is. – Sit down.

MRS WHITTAKER (*impotently*): I – I —

> *She sits down.*

LARITA: I want you to understand one thing – I deny nothing. I have a perfect right to say what I like and live how I choose – whether I've married John or whether I haven't, my life is my own, and I don't intend to be browbeaten.

MARION: I hope God will forgive you.

LARITA: Don't you rather overrate the Almighty's interest in the situation?

MRS WHITTAKER: In the face of your brazen attitude, there's nothing more to be said.

LARITA: You're wrong. There's a good deal more to be said. According to you, I ensnared John in my toils in order to break away from my old life and better my position. If that were the case, what do you mean by deliberately trying to crush down my efforts to reform myself? How do you reconcile that with your stereotyped views of virtue and charity? But you needn't worry; I didn't marry John to reform myself. I don't consider my position in this house a step up, socially or spiritually. On the contrary, it's been probably the most demoralising experience that's ever happened to me.

MRS WHITTAKER: You're a wicked, wicked woman.

LARITA: That remark was utterly fatuous and completely mechanical. You didn't even think before you said it – your brain is so muddled up with false values that you're incapable of grasping anything in the least real. Why am I a wicked woman?

MRS WHITTAKER: You betrayed my son's honour by taking advantage of his youth and mad infatuation for you. He'd never have married you if he'd known.

LARITA: I suppose you wouldn't consider it betraying his honour if he'd had an affair with me and not married me?

MRS WHITTAKER: It would certainly have been much more appropriate.

LARITA: Unfortunately, I don't consider John worthy of me in either capacity – I realised a long time ago that our marriage was a mistake, but not from your point of view – from my own.

MARION: It's easy to talk like that now.

LARITA: It isn't easy – it's heartbreaking. I love John more than I can ever say, but it's not blind love – unfortunately – I can see through him. He's charming and weak and inadequate, and he's brought me down to the dust.

MRS WHITTAKER: How dare you say such vile things! How dare you!

LARITA: It's true. You can't appreciate my feelings about it. I don't expect you to.

MARION: I should think not.

LARITA: Your treatment of all this shows a regrettable lack of discrimination. You seem to be floundering under the delusion that I'm a professional *cocotte*. You're quite, quite wrong – I've never had an affair with a man I wasn't fond of. The only time I ever sold myself was in the eyes of God to my first husband – my mother arranged it. I was really too young to know what I was doing. You approve of that sort of bargaining, don't you? – it's within the law.

MARION (*contemptuously*): Huh!

LARITA: Why do you make that peculiar noise, Marion? Does it indicate approval, contempt, or merely asthma?

MARION: Do you think this is the moment to be facetious?

LARITA: You're an unbelievable prig.

MARION: I hope you don't imagine that your insults could ever have any effect on me?

LARITA: If only you knew it, I'm at your mercy completely, but you're too silly to take advantage of it – you choose the wrong tactics.

MARION: We're certainly not experienced in dealing with women of your sort, if that's what you mean.

LARITA: It *is* what I mean – entirely. I'm completely outside the bounds of your understanding – in every way. And yet I know you, Marion, through and through – far better than you know yourself. You're a pitiful figure, and there are thousands like you – victims of convention and upbringing. All your life you've ground down perfectly natural sex impulses, until your mind has become a morass of inhibitions – your repression has run into the usual channel of religious hysteria. You've played physical purity too high and mental purity not high enough. And you'll be a miserable woman until the end of your days unless you readjust the balance.

MARION (*rising impetuously*): You're revolting – horrible!

LARITA: You need love and affection terribly – you'd go to any lengths to obtain it except the right ones. You swear and smoke and assume an air of spurious heartiness because you're not sure of your own religion and are afraid of being thought a prude. You try to establish a feeling of comradeship by sanctimonious heart-to-heart talks. All your ideals are confused and muddled – you don't know what to ask of life, and you'll die never having achieved anything but physical virtue. And God knows I pity you.

*MARION, with as much dignity as she can command, walks into the library without a word, and slams the door.*

MRS WHITTAKER: You're achieving nothing by all this.

LARITA: How do you know?

MRS WHITTAKER: Because you're a moral degenerate – lost to all sense of right and wrong.

LARITA: I respect you for one thing, anyhow – you *are* sure of yourself.

MRS WHITTAKER: I don't want your respect.

LARITA: You're the only one here with the slightest grip. You've risen up like a phœnix from the ashes of your pride. It's quite, quite excellent – and infinitely pathetic.

MRS WHITTAKER: I don't wish to speak to you any more – until to-morrow. I shall be very grateful if you will remain upstairs this evening – I will make suitable excuses for your absence.

LARITA: You mean you're frightened that I should make a scene?

MRS WHITTAKER: That is neither here nor there – I certainly don't desire an open scandal.

LARITA: You've run to cover again. I was afraid you would.

MRS WHITTAKER: This has been painful beyond belief.

COLONEL: You're right – it has.

MRS WHITTAKER: I don't feel capable of bearing any more.

LARITA: You intend to confine me to my room like a naughty child?

MRS WHITTAKER: The simile is hardly appropriate, but I hope you will have the decency to remain there.

*She goes upstairs in silence.*

COLONEL: Lari —

LARITA: Please go away – I don't want anyone to speak to me at all for a little. I must think – think —

*She is trembling hopelessly and making a tremendous effort to control her nerves.*

COLONEL: Very well.

*He goes out into the garden.*

*HILDA, who has been standing aghast throughout the entire scene, suddenly bursts into floods of tears and rushes at LARITA.*

HILDA (*hysterically*): Lari – Lari – forgive me! I didn't mean it – I didn't mean it —

LARITA (*pushing her gently away*): Don't be a little toad, Hilda. Try to have the courage of your convictions.

*HILDA rushes out into the garden, weeping hysterically.*

*LARITA bites her lip; then, still trembling violently, she lights a cigarette and takes Sodom and Gomorrah off the bureau. She settles herself on the sofa, obviously exerting every ounce of control, and opens the book methodically; she attempts to read, but her eyes can't focus the page; she is acutely conscious of an imperfect statuette of the Venue de Milo which is smirking at her from a pedestal by the dining-room doors. Suddenly with all her force, she hurls the book at it, knocking it to the floor and smashing it.*

LARITA: I've always hated that damned thing!

## CURTAIN FALLS

*When it rises once, she has buried her face in the sofa cushion, and her shoulders are heaving, whether with laughter or tears it is difficult to say.*

# ACT III

SCENE: *The same. When the curtain rises the dance is in full swing. The actual dancing takes place in the dining-room, because the floor is better. The hall and library are the sitting-out places; the buffet is on the lower end of the veranda, just out of sight of the audience. The festoons of Japanese lanterns and fairy lights look – as* MR HARRIS *prophesied – very pretty and gay.*

*There is a group of* YOUNG PEOPLE *clustered round the buffet; their light-hearted conversation can be heard intermittently. Several people are littered about the hall.* MISS NINA VANSITTART, *attired in a strikingly original rose-taffeta frock, with a ribbon of the same shade encircling her hair the wrong way    giving more the impression of a telephone apparatus than a head ornament – is seated on the sofa, basking enthusiastically in the illuminating conversation of the* HON HUGH PETWORTH, *healthy young man, whose unfortunate shape can be luckily accounted for by his athletic prowess. He has had the forethought to wear white gloves which have wrinkled up slightly, displaying below his cuffs a mercifully brief expanse of blood-red wrists.*

HUGH: It was a frightful rag.

NINA: I wish I'd been there.

HUGH: If you'd seen old Freddie fall off the roof of the taxi —

NINA (*delightedly*): I should have *died* – I know I should!

HUGH: And you should have seen the way old Minky Taylor lammed into the commissionaire chap outside the Piccadilly —

NINA (*with whole-hearted sincerity*): Oh, lovely!

*A cherubic boy –* BOBBY COLEMAN *by name – approaches them.*

BOBBY: I say, Nina – this is us.

NINA: What number is it?

BOBBY: Nine.

NINA (*rising*): I'll leave my bag here. Keep your eye on it, Hughie.

261

HUGH: I'm supposed to be dancing this with Lucy.

NINA: Never mind; it will be all right there.

> HUGH *rises automatically, and subsides again as* BOBBY *and* NINA *go into the dancing-room. Two* YOUNG PEOPLE *walk across and out on to the veranda.*

1ST YOUNG PERSON: Jolly good tune, that.

2ND YOUNG PERSON: Lovely.

1ST YOUNG PERSON: The garden looks awfully pretty, doesn't it?

2ND YOUNG PERSON: Yes, awfully pretty. (*They go off.*).

> HILDA *comes out of the library. She is wearing such a pretty blue dress, with stockings to match.*

HILDA (*to* HUGH): Why aren't you dancing?

HUGH: I'm supposed to be – with Lucy. Have you seen her anywhere?

HILDA: Yes, she's in the library. I'm looking for Philip Bordon. Have you seen him anywhere?

HUGH: No. I'll go and get Lucy. Will you dance later?

HILDA: Missing two.

HUGH: Righto. (*He goes off.*)

> HILDA *goes towards the veranda and meets* PHILIP *entering.*

HILDA: Oh, there you are. This is ours.

PHILIP: Oh – is it?

HILDA: Yes – nine. You said so this afternoon.

PHILIP: Where's Larita? – Mrs John —?

HILDA: She's upstairs with a bad head – she's not coming down at all.

PHILIP: I say – what a shame! (*Despondently.*)

HILDA (*with meaning*): Yes, isn't it?

PHILIP (*resigned*): Come on.

> *They go into the dancing-room. The music stops, and everyone can be heard clapping. Then it goes on again.*
>
> HUGH *comes out of the library with* LUCY, *a pretty girl with badly-bobbed hair; her dress is awfully pretty – yellow, with shoes and stockings to match. They go into the dancing-room. They meet* SARAH *and* CHARLES *coming out, and exchange a few meaningless words.* SARAH *flops down on the sofa.*

CHARLES: Do you want an ice or anything?

SARAH: No, thanks.

CHARLES (*sitting down*): That dining-room's far too small and hot to dance in. Why didn't they have the band here?

SARAH: The floor's better in there.

CHARLES: I hadn't noticed it.

SARAH: I'm worried, Charles – about Larita.

CHARLES: Yes – I know.

SARAH: I tried to slip up and see her when we arrived, but Marion stopped me; she said she'd asked particularly to be left alone.

CHARLES: I'm extremely disappointed – I wanted to see her too.

SARAH: Something's happened – I'm sure of it.

CHARLES: What could have?

SARAH: I don't know exactly, but I've got a feeling.

CHARLES: What shall we do about it?

SARAH: Nothing, yet – but I mean to see her somehow, before we go.

CHARLES: John seems quite happy.

SARAH: Mrs Whittaker doesn't, though, and I haven't seen the Colonel.

CHARLES: They're a tiresome family.

SARAH: Very.

CHARLES: Have you danced with John?

SARAH: Yes – just after we got here.

CHARLES: Did he say anything?

SARAH: Only that she'd got a racking headache and was in bed.

CHARLES: You'd have been able to tell from his manner if anything was wrong.

SARAH: He's either being cleverer than I thought him, or he just doesn't know.

CHARLES: She seemed all right this afternoon, didn't she? – You were here?

SARAH: Yes – more or less.

CHARLES: How do you mean – more or less?

SARAH: I'm furious with John.

CHARLES: Why?

SARAH: He's making her utterly wretched.

CHARLES: That was inevitable.

SARAH: I don't see why.

CHARLES: She's all wrong here – right out of the picture.

SARAH: I know, Charles; but he oughtn't to let her down – it's filthily mean of him.

CHARLES: He can't help it – he doesn't see anything.

SARAH: But he should see. If she's unhappy here, he must take her away.

CHARLES: That wouldn't do any good – ultimately.

SARAH: It was all a fiasco, from the first. I knew that directly I saw her. But still, he ought to play up and stand by her.

CHARLES: I can't imagine anyone of her intelligence being silly enough to marry him.

SARAH: She adores him.

CHARLES: Yes, but – she might have known it would end badly.

SARAH: It hasn't ended badly yet.

CHARLES: It will.

SARAH: Don't be so certain.

CHARLES: You're just as certain.

SARAH: Oh, Charles, I wish she'd been a cheap, loud-voiced cat – it would have been funny then.

CHARLES: Would it?

SARAH: Well, less difficult, anyhow. There would be some excuse for John.

CHARLES: That's what's worrying you, is it?

SARAH: Of course. I used to be awfully fond of him, but he's shrunk over this beyond all recognition – gone tiny.

CHARLES: An observant mind is painful sometimes, isn't it?

SARAH: Damnably.

CHARLES: Would you like to marry me, Sarah?

SARAH: Don't make me laugh, Charles – just now.

CHARLES: I believe I mean it.

SARAH: You're a darling – but you don't. The intoxicating atmosphere of this revelry has gone to your head.

CHARLES: Perhaps.

SARAH: You're not in the least in love with me.

CHARLES: I don't know.

SARAH: But it is frightfully sweet of you to ask me, and I do appreciate it.

CHARLES: We might be awfully happy together.

SARAH: We probably should, but something would be wrong somewhere.

CHARLES: I wonder.

SARAH: You know perfectly well —

CHARLES: I've been paying pretty marked attentions to you during the last six months – surely that proves something?

SARAH: It proves that you like being with me very much, and I like being with you.

CHARLES: Well, then —?

SARAH: Marriage would soon kill all that – without the vital spark to keep it going.

CHARLES: Dear, dear, dear. The way you modern young girls talk – it's shocking, that's what it is!

SARAH: Never mind, Charles dear, you must move with the times.

CHARLES: I didn't know you thought so highly of the vital spark, anyhow.

SARAH: Of course I do. It's a fundamental instinct in everybody. Being modern only means twisting things into different shapes.

CHARLES (rising): The garden looks awfully pretty, doesn't it?

SARAH (also rising): Oh, yes, frightfully pretty.

CHARLES (as they move away): All those coloured lights and everything – so attractive.

SARAH: Terribly sweet!

CHARLES: It's extraordinary how pretty a garden can look.

SARAH: Oh, shut up! (They go off on to the veranda.)

> FURBER crosses the hall, with a tray of clean glasses. The music stops, and desultory clapping can be heard. Several couples belch out of the dining-room, among them MARION with HENRY FURLEY, an earnest young man with a pinched face and glasses. MARION, for some obscure reason, is in white, with a black Indian scarf speckled with gold, and gold shoes which hurt her a little. They walk across, talking. MARION is being painfully jolly and gay – she slaps PHILIP BORDON heartily on the back in passing.

MARION: We'll have you turned out if you twirl about like that, you know.

PHILIP (with equal jocularity): I shan't go quietly.

MARION: I bet you won't.

> *Several people laugh at this volley of wit, including the perpetrators of it.*
>
> *To* MR FURLEY.

Damned good tune that.

FURLEY: Yes, I enjoyed it.

MARION: You lugged me round like a Trojan.

FURLEY (*politely*): Not at all.

MARION: You know some tricky steps – we'd do well on the stage.

FURLEY (*laughing*): Yes, wouldn't we?

MARION: Be a good chap and get me a glass of something – I'm dry as a bone.

FURLEY: Claret-cup?

MARION: Yes, rather. That'll do. I'll wait here.

> *She sits down, up-stage, and fans herself with her hand.*
>
> MR FURLEY *departs in search of claret-cup.*
>
> *Two* YOUNG PEOPLE *who have been sitting on the stairs, rise.*

GIRL: You really are awful – I don't believe a word of it.

BOY: It's true – I swear it is.

> *They both go into the dancing-room, where the music has restarted.*
>
> MRS WHITTAKER *comes in, wearing a good many brooches on a mauve dress; she also has a diamenté butterfly in her hair. She is accompanied by* MRS HURST, *a tall, handsome woman in black.*

MRS WHITTAKER: But you really mustn't – it's quite early yet.

MRS HURST: I'm just going to slip away without anybody noticing. Sarah can collect our party and come home when she wants to.

MRS WHITTAKER: Of course, if you're really tired —

MRS HURST: I'm so sorry your daughter-in-law is so seedy.

MRS WHITTAKER: It is tiresome, isn't it? – Poor Larita.

MRS HURST: Tell her how disappointed I was not to have seen her, won't you?

MRS WHITTAKER: Certainly.

> MRS PHILLIPS, *a pale white-haired woman, approaches.*

MRS PHILLIPS (*effusively*): There you are, Mrs Whittaker! It's all going off most successfully, isn't it?

MRS WHITTAKER: Yes; I think the young people seem to be enjoying themselves.

MRS PHILLIPS: So fortunate that it kept fine.

MRS WHITTAKER: I've been on absolute tenterhooks all day.

MRS HURST: I was just saying what a pity poor Mrs John is missing it all.

MRS PHILLIPS: I know – it's dreadful. What *is* wrong with her, exactly?

MRS WHITTAKER: A blinding headache – she has them, you know, quite often. I'm always trying to make her go to a specialist.

MRS PHILLIPS: Poor dear! It *is* a shame – to-night of all nights.

*JOHN comes in with* MARY BANFIELD, *a dark girl with whom he has been dancing.*

MRS WHITTAKER: But still, it's much better, if you do feel ill, to stay quite quiet.

MRS PHILLIPS: Oh, much, much! Do tell her how sorry I am, won't you?

*CHARLES and SARAH wander in from the veranda.* MARION *has been rejoined by* MR FURLEY, *and is sipping her claret-cup.* JOHN *and* MARY BANFIELD *sit on the bottom step of the stairs and light cigarettes.*

MRS HURST: Sarah, dear, I'm just going to slip away. When you come home, you will remember to lock up and turn out all the lights, won't you?

SARAH (*joining the little group with* CHARLES): All right, mother.

MRS PHILLIPS: The Chinese lanterns look so pretty, don't they?

CHARLES (*amiably*): Perfectly charming – quite Venetian.

SARAH: Mrs Whittaker, I'm so sorry about Lari. Do you think I could run up and see her?

MRS WHITTAKER (*hurriedly*): No, dear, really – she asked particularly to be left alone; you know what these headaches are —

SARAH: Yes, but —

MRS WHITTAKER: The only thing to do is just rest and keep quiet.

SARAH: Poor darling!

MRS WHITTAKER: She may have dropped off to sleep by now.

*At this moment* LARITA *appears at the top of the stairs. Her dress is dead-white and cut extremely low; she is wearing three ropes of pearls, and another long string twined round her right wrist. Her face is as white as her dress and her lips vivid scarlet. Her left arm positively glitters with diamond, ruby and emerald bracelets; her small tiara of rubies and diamonds matches her enormous ear-rings; she also displays a diamond anklet over her cobweb fine flesh-coloured stocking. She is carrying a tremendous scarlet ostrich-feather fan. There is a distinct gasp from everybody.* MARION *rises and drops her glass of claret-cup.*

CHARLES: Marvellous – marvellous.

MRS PHILLIPS: Well.

LARITA: Get out of the way, Marion dear, or I shall tread on you.

MARION: Larita – I —

MRS WHITTAKER: My dear Larita, this is a surprise.

LARITA: Why?

MRS WHITTAKER: We thought you weren't coming down.

LARITA: I've been dressing and doing my face, it always takes me hours.

MRS WHITTAKER: We understand you had a bad headache.

LARITA: Forgive me but that is quite untrue – you didn't understand anything of the sort.

MARION (*flustered*): Larita – I —

LARITA: If you have been building up a few neat social lies on my account, it is very unwise of you – I don't live according to your social system.

SARAH (*kissing her*): You look perfectly lovely, Lari, and I'm frightfully glad to see you.

LARITA: I'm dying for something to eat – I didn't feel inclined for any dinner and now I'm starving – Oh, get me a sandwich or something, Johnnie. There's a darling.

JOHN: What's the matter – I don't understand —

LARITA: And some champagne – (*There is a blank pause.*) If there isn't any, plain water will do.

JOHN: Oh, all right.

LARITA: How divine the garden looks. Hello, Charles Burleigh, I hoped you were coming – I haven't seen you for ages.

MRS PHILLIPS: We were just sending you up messages of sympathy – we understood you were prostrate.

LARITA: So I was – my maid has been massaging me – perfect agony.

MRS WHITTAKER: Well, anyhow I'm sure I'm glad you're better now – and changed your mind about coming down.

LARITA: Why do you persist in this ridiculous fallacy of my being ill? This afternoon you had the impertinence to command me to remain in my room. That was quite unpardonable and you must take the consequences. I have nothing more to say to you. (JOHN *enters with sandwich.*) Thank you, Johnnie.

MRS WHITTAKER: Marion, I'm sure the band ought to be given something to eat and drink – they've been playing for such a long time.

MARION: Righto, mother – I'll see Furber about it.

*She looks at* LARITA *contemptuously.*

LARITA: How charming you look, Marion – and what a lovely scarf. I'm sure it came from India.

MARION, *ignoring her, goes on to the veranda.*

MRS HURST: I really must be off now.

MRS PHILLIPS: I don't think I can tear myself away – yet —

MRS HURST: Good-bye and thank you so much.

MRS PHILLIPS (*seating herself beside* LARITA): I must stay a little longer.

MRS WHITTAKER: Please do – It's so early.

*She walks towards the door with* MRS HURST.

LARITA (*to* MRS PHILLIPS): How is your girl, Rose Jenkins, progressing in London, Mrs Phillips? You seemed so worried about her when you came to tea last week.

MRS PHILLIPS: I really don't know – I'm afraid she's a hopelessly bad character.

LARITA: I'm sure she'll get on in the profession you've sent her to.

MRS PHILLIPS (*stiffly*): I sent her to no profession.

LARITA: How stupid of me! I thought you had.

MRS PHILLIPS, *sensing underlying meaning, moves away.*

JOHN: Lari, why on earth are you dressed up like this?

LARITA: I just felt like it, Johnnie. I'm wearing all the jewellery I've got in the world – it's a heavenly sensation.

*She jingles her bracelets.*

JOHN: It looks ridiculous.

LARITA: Don't be an ass, John.

JOHN: But it does – honestly.

LARITA (*brushing him with her fan*): Run away and dance if you can't be pleasant to me.

JOHN: But look here, Lari —

LARITA (*with suppressed fury*): Perhaps you don't realise that I'm serious?

JOHN: Oh, all right – if you're going on like that.

*He slams off in a rage.*

LARITA: John's lost grip of things terribly lately, hasn't he?

SARAH: Lari dear, what's happened?

LARITA: Lots and lots and lots of things.

SARAH: Are you upset?

LARITA: You don't suppose I should do this – ordinarily – do you?

SARAH: Tell me.

LARITA: Not yet, Sarah – later on.

PHILIP BORDON *rushes up.*

PHILIP: I *am* glad you're all right.

LARITA: Thank you.

PHILIP: You've cut both the dances you promised me by coming down late.

LARITA: I'm so sorry. Let's have this one.

PHILIP: Rather!

LARITA (*to* SARAH): Later on, dear.

CHARLES: Next dance, please.

LARITA: Missing eight.

CHARLES: No – the next one.

LARITA: All right.

*She goes into the dancing-room with* PHILIP.

CHARLES: You must say she's magnificent.

SARAH: She's wretched.

CHARLES: I've never seen such an entrance in my life.

SARAH (*smiling*): Poor Mrs Whittaker.

CHARLES: Serve her right.

SARAH: I wonder what Lari's object is – in all this.

CHARLES: Swan song.

SARAH: Charles – what *do* you mean?

CHARLES: Wait and see.

SARAH: Come and dance, then.

CHARLES: I feel pleasantly thrilled.

SARAH: Well, you ought to be ashamed of yourself.

> *They go into the dance-room.* NINA VANSITTART *and* HUGH
> PETWORTH *are standing by the dancing-room door.*

NINA: That's her in white.

HUGH: Phew!

NINA: I've never seen anything like it.

HUGH: Look at her pearls.

NINA: Downright vulgar, I call it.

HUGH: Come on in. (*They go in.*)

> MRS WHITTAKER *intercepts* MARION *coming from the veranda, and*
> *draws her aside.*
>
> FURBER *goes into the dance-room with drinks for the band.*

MRS WHITTAKER: This is outrageous! How dare she!

MARION: Nothing can be done.

MRS WHITTAKER: I'm so ashamed.

MARION: If I can get her alone I'll give her a piece of my mind.

MRS WHITTAKER: No, no; ignore her – don't say a word. We
don't want a repetition of this afternoon.

MARION: We shall never hear the last of it. Did you see Mrs
Phillips' face?

MRS WHITTAKER: I'm sure I don't know what I've done to be so
humiliated.

MARION (*fearing a breakdown*): Mother – for Heaven's sake —

> HILDA *rushes in from the dance-room.*

HILDA (*frantically*): Mother – Lari's come down! She's dancing!

MARION: Yes, yes, we know.

HILDA: I've been telling everybody she was ill.

MRS WHITTAKER: Don't speak so loudly, Hilda.

HILDA: She looks a sight. What are we to do?

MRS WHITTAKER: Nothing. Ignore her completely – behave as if
she wasn't there at all, and don't discuss her with anybody.

HILDA: But everybody's talking about her.

MARION: I don't wonder.

HILDA: It's too awful.

FURBER *approaches them.*

FURBER: The sit-down supper's ready in the tent now, ma'am.

MRS WHITTAKER: Well, tell everybody. You'd better stop the band.

MARION: No, there won't be room if they all troop out. I'll go in and just tell some of them.

MRS WHITTAKER: Yes, do.

HILDA: I'll come too.

MRS WHITTAKER: Remember, Hilda – don't be aware of anything unusual at all.

HILDA: All right.

HILDA *and* MARION *go into the dance-room.*

MRS WHITTAKER *passes her hand hopelessly across her forehead.*

JOHN *comes in.*

JOHN: Mother – I'm fearfully sorry about this.

MRS WHITTAKER: Don't John – don't.

JOHN: But I don't understand – it's so unlike Lari to make an exhibition of herself like this.

MRS WHITTAKER (*bitterly*): Unlike her!

JOHN: Something's happened. What is it?

MRS WHITTAKER: Don't worry me now, John; can't you see I'm at my wits' end?

JOHN: I mean to find out.

*Several people come in, among them* SARAH *and* CHARLES.

MRS WHITTAKER *goes out to the supper-tent.*

SARAH (*lightly*): Don't look so gloomy, John.

JOHN: Something's happened to Lari – what is it?

SARAH: She's dancing at the moment with Philip Bordon.

JOHN: Why did she pretend to have a headache, and not come down to dinner or anything?

SARAH: She didn't feel like it, I suppose.

JOHN: I'm going to find out what's wrong.

SARAH (*taking his arm*): No, you're not; you're going to give me some supper. Come along, or there won't be any room.

JOHN: But Sarah —
SARAH: Come *along*.

> *She drags him off, throwing a meaning look at* CHARLES *over her shoulder.* CHARLES *nods, and lights a cigarette.*
> BOBBY COLEMAN *walks across with a* GIRL.

BOBBY: I think she looks jolly attractive.
GIRL: Fancy all those bracelets, though! (*They go off.*)

> LARITA *comes in with* PHILIP, *followed at a discreet distance by* HILDA, *scowling malignantly.*

LARITA: No – I couldn't eat a thing at the moment. If I'd known supper was so close I should never have had that sandwich.

> *She sits down on sofa.*

PHILIP: Can I get you anything to drink?
LARITA: No, thanks – nothing. Go and have supper with poor little Hilda, and we'll dance again afterwards.
PHILIP: But, I say —
LARITA: Please! I want to rest for a minute.
PHILIP: Oh, very well.

> HILDA *marches out, with her head in the air.* PHILIP *follows despondently.*

LARITA (*to* CHARLES): Come and talk to me.
CHARLES: I've been wanting to do that.
LARITA: How sweet of you. Where's Sarah?
CHARLES: With John – having supper.
LARITA: Oh!

> *She opens her cigarette-case and offers him one.*

CHARLES: Thanks.

> *He lights hers and his own.*

LARITA: Such a good floor, don't you think?
CHARLES: Perfectly awful.
LARITA: I wonder if your attention has been called to those fascinating Japanese lanterns?
CHARLES: Several times.
LARITA: You must admit it's a fine night, anyhow.
CHARLES: How you've changed.
LARITA: Changed?

CHARLES: Yes. Meeting you just now and then, as I've done, makes it easier to observe subtle differences.

LARITA: In what way have I changed?

CHARLES: You're dimmer.

LARITA: Dimmer! – with all these?

*She jingles her bracelets.*

CHARLES: Yes, even with those.

LARITA: You wouldn't have thought me dim if you'd seen me this afternoon.

CHARLES: Why, what happened?

LARITA: Several things.

CHARLES: I don't want you to think I'm angling for your confidence, but I *am* interested.

LARITA: I know that. It's interesting enough. Do you remember saying, the first day I met you, that one was disillusioned over everything?

CHARLES: You've been disillusioned lately?

LARITA: Yes – I didn't know I was capable of it.

CHARLES: That's one of the greatest illusions of all.

LARITA: You've been awfully nice to me.

CHARLES: Why not? We speak the same language.

LARITA: Yes – I suppose we do.

CHARLES: And naturally one feels instinctively drawn – particularly in this atmosphere.

LARITA: English country life. (*She smiles.*)

CHARLES: Yes, English country life.

LARITA: I wonder if it's a handicap having our sort of minds?

CHARLES: In what way?

LARITA: Watching ourselves go by.

CHARLES: No, it's a comfort in the end.

LARITA: I'm face to face with myself all the time – specially when I'm unhappy. It's not an edifying sensation.

CHARLES: I'm sorry you're unhappy.

LARITA: It can't be helped – you can't cope adequately with your successes unless you realise your failures.

CHARLES: It requires courage to do either.

LARITA: I've always had a definite ideal.

CHARLES: What is it?

LARITA: One should be top-dog in one's own particular sphere.

CHARLES: It's so difficult to find out what *is* one's own particular sphere.

LARITA: I'm afraid that's always been depressingly obvious to me.

CHARLES: You feel you've deviated from your course.

LARITA: Exactly – and it's demoralised me.

CHARLES: Why did you do it?

LARITA: Panic, I believe.

CHARLES: What sort of panic?

LARITA: A panic of restlessness and dissatisfaction with everything.

CHARLES: That's a black cloud which descends upon everyone at moments.

LARITA: Not everyone – just people like us.

CHARLES: When you live emotionally you must expect the pendulum to swing both ways.

LARITA: It had swung the wrong way with a vengeance when I met John. Marrying him was the most cowardly thing I ever did.

CHARLES: Why did you?

LARITA: I loved him quite differently. I thought that any other relationship would be cheapening and squalid – I can't imagine how I could have been such a fool.

CHARLES: Neither can I.

LARITA: Love will always be the most dominant and absorbing subject in the world because it's so utterly inexplicable. Experience can teach you to handle it superficially, but not to explain it. I can look round with a nice clear brain and see absolutely no reason why I should love John. He falls short of every ideal I've ever had – he's not particularly talented or clever; he doesn't *know* anything, really; he can't talk about any of the things I consider it worth while to talk about; and, having been to a good school – he's barely educated.

CHARLES: Just a healthy young animal.

LARITA: Yes.

CHARLES: Perhaps that explains it.

LARITA: If my love were entirely physical, it would; but it isn't physical at all.

CHARLES: That *is* a bad sign.

LARITA: The worst.

CHARLES: What do you intend to do?

LARITA: I haven't decided yet.

CHARLES: I think I know.

LARITA: Don't say that.

CHARLES: Very well; I'll tell you afterwards if I guessed right.

LARITA: Go, and send Sarah to me – alone; will you?

CHARLES (*rising*): All right.

LARITA (*putting out her hand*): We shall meet again, perhaps, some day.

CHARLES: I *was* right.

LARITA (*putting her finger to her lips*): Sshhh!

> CHARLES *goes out.*
> People have passed backward and forward during this scene, talking and laughing. Now the hall is practically deserted. HUGH PETWORTH *and* BOBBY COLEMAN *appear on the veranda. Seeing* LARITA *alone, they whisper and nudge each other. Finally* HUGH *comes in.*

HUGH: I say, Mrs John, will you dance?

LARITA: No, thank you – I'm rather tired.

HUGH: It's a jolly good band.

LARITA: Do you know, I don't believe I've ever met you before.

HUGH: Well, as a matter of fact, we haven't been introduced officially. My name's Hugh Petworth.

LARITA: Really. How much would you have won from your little friend if I had agreed to dance with you?

HUGH (*flummoxed*): Here, I say, you know, – I —

LARITA: You're far too young and nice-looking to be so impertinent. If I were you, I should run away and recover yourself.

HUGH (*blushing*): I'm awfully sorry.

LARITA: Don't apologise – it's quite all right.

> HUGH PETWORTH *bows awkwardly, and goes hurriedly out to rejoin* BOBBY, *who has disappeared. He cannons into* SARAH, *who is coming in.*

HUGH: I beg your pardon.

SARAH: Not at all. Hullo! Lari.

LARITA: I want to talk to you, Sarah – importantly. There isn't much time.

SARAH: Why? What do you mean?

LARITA: I'm going away – to-night.

SARAH: Lari!

LARITA: For good.

SARAH: Oh, my dear! – what on earth's the matter?

LARITA: Everything. Where's John?

SARAH: In the supper-tent.

LARITA: Listen. There was a dreary family fracas this afternoon.

SARAH: What about?

LARITA: Hilda had unearthed a newspaper cutting, disclosing several of my past misdemeanours —

SARAH: The unutterable little beast! I made her swear —

LARITA: You knew about it?

SARAH: Yes, she showed it to me three days ago.

LARITA (*slightly overcome*): Oh, Sarah! —

SARAH: I said I'd never speak to her again if she showed it to anybody, and I shan't.

LARITA: It was all very unpleasant. The Colonel stood by me, of course – John wasn't there – he doesn't know anything yet.

SARAH: But Lari dear, don't give in like this and chuck up everything.

LARITA: I must – you see, they're right; it's perfectly horrible for them. I'm entirely to blame.

SARAH: But what does it matter? The past's finished with.

LARITA: Never. Never, never, never. That's a hopeless fallacy.

SARAH: I'm most frightfully sorry.

LARITA: I wouldn't give in at all – unless I was sure. You see, John's completely sick of me – it was just silly calf-love, and I ought to have recognised it as such. But I was utterly carried away – and now it's all such a hopeless mess.

SARAH: John's behaved abominably.

LARITA: No – not really. I expected too much. When you love anybody, you build in your mind an ideal of them – and it's naturally terribly hard for them to play up, not knowing —

SARAH: But, Lari, don't do anything on the impulse of the moment.

LARITA: It isn't the impulse of the moment – I realised it weeks ago.

SARAH: It may all come right yet.

LARITA: Be honest, Sarah – how can it?

SARAH: Where are you going?

LARITA: London to-night, and Paris to-morrow. I've ordered a car. Louise is packing now.

SARAH: Where will you stay?

LARITA: The Ritz. I always do.

SARAH: I wish I could do something.

LARITA (*pressing her hand*): You can.

SARAH: What?

LARITA: Look after John for me.

SARAH (*turning away*): Don't, Lari.

LARITA: I mean it. You're fond of him – you ought to have married him, by rights. He needs you so much more than me. He's frightfully weak, and a complete damn fool over most things, but he has got qualities – somewhere – worth bringing out. I'm going to arrange for him to divorce me, quietly, without any fuss.

SARAH: I don't love him nearly as well as you do.

LARITA: All the better. Women of my type are so tiresome in love. We hammer at it, tooth and nail, until it's all bent and misshapen. Promise me you'll do what I ask.

SARAH: I can't promise; but if circumstances make it possible, I'll try.

LARITA: All right – that'll do.

SARAH: Shall I see you again – ever?

LARITA: Yes, please.

SARAH: Well, we won't say good-bye, then.

LARITA: It's such a silly thing to say.

*She gets up.*

SARAH: Good luck, anyhow.

LARITA: I'm not sure that that's not sillier.

JOHN *comes in.*

JOHN: Sarah, I've been looking for you everywhere.

278

SARAH: Well, you've found me now.

JOHN: Lari, I'm sorry I was beastly just now – about your dress. You are rather a Christmas tree, though, aren't you?

LARITA: It was done with a purpose.

JOHN: What purpose?

LARITA: It was a sort of effort to re-establish myself – rather a gay gesture – almost a joke!

JOHN: Oh!

SARAH: You'll find me in the garden, John.

LARITA (*quickly*): Don't go, Sarah – please. (SARAH *stops.*) I'm rather tired, so I'll say good night.

JOHN: The dance will go on for hours yet – this is only a lull.

LARITA: Yes, I know; but I'm dead.

JOHN: Oh, very well.

LARITA: Good night, darling.

> *She kisses him.*

JOHN: I'll try not to disturb you.

LARITA: I'm afraid you won't be able to help it.

SARAH: Come and dance, John.

JOHN: What's the matter, Lari? Why are you looking like that?

LARITA: I think I'm going to sneeze.

> BOBBY COLEMAN *and* NINA *rush across, laughing; he's delving into her bag and she's trying to recapture it.*
>
> JOHN *and* SARAH *go into the dance-room.*
>
> FURBER *enters from veranda.*

LARITA: Is the car ready, Furber?

FURBER: Yes, ma'am. Your maid is waiting in it.

LARITA: Get my cloak from her, will you, please?

FURBER: Very good, ma'am. (*He goes off.*)

> LARITA, *left quite alone, leans up against one of the windows and looks out into the garden. The light from the lanterns falls on her face, which is set in an expression of hopeless sadness. She fans herself, then lets her fan drop.*
>
> FURBER *re-enters with her cloak, and helps her on with it.*

LARITA: Thank you very much, Furber. You won't forget what I asked you, will you?

FURBER: No, ma'am.

LARITA: Then good-bye.

FURBER: Good-bye, ma'am.

*He holds open the door for her, and she walks out. There is a burst of laughter from the veranda. The band continues to play with great enthusiasm.*


CURTAIN

If you enjoy the work of 'The Master', why not join
the Noël Coward Society? Members meet on the
anniversary of Coward's birthday at the Theatre Royal,
Drury Lane to see flowers laid on his statue by
a star such as Sir John Mills, Alan Rickman or
Vanessa Redgrave. Groups go to Coward productions,
places of interest and celebrity meals.

Members receive a free copy of our regular colour
magazine, *Home Chat*, as well as discounts on
theatre tickets, books and CDs. All are welcome to join –
serious students, professional and amateur performers,
collectors of memorabilia or simply fans.

Visit our regularly updated website: www.noelcoward.net
for a membership form
or write to the Membership Secretary:

Noël Coward Society
29 Waldemar Avenue
Hellesdon
Norwich NR6 6TB
UK